Alice Lethiel
Tarentum, Pa.
June 1991

from Matt & Sue B.D. money

$6.95
E.R. Hamilton
Book seller

W9-ALZ-755

For SON
2002
AML

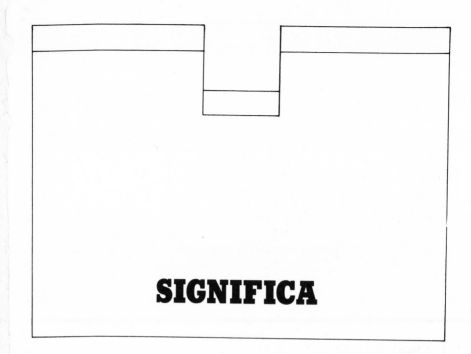

SIGNIFICA

Irving Wallace
David Wallechinsky
and Amy Wallace

SIGNIFICA

E. P. DUTTON, INC. ◻ NEW YORK

*Published in the United States by
E. P. Dutton, Inc., 2 Park Avenue, New York, N.Y. 10016*

*Library of Congress Cataloging in Publication Data
Wallace, Irving
The book of significa.*

*1. Curiosities and wonders. I. Wallechinsky, David.
II. Wallace, Amy. III. Title.
AG243.W35 1983   031'.02   83-5708*

ISBN: 0-525-24192-2

*Published simultaneously in Canada by
Fitzhenry & Whiteside Limited, Toronto*

C O B E

*Book Design: Nancy Etheredge
Production Manager: Stuart Horowitz*

10 9 8 7 6 5 4 3 2 1

First Edition

To
Walter Anderson
With Thanks

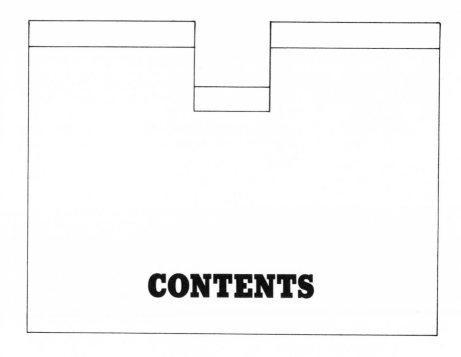

CONTENTS

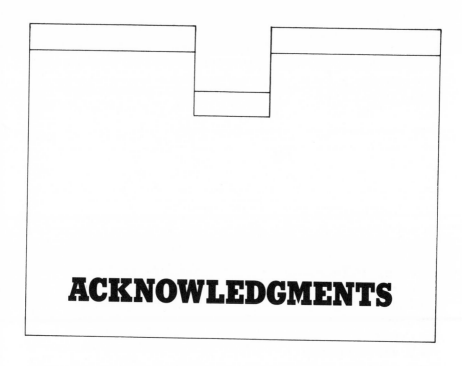

ACKNOWLEDGMENTS

First and foremost, we want to thank Bruce Felton, coauthor of *Famous Americans You Never Knew Existed*, and Ann Elwood, coauthor of *The Macmillan Illustrated Almanac for Kids*, for their contributions to the writing of this book.

Our thanks, also, to—

Lee Clayton, editor of the "Significa" column, and Carol Orsag-Madigan, editor of both the column and the book.

Vicki Scott, who served as associate editor.

Helen Ginsburg, Loreen Leo, Karen Pedersen, and Anita Taylor, who served as our chief researchers.

Carol Gershfield, who served as photo editor.

We would also like to thank Carol Dunlap, William DeGregorio, Richard Berkeley, John and Suzanne Doria, Michael J. Toohey, Sue Ann Power, Diane Brown Shepard, Linda Schallan, Annette Brown, and Aleen Stein.

And special thanks to Anita Gross, Roger Niles, Doris Schortman, Martin Timins, Ira Yoffe, and the rest of our friends on the staff of *Parade* magazine.

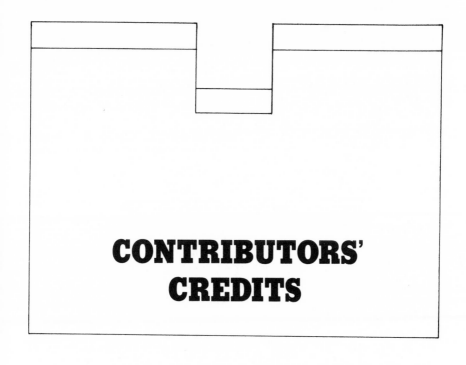

CONTRIBUTORS' CREDITS

These are the readers of *Parade* magazine who submitted ideas for "Significa" that we liked, verified, researched, and wrote up for the column and this book:

Herbert Albin, Trenton, S.C., p. 136; Richard D. Anderson, Dade City, Fla., p. 52; John K. Aulthouse, Sr., Hanover, Pa., p. 139; Margarita Avery, Sioux City, Iowa, p. 138; Elaine Bachorski, Pittsburgh, Pa., p. 157; Jim Banning, Manteca, Calif., p. 208; Elisabeth H. Barnett, West Palm Beach, Fla., p. 355; Robert G. Barto, North Arlington, N.J., p. 170; Charles Bates, Albuquerque, N.M., p. 47; Patricia Bearup, Montague, Mich., p. 256; Dorothy Becker, New Castle, N.H., p. 83; Eleanor H. Bell, Topeka, Kans., p. 229; Carlyle R. Bennett, E. Windsor Township, N.J., p. 326; Harold Benson, Mocksville, N.C., p. 103; Bonnie E. Berger, Westchester, Ill., p. 230; Bruce W. Bergondy, Hayward, Calif., p. 314; Esther and Harry Biederman, Tarzana, Calif., p. 308; G. Bissell, Liverpool, N.Y., p. 209; June Bistodeau, Three Rivers, Mich., p. 331; T. W. Black, Stuart, Fla., p. 48; Mike Blaine, Evansville, Ind., p. 164; Glenn G. Boyer, Bisbee, Ariz., p. 1; Edward Brook, Baltimore, Md., p. 29; Lois J. Brophy, Rockford, Ill., p. 268; Geraldine Y. Brosman, Glenburn, N.D., p. 159; Janice Brown, Florissant, Mo., p. 263; Simon H. Budman, Boston, Mass., p. 242; Rachel M. Burgess, Wheeling, W. Va., p. 97; Michael C.

147; Beth Scott, River Falls, Wis., p. 347; Evelyn Scott, New Carlisle, Ohio, pp. 46, 311; Anthony Seiler, Washington, D.C., p. 225; W. L. Sellers, Grand Marais, Mich., p. 254; Robert E. Shearn, Milpitas, Calif., p. 162; Gerald A. Shepherd, San Diego, Calif., pp. 69, 146; Dorothy A. Shirley, Pacific City, Oreg., p. 348; Carolyn Shriver, Honolulu, Hawaii, p. 159; Wayne A. Silkett, Annandale, Va., p. 109; Michael A. Simms, Baltimore, Md., p. 329; Stephanie Slahor, Palm Springs, Calif., p. 99; Dan Snipes, Pendleton, S.C., p. 13; Milton Steinberg, Binghamton, N.Y., p. 320; David F. Stevens, Chicago, Ill., p. 232; Terry Stewart, Spring Valley, Wis., p. 238; Terry L. Stibal, Mount Vernon, Ill., p. 166; Aline M. Stomfay-Stitz, Rockford, Ill., p. 64; Joe Stoner, Arlington, Va., p. 140; John E. Sturm, Bayville, N.J., p. 223; B. E. Suits, Doyline, La., p. 10; Patrick Sullivan, Daytona Beach, Fla., p. 198; Dave Summers, Holly, Mich., p. 177; Arnold M. Sweig, Plainville, Conn., p. 126; Wallace Tangwall, Chicago, Ill., p. 137; Allan E. Thomas, Boise, Idaho, p. 258; Carson J. Thompson, Havertown, Pa., p. 291; James Toutloff, La Porte, Ind., p. 145; Anthony Travers, Arlington, Mass., p. 303; J. Gordon Vaeth, Washington, D.C., p. 344; J. Van Burik, Washington, N.J., p. 80; Thomas Vaughan, Bisbee, Ariz., p. 321; Jaime Velasquez, Cerritos, Calif., p. 30; Donna M. Vincent, Baton Rouge, La., p. 313; Fran Wallace, Knox, Ind., p. 22; William Walsdorf, Leavenworth, Wash., p. 92; Joe Wanner, Kutztown, Pa., p. 10; William Wartofsky, Potomac, Md., p. 194; Clyde W. Watson, Piedmont, S.C., p. 176; John I. White, Chatham, N.J., p. 148; Stanley White, Honolulu, Hawaii, p. 160; Flora Whites, Arlington, Tex., p. 28; Noel Wical, Columbus, Ohio, p. 42; Catherine Williams, Argos, Ind., p. 218; Edgar Williams, Toledo, Oreg., p. 332; L. Williams, Oakland, Calif., p. 152; Carol Wilox, Morgantown, W. Va., p. 282; J. G. Wilson, Anderson, S.C., p. 259; Stan Wilson, Baltimore, Md., p. 286; Steve Woit, Framingham, Mass., p. 206; Mrs. Randy Wooldridge, Ravenna, Ohio, p. 282.

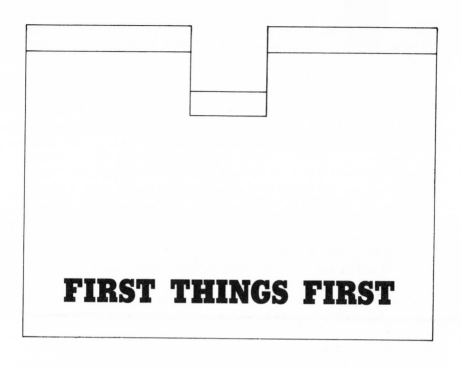

FIRST THINGS FIRST

It all began with a telephone call from New York by a man who introduced himself as Walter Anderson, the recently appointed editor of *Parade* magazine, America's leading Sunday newspaper supplement. Anderson wanted to talk to us about doing a weekly column for him. We were grateful, but we told him we were far too busy with the books we were writing. Anderson said he would like to come out and see us in person, and explain what he had in mind. We agreed to meet with him at our home in Los Angeles.

Five days later, Walter Anderson arrived to talk to us. He was a young man, bursting with ideas and enthusiasm. He explained to us that *Parade* magazine appeared every Sunday in 130 different newspapers in the United States, including such major papers as the *Washington Post, Detroit Free Press, Chicago Sun-Times, Boston Globe, Newark Star-Ledger, Houston Post,* and *New Orleans Times-Picayune.* In all, *Parade* had a circulation of 22 million copies weekly, the greatest circulation of any magazine in America.

"As its editor, I'm looking for new features," said Anderson. "And one feature I want to start is a full-page weekly column of strange and unusual facts. When I wondered who could do such a column, I was told by Don Wright, the artist, that the three of you were the best. So I read your books, *The People's Almanac* and *The Book of Lists,* and I agreed with what I had heard. That you were the ones to do the column for me."

We discussed the matter with him for three hours, and at the end of that time we told him that we were considering some other book projects but would have a decision about the column before Christmas Day of 1980. On December 22, 1980, we called Walter Anderson at his office in New York and told him we had decided to do the weekly full-page column for one year to see if we could manage it and to see if it would prove to be popular.

Anderson was more enthusiastic than ever, and he infected all three of us with the same sense of excitement. The details were quickly worked out. We would do four stories of unusual facts a week. And we would invite the readers in 22 million homes who read *Parade* each Sunday to submit ideas for our column, paying for those we accepted.

We started to prepare the first columns, but we needed a name for them. David suggested "Significa." He recalled when and where that word had come about. At a dinner party, some time before, we had met Gary Owens, the extremely gifted radio performer. Owens had told us, "I've been using excerpts from *The Book of Lists* on my show for a long time. I'm grateful to you all. But I refuse to classify them as mere trivia. They are far more. I like to call them 'significa,' because that's what they are, significant unusual facts. I suggest you begin to use that word, that's the right word." Immediately we agreed that "Significa" would be the name of our weekly column.

Our first "Significa" column was published nationwide on May 10, 1981. Typical items in that first column: a Donald Duck cartoon strip had once given a Danish manufacturer a means of actually salvaging a sunken ship (we had telephoned the manufacturer in Copenhagen to verify this); the Bayer Company at one time had sold heroin as a cough medicine; a U.S. 1812 war veteran had once been mocked and jailed for growing a beard; and when Argentine dictator Juan Peron went into exile in Madrid, he had the embalmed corpse of his beloved wife Evita (dead nineteen years) placed at his dinner table nightly. Yes, we were on our way, and we have been going strong with "Significa" ever since.

Now we are pleased to present two years' worth of our best "Significa" items in book form. But this book is not merely a collection of reprints. Perhaps 30 percent of the writing in this book is new and has never appeared in our columns. The material in three out of every ten items has been expanded with colorful new facts, and includes corrections and updates sent to us by our more knowledgeable readers.

This is, whenever possible, an oddity book about *significant* offbeat facts that have eluded standard history books and biographies, even as a mention in footnotes. And, more often than not, these overlooked facts have something to say about our lives, our backgrounds, the human condition.

In our personal reference library of over 40,000 books, we may have one of the largest private collections of oddity volumes anywhere in the world. Oddity books are not a modern innovation. There was an oddity book published less than 200 years after printing first began. It was called *The Wonders of the Little World*, written by Nathaniel Wanley in 1634. There are numerous others that go way back, including six different volumes of *Kirby's Wonderful and Eccentric Museum* by R. S. Kirby published between 1803 and 1820; *The Cabinet of Curiosities*, anonymous, 1824; *Credulities Past and Present* by William Jones, 1880; the three volumes of *Curious Questions* by Sarah H. Killikelly, 1886; and *Historic Oddities and Strange Events* by S. Baring-Gould, 1889.

Then in modern times came Robert Ripley, the great popularizer. He was a little-known sports cartoonist on the *New York Globe* when one day in December 1918—for lack of something to draw—he did a cartoon depicting nine unusual sports events with sketches and captions ("A. Forrester ran 100 yards backwards in 14 seconds"). He titled it "Chumps and Champs." The sports editor, Walter St. Denis, didn't like the name so together they concocted the title "Believe It or Not." When the cartoon brought in a few letters, the editor asked Ripley to draw another one full of "crazy stunts." Response was good, and soon Ripley was doing the cartoon twice a week, and then daily. Eventually, Simon and Schuster prodded Ripley into collecting his best cartoons for a book, and in 1929 *Believe It or Not* became a national best-seller. When William Randolph Hearst saw the book, he signed Ripley for his powerful King Features Syndicate. Eventually, Ripley was earning a half million dollars a year. By the time of Ripley's death in 1949, the name Ripley and the word "oddity" had become synonymous.

Ripley was followed by some excellent oddity hunters, who gained varied degrees of popularity. Among these were John Hix, Douglas Storer, Freling Foster, and, in a more scholarly vein, George Stimpson.

When we joined the field, we decided to make our column different in three major ways. First, we did not intend to limit ourselves to trivial oddities. At the outset we offered a definition of what we were attempting to present: "**significa** (sig-nif´-i-kǎ) *n:* unusual or little-known facts which have too much significance to qualify as mere trivia." To be sure, there is some trivia in this book, but we have tried to devote ourselves to offbeat facts that were meaningful in some way.

Second, we sought a broader reader input in terms of ideas than any other oddity compiler since the heyday of the original Ripley. Every week we invited readers who perused "Significa" to send us their suggestions and sources for offbeat facts. Unfailingly, we received about 400 letters a week, many of them offering material so fresh and varied that we've been able to achieve a diversity no authors could have achieved on their own.

Finally, more than any other oddity column or book we know of, "Significa" has been painstakingly researched to make sure that so-called facts are real facts, accurate facts. Many modern oddity books we have sampled, and checked, have been riddled with inaccuracies. Perhaps the master of them all, Robert Ripley himself, was one of the worst offenders. Too often he sacrificed truth for sensationalism. As Ripley's friend and biographer, Bob Considine, wrote on the master:

> Some of "Ripley's Believe It or Not" rested on rather flimsy evidence. . . . It is an insight into Ripley's obsession, his search for the curious, that he accepted anything in print as authentic. It wasn't that Bob didn't know better; it was simply one of the rules he adopted for the game. . . . As long as he could cite an authority for something he printed, he felt he was off the hook, regardless of how feeble the authority might be on investigation.

(After Ripley's death, those who inherited his cartoon—including the successors who create it today—have adhered to the highest standards of accuracy.)

No one can be perfect in regard to accuracy. One can only try as hard as possible. For all our efforts to verify an unusual fact found by us or our readers, we have been brought up short a number of times. There will occasionally be a reader with even more authoritative information, to chide and question a slip we have made. But still we think we have set up the stiffest research standards in years. Whether we stumble on ideas of our own or use the dozen most fascinating suggestions out of the 400 that come in during any given week, we assign them to one or two of our eight researchers to check. If at least two or three other sources—primary sources, whenever possible, and independent of each other—back up a fact we are investigating, we accept it and prepare it for our column and this book.

Some of the best so-called facts offered us simply didn't stand up under accuracy checks. A doctor told us that Karl Marx had defended and advocated black slavery. We checked it out. Not true, not really true. Several readers told us that Leonardo da Vinci in his painting *The Last Supper* had used the same model for Jesus and for Judas. The source given was a certain Bible. The Bible publisher wrote us that the so-called fact was probably fiction. We had heard that a large eagle in Scandinavia had picked up a four-year-old girl and flown off, carrying her over a mile. We could not verify this so we consulted a leading ornithologist, Roger A. Caras, and he wrote us, "In my opinion, no eagle has ever picked up a child of any size and carried it a dozen feet, much less into the air. I have watched scores—no! hundreds—of eagles, and they frequently have trouble carrying off a three- or four-pound fish." We had read somewhere that in 1931 Yugoslavia issued a postage stamp honoring Gavrilo Prinzip, assassin of Archduke Ferdinand at Sarajevo, the murderer who helped start World War I. We went to two of the leading stamp companies for confirmation. There was no such stamp and never had been one. A reader sent us a series of Universal Pictures interoffice memos revealing that Charlie Chaplin was considered a disappointment in his first screen test in 1913, and that the studio would consider him only if he would drop his derby, his mustache, and his name, and change his crazy walk. We checked this out. The memos were an inside joke that had gained outside acceptance. We considered using one of the classical oddities of all time. It involved a hoax which Russian Field Marshal Grigori Potëmkin had tried to pull off on his onetime lover, Empress Catherine the Great. Potëmkin had been sent to the Crimea to develop and modernize that backward land. In 1787, Catherine decided to inspect the villages and people from a riverboat. Since Potëmkin had failed to improve the area, he hurriedly gave the villages two-dimensional false fronts, and dressed the people for this one day in new clothes, so that the Empress would not discover the squalor behind the facades. Yes, a classic, the Potëmkin villages, but alas not true. The story was started by a gossipy French observer, who distorted what he had seen. All the other firsthand international observers agreed that Potëmkin had, indeed, raised the local standard of living, and no false fronts had been necessary. We had to drop the time-honored oddity as untrue.

We hope our readers will find that everything else that survived our fact checking to surface in this book is true. And we also hope these facts are full of wonder and surprise, and offer some enlightenment and fun as well.

Finally, we want to offer the readers of this book the same invitation we offer the readers of our column.

If you know an unusual fact that might fit into "Significa," the column and the book, please send it to us with the exact source of your information. If we don't already have it and if we print it, we will send you $50. We look forward to reading any other comments you might have. Because of the volume of mail, we cannot reply to the letters we don't use. But thank you one and all.

Write to: *The Book of Significa*
     P.O. Box 49699
     Los Angeles, Calif. 90049

I.W., D.W., & A.W.

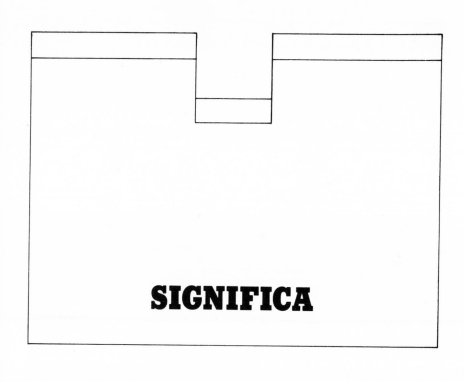

SIGNIFICA

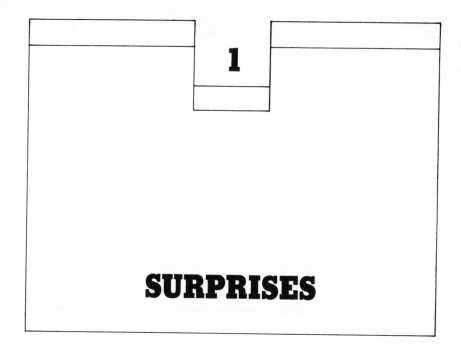

1

SURPRISES

HIDDEN SIDE OF HELEN KELLER

Helen Keller is famous throughout the world as the blind and deaf girl who learned to speak, read, and write. What is little known is that for much of her life Helen Keller was an active socialist and political radical.

She first learned of socialism when she read a Braille edition of H. G. Wells's *New Worlds for Old.* In 1909, when she was twenty-nine, Helen Keller joined the Socialist Party in Massachusetts and proudly displayed a red flag in her study. Finding the socialists "too slow," however, she later switched allegiance to the more militant Industrial Workers of the World (IWW).

In 1915 she wrote to President Wilson, urging him to stay the execution of IWW organizer Joe Hill. She also wrote in favor of birth control and women's suffrage and supported the creation of a Women's Party. She opposed U.S. involvement in World War I, charging that only the rich would gain from it, and called instead for a revolution.

By speaking out against injustice, Keller became an inspiring symbol—at least to one Hollywood director, George F. Platt, who brought her to California to film the story of her life as a crusader for the handicapped. Keller appeared in part of the film. Titled *Deliverance,* it premiered in 1919, but was a box-office failure.

The radical Helen Keller

In financial difficulty, Helen Keller took to the vaudeville circuit the following year. With her teacher, Mrs. Anne Sullivan Macy, she toured the Eastern states and Canada until the spring of 1924. After two twenty-minute lectures daily, Keller answered questions from the audience. She said of the experience, "I liked it . . . not only for the excitement of it, but also for the opportunities it gave me to study life."

Until her death in 1968, Helen Keller devoted much of her energies to helping the blind, but she continued to support political causes, including the 1924 Progressive Party presidential candidacy of Robert LaFollette.

In 1933 Helen Keller's books were burned by the Nazis because of their socialist content.

THE U.S. FIRED FIRST SHOT AT
PEARL HARBOR

It was the Japanese sneak attack on the United States naval base at Pearl Harbor, Hawaii, that all but destroyed America's Pacific Fleet and brought the United States into World War II. Yet, the first shot at Pearl Harbor was fired by the United States, not Japan.

Just before daybreak of December 7, 1941, a small American minesweeper signaled the U.S. World War I destroyer, *Ward*, a 1,000-ton patrol vessel, that it had spotted an unidentified submarine sliding toward Pearl Harbor. Almost four hours later the *Ward*'s lookouts picked up sight of the conning tower of a green, two-man midget submarine trailing behind an American supply ship. The skipper of the *Ward*, Lt. William W. Outerbridge, called his crew to their battle stations. "Commence fire!" he barked. The midget submarine was fifty yards away when a shell from the No. 3 gun blasted the conning tower. The stricken sub spun crazily, erupted, and sank. The *Ward* dropped four depth charges on it to seal its grave. The first shots of Pearl Harbor had been fired at 6:45 A.M.—the United States had fired them—and their victim was a Japanese submarine, which was to have been part of a planned attack.

One hour and ten minutes later, the Japanese came over Pearl Harbor full force and did their own firing. Two waves of 353 Japanese aircraft—dive-bombers, torpedo planes, fighters, high-level bombers—shattered Pearl Harbor, killing 2,335 sailors and soldiers, sinking or disabling 19 major U.S. ships, and wiping out 150 planes on the ground, during what President Roosevelt called the day "which will live in infamy."

The Japanese caught up with the *Ward* exactly three years later, when on December 7, 1944, kamikaze pilots attacked and sank it off the Philippines.

WHITEWASHING THE WEST

The media image of the cowboy as a white, native-born hero is not accurate. In the heyday of the cowboys, one in seven was black and one in seven was Mexican. Some were Indians, and others were English.

Many blacks worked as cowboys on Texas ranches before the Civil War, mostly as slaves. In the first thirty years after the war, about 5,000 of them rode out of Texas and up the Chisholm Trail with the cattle drives to escape the faltering economy and the backlash to Reconstruction politics. Among those who made their mark were:

☐ Isom Dart, who was born into slavery in Arkansas and later led a checkered career as a rodeo clown, cattle rustler, prospector, and broncobuster.

☐ Bill Pickett, a black rodeo star who became famous throughout the West as Will Pickett the Dusky Demon. He invented bulldogging (throwing a bull to the ground by its horns) and remained the only cowboy to employ the unique method of using his teeth to bite into the animal's upper lip as he wrestled it off its feet.

☐ Nat Love ("Deadwood Dick"), who was born in a Tennessee slave cabin. He went to Dodge City at age fifteen, worked as a cowboy, and ended up in the rodeo. A colorful character, he ordered drinks for his horse in a Mexican bar and boasted of having fourteen bullet wounds. In his autobiography, he wrote of the West: "There a man's work was

Cowboy Nat Love

to be done, and a man's life to be lived, and when death was to be met, he met it like a man." This was a perfect expression of the Western myth that later excluded Nat Love and other blacks, Mexicans, Indians, and Englishmen.

ENCORE FOR EVITA

In 1971, a friend of ours visiting in Madrid had dinner with Juan Peron, the exiled former president of Argentina. What our friend found weird about the evening were the two other persons at the table—one being Peron's new wife, Isabel, the hostess, and the other being his second wife, Eva, who had died nineteen years earlier.

You heard us right. That's what happened, and here is how it came about.

When thirty-three-year-old Eva "Evita" Peron died of cancer in 1952, her husband ordered her physician, Dr. Pedro Ara, to embalm her immediately. Dr. Ara replaced her blood with alcohol, then glycerine. He took almost a year putting the finishing touches on his embalming, but he had preserved Evita for all time. For his handiwork, Dr. Ara was paid $100,000. When Evita lay in state in Buenos Aires, 2 million people filed past her body to pay homage. But before she could be buried, Peron was thrown out of office and went into exile in Spain.

The new Argentinian regime stored Evita's body in Room 63 of the Confederation of Labor Building in Buenos Aires. Within months, the new regime itself was ousted, and Evita's corpse vanished in the upheaval. Dr. Ara was near Room 63 when soldiers came to fetch the coffin. It was later learned that the coffin had been sealed in a packing case by anti-Peronists and stored for several months in warehouses and offices around Buenos Aires. One day it was shipped to Bonn, West Germany, where it was placed in the cellar of the Argentine embassy. From there it went to Rome, then on to Milan. Under a false name, Evita was finally buried in Lot 86 of Milan's Musocco Cemetery.

In 1971, a sympathetic Spanish intelligence officer informed Peron of his wife's resting place. Peron had the embalmed body exhumed and sent to him in Madrid. When the seventy-four-year-old ex-dictator had the coffin pried open, he burst into tears, crying, "She is not dead, she is only sleeping!" Her features were as beautiful as on the last day he had seen her, nineteen years earlier. Thereafter, Peron and his young

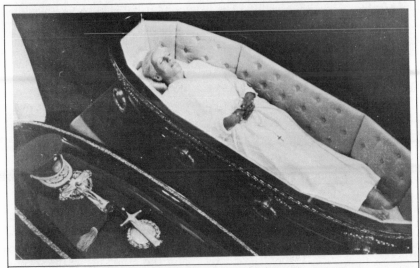

(Left to Right) Coffins of Juan Peron and his wife Eva

third wife, Isabel, would dine nightly in the company of his second wife.

A year later, Peron was summoned back to Argentina and power, but he left Evita in Madrid. When Peron himself died in 1974, Isabel became president of Argentina. She flew Evita's body home from Spain, and again thousands filed past the coffin as Evita once more lay in state, this time beside Juan Peron. Evita found a final resting place in 1976. Today, she sleeps in an underground tomb in a private section of Recoleta Cemetery in Buenos Aires.

REAGAN IN LAS VEGAS

Ronald Reagan once worked as a Las Vegas nightclub entertainer.

On February 15, 1954, the future United States president opened at the Ramona Room of the Hotel Last Frontier for a two-week engagement. It was a gamble, for Reagan was no song-and-dance man—but it paid off in capacity crowds and rave reviews. Wrote one columnist, "Rollicking Reagan proves that he can blend in with veterans of the nightclub beat—dancing, singing, and clowning, complete with pratfalls."

Reagan took the job because he needed the work. His movie career

Rollicking Ronald Reagan with the
Honey Brothers at the Hotel Last Frontier

had been slipping, yet he wasn't interested in TV or the stage and rejected several film roles he felt were unworthy of his talents. Then his
agent suggested a Las Vegas booking.

Reagan got top billing during his stint at the Ramona Room. With
wife Nancy watching the show every night from a quiet table in the rear,
he introduced the other acts, did a stand-up comic monologue, and
romped with the Honey Brothers, a team of zany slapstick comedians.
(One critic dubbed his antics "rib-busting.") The finale of the nightly
ninety-minute show was a staged wrestling match between Reagan and
the bandleader. More recently, Reagan has tangled only with members
of Congress.

Reagan was a smash hit in Las Vegas and the hotel begged him to
stay. Similar offers came in from Miami, New York, and Chicago. But
Reagan had decided he'd had his fill of nightclub performing. Both he
and Nancy had felt out of place in Las Vegas and were only too happy
to return to Hollywood. But his success in the gambling capital proved
to be just the start of things to come. Later that year he was signed on
as host of TV's "General Electric Theater" at a yearly salary of
$125,000.

J. EDGAR HOOVER'S NAZI FRIENDS

As Hitler overran Europe, FBI head J. Edgar Hoover was cooperating with the Nazis who ran Interpol.

Interpol (International Criminal Police Organization), which today has more than 100 countries as members, was begun in 1923 as a private organization composed of law enforcement agencies from participating nations. Hitler needed just such a police network for his conquest plans, and he had Interpol headquarters moved to Berlin in 1938.

The Nazis had just taken over Interpol when Hoover decided the FBI should join its ranks. He corresponded with Interpol's Nazi officials and even sent one Nazi admirer a signed photo.

In documents obtained from the FBI under the Freedom of Information Act, there is evidence that the FBI sought Interpol's aid in capturing American criminals. The notations "Jewish type" and "Jewish race" appeared on some descriptions of Americans in Interpol's police journal. FBI information did not include religious affiliation for any other American fugitives. As late as 1940, when some were warning of the Nazis' plan to exterminate the Jews in what would soon be called "the Final Solution"—the FBI label "Jewish type" persisted.

The FBI director maintained that Interpol was a neutral police agency. In fact, Interpol had two Nazi presidents from 1938 to 1941. One was hanged in 1946 for war crimes. It was not until *three days* before the Japanese attack on Pearl Harbor that Hoover stopped cooperation with the Nazi police. In 1945, at war's end, Hoover and the FBI rejoined Interpol. Hoover was its vice-president from 1946 to 1950.

Today the United States pays annual dues of about $500,000 to the organization. Interpol has refused to assist in hunting Nazi war criminals still at large, maintaining that such "political" involvement runs counter to its charter.

NO WITCHES BURNED IN SALEM

Contrary to popular belief, not one person accused of being a witch was burned in Salem, Massachusetts. During the summer and fall of 1692, however, nineteen men and women convicted of witchcraft rode in carts up Salem's barren "Gallows Hill," where they were hanged.

The trouble had begun in the kitchen of preacher Samuel Parris, whose slave Tituba entertained her master's daughter and girl friends

with fortune-telling. When the girls began suffering violent fits and weeping spells, they blamed Tituba and two others who were subsequently arrested and questioned. Tituba readily admitted she was the devil's servant. The other women pleaded innocent, but their protestations were drowned out by the shrieks and thrashings of the girls, who at this meeting and all future trials had front-row seats.

When the formal trials began in June, 170 persons crowded the Salem jail and nearby Boston prison. The youngest prisoner was five-year-old Dorcas Good, who was restrained in chains for nine months. The oldest, Nehemiah Abbot, who said he was 100 was the first to be acquitted. Among those charged were a beggar, a tavern keeper, a minister, and a wealthy merchant. At the trials, spouses were encouraged to testify against each other, children against parents. One of the accused, eighty-year-old Giles Corey, refused to enter a plea. Under a law of the day, the court sentenced him to be pressed to death. He died slowly, as stone weights were piled upon him. Curiously, the fifty-five men and women who confessed to being witches were not sentenced to death; only those who claimed innocence made the trip to "Gallows Hill."

WHEN SWASTIKAS WERE GOOD

The Nazis did not invent the swastika, nor is it an intrinsically evil symbol. The twisted cross has been around since antiquity and has usually carried positive connotations.

One of humankind's oldest symbols, the swastika probably originated in Asia. The ancient Aryans of India drew swastikas to represent the sun's motion across the sky, and this solar wheel became an emblem of the sun's goodness and regenerative power. In ancient Sanskrit, swastika means "conducive to well-being."

Swastikas have represented prosperity and happiness in other early cultures. The symbol has been found on Persian carpets, on representations of the Buddha, on antique Greek and Cretan coins, and in the Roman catacombs. Early Christians disguised their cross as a swastika to avoid religious persecution. In North America, certain Indian tribes have used the swastika to signify peace, or the four directions. Both clockwise and counterclockwise swastikas appear on the religious artifacts of many civilizations, but scholar Max Müller identified the clockwise sign as the true swastika, while the left-turning wheel is named suavastika.

Adolf Hitler, believing that the swastika was exclusively an Aryan symbol, claimed it as an emblem of "Aryan" racial superiority for Germanic and Nordic people. Although he used the symbol's ancient meaning of eternal rebirth and prosperity, he added a new and sinister element—anti-Semitism—to make clear that he meant it to signify the well-being of the German state alone.

RED CROSS—UP IN ARMS

Though the Red Cross stands for all that's humane and peace-loving, it owned and operated an arms factory for seventeen years.

The firm of Oy Sako Ab was chartered in Finland in 1921, two years after that country won its independence from Russia. In its formative years, Sako was principally a gun-repair service, its clientele mostly Civil Guard members. But in 1928, the company began turning out rifle cartridges.

During World War II, Sako made about 275 million cartridges for Finland's fighting forces. As the war drew to a close, the Russians moved quickly to grab up all munitions factories within its occupied territory. The Finns, however, devised an ingenious means of keeping it out of Moscow's grip—they gave the firm to the Red Cross.

It wasn't much of a gift. By 1945, postwar inflation, the loss of defense contracts, and other factors had severely reduced the profits of Sako's cartridge operation. The situation prompted the company to manufacture textile machinery instead of arms. But by the early 1950s, Sako—and the Red Cross—was back in the arms business.

The Red Cross held on to Sako until 1962, when it was transferred to the Finnish Cable Works, which in turn was taken over by the Finnish conglomerate Oy Nokia Ab. Today, the International Red Cross owns no arms factory. To the best of our knowledge, it's not in the market for one either.

AUDUBON—WILDLIFE KILLER

John James Audubon, the nineteenth-century naturalist, is considered the father of American wildlife conservation. A genuine lover of nature

Audubon with the gun he used to get his models

in his own way, Audubon endured hardship and neglected his family while tramping through the wilderness in search of birds. Yet he was an avid hunter who shot as many as 100 birds in a day.

Audubon's fame rests on his detailed paintings of birds and other animals. He achieved unequaled realism by using freshly killed models held in lifelike poses by wires. Sometimes he shot dozens of them to complete a single picture. Audubon refused to draw from stuffed models, and his specimens tended to lose their brilliant colors and to putrefy, requiring replacement.

But Audubon also enjoyed killing for its own sake. He was remorseful, however, after a gory buffalo hunt in 1843. He wrote in his journal: "What a terrible destruction of life, as if it were for nothing. . . . Before many years, the buffalo will have disappeared; surely this should not be permitted." Yet he went on hunting buffalo.

Today, the National Audubon Society, founded in 1905, is the premier conservation organization in the United States.

HE WASN'T ALONE IN THINKING
THE WORLD WAS ROUND

Christopher Columbus was not the only person of his time who believed the world was round. But he did believe, incorrectly, that it was much smaller than it is.

Since the twelfth century, educated people had been aware of the earth's actual shape. Columbus's plan to sail west to the Indies was not initially rejected because European royalty thought the earth was flat. It was rejected because royal advisers thought—rightly—that Asia was too far away for an easy westward sea route. Columbus, however, estimated the distance at 2,500 miles. He derived this figure from faulty equivalents of Moslem estimates of a degree of longitude, as well as a miscalculation of the eastward reach of Asia. Actually, the distance is about 12,000 miles.

Columbus didn't know of the Americas. Had they not been in his path, his trip would have ended in death on a seemingly endless sea.

THE EMANCIPATION PROCLAMATION
ACTUALLY FREED NO SLAVES

Abraham Lincoln opposed slavery but his Emancipation Proclamation emancipated no one. Lincoln called it "a fit and necessary war measure for suppressing rebellion"—not a humanitarian edict.

Issued on New Year's Day in 1863, the proclamation freed only slaves in the secessionist Southern states, excepting West Virginia and parts of Virginia and Louisiana. In other words, the Emancipation Proclamation affected only those areas where the president and the Union had no authority to enforce it. It did not apply to slaves in the North nor in the border states of Delaware, Maryland, Kentucky, and Missouri.

The proclamation satisfied abolitionists and enabled the Union forces to enlist secessionists' slaves. (By 1864, the Union forces had gained 130,000 black soldiers, sailors, and laborers.)

Many slaves escaped to the North; many were liberated as Union troops advanced. But it was not until the Thirteenth Amendment took effect in 1865 that slavery was abolished.

GRANT AND LEE—SLAVE-OWNERS

The presiding generals when the South surrendered to the North in 1865, ending the Civil War, had *both* been slave-owners. And the Southern general, Robert E. Lee, had freed his slaves *before* the Northern general, Ulysses S. Grant.

Grant's wife, Julia, owned four slaves when he married her in 1848. In 1858, Grant himself bought another slave from Julia's father, a Missouri plantation owner, but he freed the slave a year later. The only time Grant used slaves as field hands was during the four years he worked his farm, Hardscrabble. But Julia's slaves were not freed until the end of the Civil War. Mrs. Grant was an apologist for slavery all her life, and her husband stood up for her.

On the other hand, Robert E. Lee once wrote: ". . . slavery as an institution is a moral and political evil." In the late 1840s, Lee reportedly freed his own four slaves. And he released his wife's slaves, whom she had inherited from her father, in 1863—two years before those owned by Julia Grant gained their freedom.

IT'S NOT O.K.

The famous "Gunfight at the O.K. Corral" in Tombstone, Arizona Territory, on October 26, 1881, did not take place at the O.K. Corral. And it wasn't a gunfight, but more like a murder.

On one side were the three unsavory Earp brothers—Wyatt, Virgil, and Morgan—and Doc Holliday, their sidekick. As a Tombstone deputy said, Wyatt was "a tinhorn outlaw operating behind a badge." The badge belonged to brother Virgil, town marshal. On the other side were bandits Ike and Billy Clanton and their neighbors Tom and Frank McLaury. There was bad blood between the two groups.

The "gunfight" occurred in a lot next to Camillus Fly's photographic studio—ninety feet east of the O.K. Corral's back entrance. Some thirty shots were fired in just thirty seconds. Many eyewitnesses testified that the Earps gunned down the Clantons and McLaurys without provocation. Billy Clanton and the McLaurys died in the street. Ike Clanton fled. The Earps and Holliday were legally cleared.

The gunfight was erroneously placed at the O.K. Corral by Stuart Lake in his 1931 book *Wyatt Earp: Frontier Marshal.* The name stuck.

Tombstone, now a tourist town, enlarged the O.K. Corral to include the actual battle site. A good thing too. Who'd pay to see the site of "the Gunfight at Fly's Photographic Studio"?

AMELIA EARHART—POOR PILOT?

Amelia Earhart, perhaps the most famous woman flyer of all time, may have been an incompetent pilot. She had courage, but how good was she at the controls? And how careless?

Most sources say she received her pilot's license in 1922 or 1923. Elinor Smith, the "Flying Flapper of Freeport," maintains in her book *Aviatrix* that Earhart wasn't licensed until 1928, when she was thirty years old, and that Earhart's mechanics did much of the actual piloting in her early flights.

G. P. Putnam, a public relations man who later married Earhart, capitalized on her resemblance to Charles "Lucky Lindy" Lindbergh and made her famous as "Lady Lindy." Through his efforts, Earhart advertised chewing gum, cigarettes, luggage, and coats. According to Elinor Smith, Putnam signed other women pilots to contracts in which they agreed to let Earhart have the limelight.

Amelia Earhart

Earhart often flirted with death. Within months, she pancaked one plane in a field and sent another into a dangerous spin through clouds and snow. In a 1929 cross-country flight, she lost her way at least twice (once because a map, pinned to her shirt, blew off) and cracked a propeller when landing.

Elinor Smith reports that in 1929, when Earhart took over the controls of their plane, "our big, calm bird suddenly lurched out of control and wobbled all over the sky."

Pilot James G. Ray discovered Earhart to be a poor student when he instructed her in flying an autogiro. Most fliers master the craft within an hour or two, but not Earhart. She later flew the autogiro solo, but the flight ended in a crash.

On the other hand, a number of biographers have described Amelia Earhart as a skilled and courageous pilot. Said John Burke in *Winged Legend*, "She was a 'natural'. . . she was coolheaded, and she handled a plane with the same sure, steady hands with which she managed an unruly horse."

In 1937, after cracking up a plane in Honolulu, Earhart began a round-the-world flight with navigator Fred Noonan. On the lap from New Guinea to Howland Island in the central Pacific, her plane disappeared. Why? The Coast Guard cutter commander who was the last to communicate with her has said Earhart's flight preparations were "casual, to say the least." In her eagerness to get started, she had not waited for delivery of proper radio equipment. The Coast Guard could not give her bearings, and she was never found.

THE DAY HITLER SUED A FUTURE
U.S. SENATOR

In the late 1930s, a young American foreign correspondent stationed in Germany read the first part of Adolf Hitler's autobiography and political testament, *Mein Kampf* ("My Battle"), in German. About fifteen years earlier, while in jail for an attempted revolt against his government, Hitler had dictated his savage book to his friend Rudolf Hess. It had been published in Germany in 1925–26. In the book, Hitler had attacked democracy, set down his anti-Semitic policy, advocated banishing all Jews from Germany, and outlined the necessity for German military expansion and conquest. When the young foreign correspondent returned to the United States, he found that a severely abridged English version of *Mein Kampf*, published by Houghton Mifflin Company of Boston, was on sale. The American journalist was aghast. "I was outraged by the U.S.-edited version of *Mein Kampf*, which deliberately skirted the full impact of Hitler's plans for world conquest," he told us recently.

To get the truth of Hitler's plan to the American public, the young correspondent—joined by a friend, Amster Spiro, a New York newspaper editor—translated those parts of Hitler's book the legal Boston publisher had left out. They blurbed it "Adolf Hitler's Own Book . . . A new unexpurgated translation condensed . . . Hitler's 10-year plan for the conquest of Europe." The American pair published the book themselves, without permission, in paperback. When Hitler heard of this, he hit the ceiling.

"The suit for copyright infringement was filed against us locally by Hitler's American publishing agents, who easily obtained an injunction against us," the former newsman admitted to us. "We obviously were guilty and didn't bother—nor could we afford—to contest it! We had by then sold half a million copies, anyway."

The young American correspondent sued by Hitler? His name was Alan Cranston, today the Democratic U.S. Senator from California.

BLACK AMERICAN AT THE NORTH POLE

The first American to set foot on the North Pole was not Robert E. Peary but his assistant, a black man named Matthew Alexander Henson.

Henson, who worked with Peary for twenty-two years, had always craved adventure. As a teenager he had sailed the South Seas on a three-masted merchant ship. When he met Peary, however, he was working in a Washington, D.C., hat shop. Peary came in looking for a sun helmet, immediately took a liking to the wiry Henson, and hired him as his valet.

There actually was some doubt that a black man, being of a tropical race, could survive in the Arctic—such was the racial prejudice of the time. Henson saved his employer from almost certain death on two occasions—first, protecting him from a rampaging musk ox, and second, rescuing him in the wilderness when Peary suffered from gangrene and lost eight toes.

The 1909 attempt to reach the North Pole was Peary's last, desperate try at achieving his dream. For the final 132-mile leg of the trip, he took with him only four Eskimos and the forty-two-year-old Henson. Peary later said—in a patent insult to the man he "could not do without"—that Henson was chosen because, being black, he lacked the "initiative of the white assistants in finding his way back to the land and it would be unfair to send him back alone."

Matthew
Alexander Henson

For most of the punishing five-day dash, Peary, hampered by his lack of toes, rode in a dog sled. On the last day, he sent Henson and the Eskimos ahead to break a trail, telling them to stop short of the goal. They didn't. On April 6, Henson and the Eskimos reached the North Pole and gave a cheer. When Peary arrived, he was angry at being upstaged. Yet they went through the ceremonies and tasks as planned, then left behind a strip of flag in a container with an edict that Peary had taken the North Pole for the United States.

Afterward, Peary—not Henson—raced back to announce the accomplishment, while his assistant and the Eskimos froze their heels in a temporary camp.

Heading the expedition brought Peary fame and honors from many scientific institutions. He accepted the awards without mentioning his assistant's accomplishment, and Henson never asked to share the limelight.

Another explorer appeared, however, to contest Peary's claim. Dr. Frederick Cook bitterly protested that he had reached the Pole almost a year earlier, on April 21, 1908. The controversy grew, and it came out that while Peary's documentation was suspect, Cook's was nonexistent. By the end of 1909, Peary emerged as the official victor in the race. But because neither man could prove he had actually stood on that spot of frozen sea atop the North Pole, the question of who got there first—if indeed either of them did—remains open to this day.

THOREAU FOREST FIRE

Nature-lover Henry David Thoreau, author of *Walden, or Life in the Woods*, carelessly caused a forest fire—and exhibited little remorse over it. Oddly enough, a study of trees indirectly contributed to his death at age forty-four.

In 1844, Thoreau, then twenty-six, and a friend were camping on the bank of the Sudbury River in Massachusetts. They lit a fire in a tree stump to cook some fish and the flames spread over Fair Haven Hill and charred 300 acres of forest land.

His study of seed transportation and the succession of forest trees—his major contribution to science—may have been compensation for the destruction he caused. In December 1860, while studying tree rings on the stumps of the trees on Fair Haven Hill, Thoreau caught cold, triggering the latent tuberculosis that killed him two years later.

THE STAMP THAT BUILT THE PANAMA CANAL

A postage stamp was largely responsible for the building of the Panama Canal. The present site of the Panama Canal was probably determined by a Nicaraguan postage stamp sent to members of the U.S. Congress by an obsessed Frenchman, engineer Philippe Jean Bunau-Varilla.

The U.S. Congress had planned to construct a canal in Nicaragua. But Bunau-Varilla had worked earlier on the French Panama Canal project until its failure in 1889, then devoted himself to selling French rights to the United States. Grandly mustachioed, vain, and short, he had, according to President Theodore Roosevelt, "the look of a duelist."

The United States fully realized the urgent need for a canal across the midsection of the Americas when the battleship *Oregon*, desperately needed for the Spanish-American War, took sixty-eight days to travel from San Francisco around South America to the Caribbean. By 1899 a bill was pending in Congress to build such a canal, but through Nicaragua, not Panama. This put Bunau-Varilla in a tizzy.

Then, a fateful event: on May 8, 1902, Martinique's Mount Pelée

erupted, killing 30,000 people. About a month later, Nicaragua's Momotombo also erupted. The tragedies provided a golden opportunity for Bunau-Varilla. He found nearly 600 Nicaraguan postage stamps issued in 1900 illustrating a smoking Momotombo and sent them to Congress. The implicit question: Why not consider building a safer canal through a country without volcanos—Panama, for instance? And, in 1904, Congress so voted.

A FAKER NAMED PAUL REVERE

Paul Revere—immortalized for his Midnight Ride in 1775 to alert the American colonists that the redcoats were coming—was, of course, an excellent silversmith. He also fashioned teeth, manufactured munitions, and was well known as an artist-engraver. Less well known about Revere as an artist was that he forged other artists' pictures.

Revere's most notorious pilferage was his most popular print—the Boston Massacre of 1770. This was actually first rendered by colonial artist Henry Pelham, who labeled his engraving "An Original Print . . . taken on the Spot." Paul Revere copied the Pelham print before it was offered for sale, signed it, and started selling it. Pelham was stunned and on March 29, 1770, wrote Revere that he had "coppied [sic] it from mine" and charged that Revere had taken "undue advantage" of him. Pelham also complained that Revere had treated him as "if you had plundered me on the highway" and accused Revere "of one of the most dishonourable Actions you could well be guilty of." Revere's print of the Boston Massacre had become a big seller by the time Pelham got his original to the public.

This was not Paul Revere's only fraud. Assigned to do a portrait of Indian fighter Benjamin Church for a 1772 book, Revere copied an unknown artist's portrait of English poet Charles Churchill. People recognized the similarity, but Revere insisted it was Church, and that it was done by himself. Before that, Revere had taken credit for a number of copyrighted British political cartoons that he had stolen and sold under his name. In fact, it's hard to find an originally designed Revere engraving.

SOUTH AFRICA'S BLACK PRIME MINISTER

Louis Botha, the first prime minister of the Union of South Africa, was actually descended from a black slave, Lijsbeth van die Kaap. In the late seventeenth century, Lijsbeth had five daughters, three by an Indian and former slave, Louis van Bengale, and two by Johann Herfst, a German settler. Four of these daughters married white men.

According to research released by Professor Leon Hattingh of the Institute for Historical Research of the University of West Cape, General Louis Botha, who became South Africa's first prime minister in 1910, was one of Lijsbeth's descendants, as are more than 200,000 living Afrikaners—who consider themselves to be "pure white."

Hattingh's research team also revealed that the average "white" Afrikaner is really 7 percent black.

General
Louis Botha

"FATHER OF TRAFFIC SAFETY" NEVER DROVE

William Phelps Eno, the man responsible for modern traffic regulations, never drove a car.

Called "the Father of Traffic Safety," Eno originated stop signs, one-way streets, taxi stands, pedestrian safety islands, traffic rotaries, and the first manual of police traffic regulations. His warnings about the dangers of noise pollution prompted a ban on car horns in Paris in the 1930s.

Eno was born in New York City in 1858. In those days, automobiles were only a dream, but massive traffic jams were a daily reality because of the absence of traffic regulations. Just a dozen horse-drawn vehicles, Eno once observed, could tie up traffic for blocks.

In 1900, disgusted with the roadway chaos, Eno published an article

William Phelps Eno

titled "Reform in Our Street Traffic Urgently Needed." It instantly established his reputation as a traffic safety expert. He continued to write numerous articles on the subject and later served as a consultant overseas. He is responsible for the circular traffic pattern around the Arc de Triomphe in Paris. In 1921 he established a nonprofit study center in Saugatuck, Connecticut—still active today as the Eno Foundation for Transportation, Inc.

Eno, a lifelong lover of horseback riding, placed little faith in the auto when it first appeared and didn't think it would last. When motor transportation became a necessity, he relied on his chauffeur. He died in 1945, never having learned to drive.

WHEN HO HAD U.S. SUPPORT

During the Vietnam War, the U.S. government's No. 1 enemy was Ho Chi Minh. But only two decades earlier, the United States heartily supported the Vietnamese leader and his followers.

At the end of World War II, the United States held a staunch anticolonial line and opposed France's efforts to reestablish sovereignty over Indochina. The French also were repudiated by the Vietminh, the Marxist party founded by Ho Chi Minh. Gen. Philip E. Gallagher, a U.S. adviser to the Chinese army, arrived in Vietnam in the summer of 1945 and established a warm rapport with Ho. His speech at a rally in Hanoi that October was broadcast over Vietminh Radio.

Within weeks of the broadcast, however, Washington switched sides. The Vietminh fell from America's good graces, never to return. Yet even today, a reminder of that early friendship endures. The Vietnamese proclamation of independence, issued on September 2, 1945, begins: "All men are created equal. They are endowed by their Creator with certain unalienable rights; among these are life, liberty, and the pursuit of happiness." The source—the U.S. Declaration of Independence.

UNLIKELY MEMBERS OF THE KKK

Although the very words Ku Klux Klan have been synonymous with bigotry and violence for more than a century, not *all* members of that organization have been black-baiting rednecks. Among other notables, a U.S. president and two Supreme Court justices have joined.

The Klan was founded in 1865 in Pulaski, Tennessee, primarily to scare blacks away from voting. It was soon disbanded, but a second KKK—more violent and openly racist—was formed in 1915. Today, it is 10,000 strong. Among its less typical members over the years have been:

☐ Harry Truman, thirty-third president: Truman joined in 1922 only because he needed the KKK's backing to be elected judge in Jackson County, Missouri. When the Klan demanded that Truman appoint no Catholics or Jews to county offices, he angrily resigned and got back his $10 entry fee.

☐ Hugo Black, U.S. Supreme Court justice, 1937–71: Alabama-born Black signed up with the Klan in 1923 in Birmingham. Like Truman, his motivation was political, and he stayed in the group for only two years. Later, as a Supreme Court justice, Black was known for his liberal views.

☐ Edward D. White, chief justice of the United States, 1910–21:

Chief Justice Edward D. White
of the U.S. Supreme Court   President Harry Truman

24

White took part in Klan activities in Louisiana during the Reconstruction era. "I was a member of the Klan," he confessed at a 1915 White House screening of the film *The Birth of a Nation*.

○ Gutzon Borglum, sculptor: Idaho-born Borglum—who created South Dakota's famous Mount Rushmore memorial—was a member of the Klan's Imperial Kloncilium, or national executive board, in the 1920s.

○ Mary Bacon, jockey: Bacon had been a closet Klanswoman until her much-publicized appearance at a KKK rally in Louisiana in 1974. TV film crews recorded her derogatory remarks about blacks, and she lost several contracts for TV commercials.

THE STAGECOACH DRIVER'S LIFELONG
SECRET

One of the toughest stagecoach drivers of the Old West, Charlie Parkhurst, kept up a lifelong masquerade. No one knew, until after Charlie's death, that "he" was a woman.

As a youngster, Charlie dressed as a boy and ran away from a New Hampshire orphanage. He became a stableboy in Worcester, Massachusetts, where he learned to drive a team of horses.

In 1851, during the Gold Rush, Charlie went to work for the California Stage Company and quickly became known as one of the bravest, fastest, and safest drivers in the Sierras. About five feet seven, tanned, with broad shoulders, a chewer of tobacco and a gambler, Charlie looked the part. Once, this legendary master of the whip raced a team across an unstable bridge, reaching the other side just before it collapsed. Another time, stopped by highwaymen, Charlie shot the leader and escaped with passengers and goods intact.

In the late 1860s, illness forced the old driver's retirement to a cabin near Watsonville, California. On December 31, 1879, neighbors found Charlie dead. Only when dressing the body for burial did they discover the well-kept secret—that tough Charlie had really been a woman.

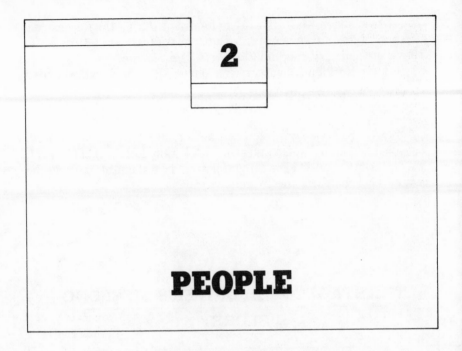

2

PEOPLE

MAN IN THE ZOO

The Bronx Zoo in New York City has the dubious distinction of being the only American zoo ever to exhibit a human being in a cage.

Ota Benga, a twenty-three-year-old Congolese Pygmy, had been brought to the United States by the African explorer Samuel Verner to appear at the 1904 St. Louis Exposition. When a tribal war prevented Benga from being returned to his people, Verner gave the four-foot-eleven African to Bronx Zoo director William Hornaday. He exhibited Benga in a cage with an orangutan named Dohong and a parrot.

The display drew an immediate protest from the New York black community and from churchmen who saw it as an attempt to prove the Darwinian theory. A group of outraged black clergymen formed a committee and appealed fruitlessly to New York's mayor and to the New York Zoological Society.

The committee declared the exhibit degrading. Hornaday maintained that Benga was happy and quite comfortable and absolutely free. He was kept in the cage simply to take care of the animals and to show visitors "how they did things in Africa." Benga's own thoughts are unrecorded—he neither wrote nor spoke English.

After threatening legal action, the black clergymen did force the

Ota Benga with
a fellow inmate
of the Bronx Zoo

release of Benga. But even out of his cage, he attracted tourists like a magnet as he strolled about the zoo in a natty white suit and canvas shoes, drinking soda water and helping the keepers with their chores. He still slept in the primate house.

Soon crowds began to beset and annoy him, precipitating several incidents. Once he was forced to keep a tormenting mob at bay with his bow and arrows until he could escape and take refuge in the monkey house. One visitor was slightly wounded.

Eventually Benga left the zoo, becoming the ward of various individuals and institutions. Unhappy in his adopted land and lacking funds for the trip home, he committed suicide in 1916 near Lynchburg, Virginia.

LITTLE MARY ELLEN

Before 1875, U.S. authorities had no legal means to interfere in cases of battered children. The laws were changed with the help of the Society for the Prevention of Cruelty to Animals (SPCA).

A nine-year-old named Mary Ellen became the exemplar of the battered children's plight. Indentured to Francis and Mary Connolly (and rumored to be the daughter of Mary's ex-husband), the girl was whipped daily, stabbed with scissors, and tied to a bed. Neighbors reported the situation to Etta Wheeler, a church worker, in 1874. When Wheeler found that there was no lawful way to rescue the child from her brutal guardians, she went to Henry Bergh of the SPCA for help.

Under the premise that the child was a member of the animal kingdom, the SPCA obtained a writ of habeas corpus to remove Mary Ellen from her home. On April 9, 1874, she was carried into the New York Supreme Court, where her case was tried. She was pitifully thin, with a scissor wound on her cheek. Mrs. Connolly was sentenced to a year in prison. Mary Ellen was given a new home. The following April, the New York Society for the Prevention of Cruelty to Children (NYSPCC) was incorporated.

Before-and-after photos of Mary Ellen (as a pathetic waif upon her rescue and as a healthy child a year later) still hang at the New York SPCA, framed along with Mrs. Connolly's scissors.

SPCA's before-and-after photos of Mary Ellen,
with the scissors used to punish her

THE CLERGYMAN SALOONKEEPER

Most churches at the turn of the century shared one priority: combating the vice of drunkenness. Henry C. Potter, Protestant Episcopal Bishop of New York, found a novel solution—he opened a saloon.

You can't blame working people for visiting bars, said Bishop Potter, in an address to a 1902 religious convention. The wealthy can afford fashionable clubs for relaxation, conversation, and companionship. The poor can afford only saloons. If these are indecent, the church should try to improve them, not shut them down.

With Potter's support, a group of businessmen opened the Subway Tavern at Mulberry and Bleecker Streets in Manhattan as a club where a respectable workingman could take his family. Soda water and beer were served in the front. Hard liquor was served in the rear, where ladies were not permitted. Lunch was free. Drunkenness was not allowed.

Bishop Potter dedicated the tavern on August 2, 1904. He contemplated the rows of whisky, gin, and brandy bottles, delivered a speech, and led the crowd in a hymn. Customers drank to his health, but he refused to imbibe.

Despite opposition from scandalized church groups, Potter almost proved his point—three of the rowdier neighborhood bars lost customers to the Subway Tavern and shut their doors. As the novelty of a church saloon wore off, however, so did business. Within two years, Potter's pub had closed.

THE FIRST AMERICAN PRINCESS OF MONACO

The late Grace Kelly was not Monaco's first American princess. The first American princess was Alice Heine, and she was, it might be added, a real Jewish princess.

She was born in New Orleans in 1858, the daughter of a wealthy banker who took her to Paris when she was sixteen in search of a wealthy husband. She found one—Duc Armand de Richelieu—but he died after five years of marriage, leaving his young widow with an estate of $15 million.

Alice had barely begun mourning her husband when she met and fell in love with Prince Albert of Monaco on the Portuguese island of Madeira. She married him in 1889 and returned with him as his princess to the tiny Mediterranean principality in 1890.

Then as now, Monaco's fame rested on its gambling casinos, but Princess Alice attracted opera, theater, and ballet to the country and transformed it into a major cultural center. Although her husband supported her efforts, she was hardly as sympathetic to his first love—the sea; she even refused to set foot on the two yachts he named for her. Over the years, the royal couple found other things to differ about as well, and in 1902 they separated.

Although Alice's parents had converted her to Catholicism when she was a child, she never lost sight of her roots. One of the causes of the breakup of her marriage was a popular young British-Jewish songwriter and singer named Isidore Cohen. Later, as the dowager princess, she divided her time between her home in France and a London apartment where she entertained noted artists, writers, and political leaders. She died in Paris in 1925 at the age of sixty-seven.

JOHNNY APPLEWEED

Can't get rid of the pesky dog fennel weed infesting your property? You can blame Johnny Appleseed, the Yankee nurseryman who planted it—along with his famous apple orchards—across America in the early pioneer days.

John Chapman, better known as Johnny Appleseed, took his sack of apple seeds to Ohio around 1800, sowing them along roadways, by rivers, and in forest clearings. Wearing a burlap coffee sack for a shirt and a tin mush pan for a hat, the barefoot eccentric became well known to settlers throughout the wilderness.

Appleseed was a great believer in the power of medicinal plants and encouraged their use. It was a common belief in his day that dog fennel relieved fever—so, with the best of intentions, Appleseed scattered the seeds throughout Ohio and Indiana. The foul-smelling weed spread from barnyard to pasture, sometimes growing as high as fifteen feet. Today, exasperated midwestern farmers still cannot rid their fields of the plant they half humorously call "Johnnyweed."

THE QUEEN WAS A MECHANIC

At eighteen, Britain's dignified Queen Elizabeth II was a grease monkey.

Wanting to contribute to the war effort in 1944, the eighteen-year-old Princess Elizabeth joined the Auxiliary Territorial Service for a course in heavy mechanics. Officially, she was No. 230873 Second Subaltern Elizabeth Alexandra Mary Windsor.

Her commander picked the princess up at Windsor Castle on her first day and drove her to the training center at Camberly, where a jacked-up car without wheels awaited her. At that time, she couldn't even drive. During her training, in which she learned to strip and service engines and drive military vehicles, she was treated "like any other"—except that she slept each night at Windsor Castle.

On final test day, King George VI found his daughter in greasy overalls under a car. Returning a short while later, he asked, "What, not got it going yet?" To her chagrin, the engine wouldn't start. The king had secretly removed the car's distributor.

Princess Elizabeth struggles with a stubborn tire during wartime duties

The princess's commander gave her a positive evaluation: "Her Royal Highness is a very good and extremely considerate driver."

THE SOLDIER WHO FLED THE ALAMO

Of the more than 180 defenders of the Alamo, only one man, Louis "Moses" Rose, escaped to tell the story of the bloody siege in the winter of 1836.

Bolstered by the hope that reinforcements would arrive at any moment, the tiny garrison of Texas patriots had for days held off more than 5,000 Mexican troops led by General Antonio López de Santa Anna. However, it eventually became clear that no help was forthcoming and that defeat was imminent.

The garrison's commander, Colonel William Barret Travis, assembled his men to advise them of the hopeless situation. In an inspired speech, he extolled the virtues of dying for Texas, then he drew a line in the dust with his sword. Those who wished to fight and die in glory and honor, he said, should step across the line. One by one, all crossed—except Moses Rose.

A fifty-year-old French veteran who had fought with Napoleon, Rose professed to know more about violent death than did the twenty-seven-year-old Travis. "I am not prepared to die," Rose said, "and shall not do so if I can avoid it." He vaulted a wall and fled through enemy territory, barely eluding capture. Several days later, he found shelter with a sympathetic farmer who listened to his amazing tale. By this time, all the defenders of the Alamo were dead. The victorious Mexicans spared only the noncombatants—a few women, children, and slaves.

Rose lived fourteen more years, running a butcher shop in Nacogdoches, Texas. Eventually he went to live near Logansport, Louisiana, where he died in 1850.

THE OTHER JONAH

The biblical story of Jonah being swallowed by a whale—just an ancient fish story? Don't be too sure. As recently as ninety-two years ago, a human being was swallowed by a whale—and lived.

In February 1891, a young English sailor named James Bartley was a crew member on the whaling ship *Star of the East*, which ranged the waters off the Falkland Islands in the South Atlantic, searching for marine leviathans. Suddenly, three miles out, the sailors spotted a sperm whale that later proved to be eighty feet long and weigh eighty tons. Two boats with crew members and harpooners—one of them Bartley—were dispatched to kill the whale. As they closed in, one harpooner catapulted his eight-foot spear toward the sea beast. The instant it struck, the whale twisted and lashed out with its fanning tail. The tail slammed into one boat, lifted it into the air, and capsized it. But the sailors soon subdued and killed the wounded mammal.

When the boat was righted, Bartley and another crewman were missing and written off as drowned. The crew pulled the carcass of the whale alongside *Star of the East* and worked until midnight removing the blubber. The next morning, using a derrick, the sailors hoisted the whale's stomach on deck. According to M. de Parville, science editor of the *Journal des Débats*, who investigated the incident, there was then a movement in the whale's belly. When it was opened, Bartley was found unconscious. He was carried on deck and bathed in seawater. This revived him, but his mind was not clear and he was confined to the captain's quarters for two weeks, behaving like a lunatic.

Within four weeks, Bartley had fully recovered and related what it had been like to live in the belly of a whale. He remembered the whale's tail hitting his boat. Then, reported de Parville, Bartley was encompassed in darkness and felt himself slipping along a smooth passage. His hands felt something slimy all around him. The heat was unbearable—it was thought to be 104 degrees F.—and he lost consciousness. When he awoke, he was in the captain's cabin.

For the rest of his life, Bartley's face, neck, and hands remained white, bleached by the whale's gastric juices.

THE TRANSVESTITE GOVERNOR

In 1702, Queen Anne of England gave Lord Cornbury, her spendthrift cousin, a choice: either go to debtor's prison or become governor of colonial New York and New Jersey. Off to the colonies he went.

Asserting that he wanted to literally represent the queen, Cornbury was usually seen about town wearing the most elegant dresses. The well-groomed transvestite governor shocked his constituents from the beginning. Addressing one assembly, he resisted speaking of politics and instead delivered an ode to the beauty of his wife's ears. Each gentleman present was then invited to feel their shell-like contours. During his tenure, Cornbury could also be seen sneaking up behind unsuspecting men and pulling their ears.

As a governor, Lord Cornbury was a disaster. Nonpartisan corruption flourished as he freely took bribes from all sides in political disagreements. At home, he wined and dined extravagantly and ignored the debts piling up. His finery must have cost a fortune, although some of the gowns were gifts from the queen herself.

Finally, the colonists could tolerate no more and complained to

Edward Hyde Lord Cornbury
afterw. 3rd Earl of Clarendon.

Queen Anne about this "peculiar, detestable maggot." She obligingly removed him from office in December 1708, whereupon he was immediately seized by his irate creditors. In jail, Cornbury was saved when his father died, leaving him the earldom of Clarendon—and thus immunity to prosecution. With debts unpaid, he returned to England and a comfortable political career, courtesy of the queen.

THE PRINCE AND LADY DIANA: TWO CENTURIES LATER

History repeated itself—almost—when Prince Charles and Lady Diana Spencer were married on July 29, 1981, at St. Paul's Cathedral in London. The fact is that more than two centuries ago, another Prince of Wales asked for the hand of another Lady Diana Spencer in marriage. That tale had a far less happy ending.

Soon after he became Prince of Wales in 1729, Frederick Louis quarreled bitterly with his father, King George II of England. The subject was money. The high-living Frederick felt that his yearly allowance of £50,000 was barely sufficient. To bait his father and also to raise cash, Frederick arranged with the Duchess of Marlborough to marry her beautiful and accomplished granddaughter, Lady Diana Spencer, the dowry to be £100,000.

A wedding date was set, but at the last minute, Prime Minister Robert Walpole, a longtime foe of Frederick, found out about the plans through a hired informant and quashed the marriage. The following year, Frederick married Augusta Saxe-Gotha. Meanwhile, Lady Diana married Sir John Russell and became the Duchess of Bedford. Second best, but not bad.

Frederick never forgave Sir Robert and conspired against him and his partisans. In 1737, Frederick cut all ties with his father as well, after unsuccessfully petitioning Parliament for a more generous allowance. Later, he openly made peace with King George, but the great-great-great-great-great-great-grandfather of today's Prince Charles continued, until his death in 1751, to scheme against the king's ministers.

ALBERT EINSTEIN REFUSED PRESIDENCY

OF ISRAEL

Albert Einstein, the great physicist, was once offered the presidency of Israel. Although devoted to the ideal of a Jewish state, he refused the job.

On November 9, 1952, Chaim Weizmann, Israel's first president, died in office. The next day, an Israeli newspaper proposed Einstein for the job, calling him the greatest Jew alive.

Upon the instructions of Prime Minister David Ben-Gurion, Einstein was told that his election to the largely symbolic office was assured and that Israel would support his scientific work while he was in office. The seventy-three-year-old physicist declined, citing his age as one factor. More important, he said, although he knew a few things about the world, he "lacked both the natural aptitude and the experience to deal properly with people."

MARTYR TO A BEARD

He was the first man in American history thrown into jail for wearing a beard.

His name was Joseph Palmer. He had fought in the War of 1812. Palmer was a big man, a forty-two-year-old Massachusetts farmer who moved into busy Fitchburg with his wife Nancy and son Thomas in May 1830. He was average in every way save one—he affected a great flowing beard, making him resemble a biblical patriarch.

No Americans wore beards in those times. The leaders of the Revolution, the signers of the Constitution, the presidents of the United States from George Washington to James Buchanan were all beardless. The kindly Joseph Palmer was said to be the first American citizen in the East to sport whiskers.

The people of Fitchburg didn't like that crazy man with a beard. When he took a walk, children jeered, and women crossed to the opposite side of the street. Grown men heaved stones through the windows of his home. The local pastor, Rev. George Trask, denounced Palmer from the pulpit: "Let us join in prayers for the vain Mr. Palmer. He admires only his own reflection in the glass."

Several days later, four men ambushed Palmer in front of his house.

They were carrying scissors, soap, brush, and razor. They threw him to the ground, then tried to pin him down and remove his beard. Palmer managed to pull out his pocket knife and started slashing at them, injuring two in their legs. They left him and fled. The town magistrate had Palmer arrested for "unprovoked assault" and fined him. Palmer refused to pay his fine and was thrown into the jail in Worcester, Massachusetts.

There, Warden Bellows offered other prisoners lighter sentences if they would shave Palmer by force. Two tried. Palmer flattened them. Palmer smuggled letters out to his son, who had them published in the *Massachusetts Weekly Spy*. Palmer's plea to the outside world was simple: did not the Constitution give every man the freedom to wear what he wanted? Henry Thoreau, Bronson Alcott, and Ralph Waldo Emerson heard his plea and rallied round him. After a year, he was becoming a Cause, and his jailers asked him to go home. He refused unless they admitted publicly that he had the right to wear a beard. One day his jailers simply picked him up in his chair, carried him onto the street, and left him. With his beard.

Nearby was a vegetarian utopia named Fruitlands. Palmer bought it and turned it into "a sort of asylum for waifs and tramps and men with beards." Palmer died in 1875, fourteen years after President Lincoln was inaugurated wearing a beard. Palmer's gravestone may be seen today in Evergreen Cemetery, Leominster, Massachusetts. Part of the inscription reads: PERSECUTED FOR WEARING THE BEARD.

FRENCHMAN WITH RADAR EYES

He was a man who could "see" distant shapes not visible to the naked eye or through a telescope.

His name was Etienne Bottineau, and from the 1760s to the 1780s he was known in the French African colony of Île de France as the man with amazing eyesight.

Appointed beacon keeper for the island (which is now called Mauritius) in 1764, Bottineau spent the next twenty years perfecting his new art of "nauscopie." He trained his eyes—without the use of a telescope—to scan the ocean horizon for approaching ships which were not yet visible. The passage of a ship through water, he explained, disturbed atmospheric gases which then rose in a "vaporous envelope," perceptible to Bottineau's practiced eye from 100 to 600 miles away.

Island officials finally began to keep a tally of Bottineau's predictions. During one six-month period, the French beacon keeper successfully forecast the arrival of 109 unseen ships, one to four days before they docked. On two occasions when no ships appeared as forecast, it was later learned the vessels had changed course. As the governor of Mauritius put it, the statistics proved that Bottineau was neither "an imposter nor a visionary," but a true scientist.

Bottineau died in 1789 and the secret of nauscopie was lost in the turmoil of the French Revolution. In Mauritius, legend has it that a second Frenchman with so-called "radar eyes" warned of the approach of ships in 1810. Island officials failed to heed the warning, and the British navy captured the colony from France.

INCREDIBLE INFANT

Probably the most innovative exploit in espionage history was carried off by a French spy who posed as an infant.

The spy's name was Richebourg. He was twenty-three inches tall, a midget who worked as a servant for the Duchess of Orléans, mother of the future King Louis Philippe of France. When the French Revolution erupted in 1789, the House of Orléans was cut off from its Royalist friends and allies in Paris. A spy was desperately needed to pass information to the Royalists in Paris and report back on activities inside the city. It was then that the twenty-one-year-old Richebourg volunteered to be the spy.

Richebourg, dressed in infant's swaddling clothes and carried by an Orléans maid posing as a nurse, passed by the armed guards at the gates of Paris. The ruse succeeded time and again as the midget, cradled to the bosom of his "nurse," conveyed military dispatches in and out of Paris.

At the end of the Revolution, Richebourg moved to the Saint-Germain quarter of Paris. From the exiled Orléans family he received a pension of 3,000 francs a year. He lived as a recluse through the reigns of Napoleon Bonaparte, Louis Philippe, and part of the reign of Napoleon III. In 1858, the *London Times* printed an obituary upon his death at the age of ninety.

THE REAL DR. JEKYLL AND MR. HYDE

Everyone who has read the novel by Robert Louis Stevenson or seen a version of the movie knows about the fictional Dr. Jekyll and Mr. Hyde. A respectable physician in the daytime, Dr. Jekyll swallowed a potion that transformed him into the brutal, evil Mr. Hyde by night. Pretty fanciful, you might say. Not at all. He lived. He was based on a real person named Deacon William Brodie.

By day, William Brodie was a paragon of virtue in mid-eighteenth-century Edinburgh, Scotland. He owned a successful cabinet-making business, served as a town councilman, and was the deacon of the local cabinetmaker's union. A sober bachelor who usually wore white, Deacon Brodie lived quietly with his father and sister. Brodie's dark side emerged when the sun set. Attired in a black suit and black mask, the deacon was transformed into a gambler, a drunkard, and a

Deacon William Brodie as Dr. Jekyll

thief who kept two mistresses and used a portion of his loot to support his five children by them.

In 1786, at age twenty-seven, Brodie committed his first burglary when he stole £800 from a bank. During the next eighteen years, his nocturnal activities presented few problems. Brodie's secret criminal life might have continued unchecked, but ambition proved his undoing. His dream of leading a gang of cutthroats became a nightmare when he located three other robbers to assist him in his larcenous pursuits. After a carefully planned robbery of the Scottish General Excise Office was botched, one of the deacon's cohorts turned king's evidence. Brodie managed to escape to Amsterdam and was on the verge of embarking for America when he was captured. In the same courtroom where he had served as a respectable juror six months earlier, he was sentenced to be hanged.

The man of two lives plotted for a third, however, and consulted a doctor for assistance in cheating the hangman. Elaborate measures were taken to soften the noose's impact, including wiring Brodie's body so it wouldn't be jerked. An hour before he was to face the executioner on October 1, 1788, the deacon concealed a steel collar under his neckerchief to prevent strangulation. But the gallows were not to be denied, and Brodie died of a broken neck.

SEASICK LORD NELSON

Horatio Nelson (1758–1805), possibly history's greatest naval commander, was constantly seasick. At the time he defeated Napoleon's navies for his native Britain, he also was suffering from gout, recurring attacks of malaria, chest and lung pains, rheumatic fever, and mental depression. In addition, Lord Nelson was missing his right eye and an arm, which had been amputated.

Nelson relieved his excruciating gout with a vegetarian diet, but he never did overcome his seasickness. At the age of forty-three, after thirty years at sea, he wrote despairingly: "Heavy sea, sick to death—this seasickness I shall never get over." Another time, he bemoaned being so seasick "that I cannot hold up my head, but none of them [his crewmates] cares a damn for me and my sufferings." Maybe Nelson was in the wrong line of work.

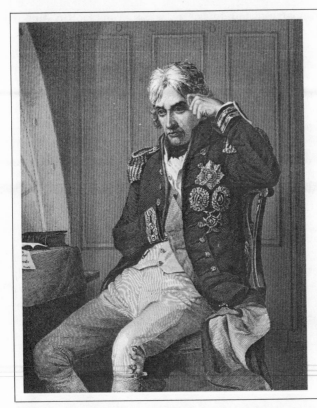

Horatio Nelson
suffering motion
sickness

THE FEMALE PAUL REVERE

During the American Revolution, a sixteen-year-old girl named Sybil Ludington took a midnight ride for the rebel cause that was more dangerous and far longer than the famed ride made by Paul Revere.

On the night of April 25, 1777, 2,000 British soldiers landed in Connecticut, marched inland to the town of Danbury, and proceeded to destroy the rebels' storehouse of food and arms. Diverted by hogsheads of rum, the redcoats thereupon got drunk, shot off their guns, and began burning the town.

At 7:00 P.M., a messenger with a bullet in his back rode up to the Ludington house, twenty miles west of Danbury, and alerted Sybil's father, who was commander of a militia regiment. Colonel Ludington had a grave dilemma: if he rode off to notify his 400 volunteers, he might not return in time to lead them in battle. Sybil offered to go in his place.

Sidesaddle on a big bay horse, she rode forty miles—twenty-six miles more than Revere—through a dangerous no-man's-land between British and American lines that was infested with deserters and hostile Indians. As she rode, she banged on doors with a stick and shouted the summons. The night almost over, she returned home and slid, exhausted, from her horse. The colonials responded to her call, and though too late to save Danbury, they joined regular Continental troops to attack the British at Ridgefield, south of Danbury, soundly defeating the redcoats and forcing them to retreat, panic-stricken, to their ships.

William James Sidis

THE CRADLE GENIUS

In 1910, the words "child prodigy" meant one thing to most Americans: William James Sidis. Born in 1898, he was the son of Sarah and Boris Sidis, the latter a Russian-born Harvard professor of abnormal psychology.

Dr. Sidis believed that geniuses were made, not born, and set out to prove his theory with his infant son. He hung alphabet blocks over the boy's crib—and within six months, William knew his ABC's perfectly. At two, he could type in English and French. At three, he studied advanced mathematics; and at five, he wrote a treatise on anatomy.

William was ready for Harvard at nine, but was considered emotionally immature and told to reapply at eleven. He did, and became the youngest student ever admitted to Harvard. He began his college years with a splash, delivering a lecture on the fourth dimension that was too sophisticated for most of his audience. At twelve, he withdrew from college, probably because of emotional strain.

Later, Sidis returned to Harvard and graduated cum laude at sixteen. He told the press: "The only way to live the perfect life is in seclusion." From that point on, except for a brief stint as a law student and then a teacher, Sidis retired from public life. He took one menial job after another, earned $15–$25 a week, refused promotions, and pursued the various passions of his life—politics, American Indian history, and the collection of streetcar transfers.

Sidis joined the Communist Party and was arrested in 1919 for leading a May Day demonstration. Eventually, he became an ardent pacifist libertarian.

But even libertarianism played second fiddle to streetcar transfers. Sidis rode streetcars constantly, tenderly hoarding the transfers. Among his few published works is the book, *Notes on the Collection of Transfers*.

In 1937, Sidis sued the *New Yorker* magazine for invasion of privacy. The magazine had published a story that portrayed him as an eccentric genius. He was quoted as saying, "The very sight of a mathematical formula makes me ill." Sidis, acting in his own defense, pleaded that he was a normal man, a mere ordinary human—and he offered to take an IQ test to prove it. Sidis lost the case, and eventually the *New Yorker* settled out of court for $600.

At the age of forty-six, William James Sidis died of a cerebral hemorrhage—perhaps a symbol of the internal combustion of his great brain.

THE ORIGINAL DUNCE

The word "dunce," meaning a "dull-witted or ignorant person," derives from one of the greatest minds of the Middle Ages.

John Duns Scotus, born in Scotland in 1265, wrote profound treatises on grammar, logic, metaphysics, and theology. He was educated at Cambridge and Oxford and pursued his master's degree in theology at the University of Paris. There, in 1303, he became embroiled in one of the most heated disputes of the day. France's King Philip IV had moved to tax the Church in order to finance his war with England; in response, Pope Boniface VIII threatened to excommunicate him. For supporting the pope, Duns Scotus was banished from France. Later he assumed a university professorship in Cologne, where he died in 1308.

The term "dunce" was coined two centuries later by Renaissance humanists and Reformation leaders who took sharp issue with Duns Scotus's teachings and his defense of the papacy. To them, any follower of Duns Scotus—a "Duns man" or "Dunce"—was a dull-witted sort, "incapable of scholarship and stupid." The definition has stuck ever since.

FREE BLACK SLAVEHOLDER

A black New Orleans planter, Andrew Durnford, was the owner of seventy-seven black slaves.

Born in 1800, Durnford was the son of a free black mother and an English aristocrat. He bought his first slave, Noel (later his business manager), for $500 in 1828, when he began work on his sugar plantation, St. Rosalie. By 1829, he had nineteen slaves.

Like many plantation owners, Durnford fretted about slave prices and fed his slaves poorly, though he treated them well otherwise. His attitude toward slavery was ambivalent. He did not really believe it was right, yet slaves provided the best—and cheapest—plantation help. "Self-interest is à la mode," he wrote. He supported the effort to help freed slaves colonize in Liberia, Africa, but he probably did not participate in the program. According to his biographer, David O. Whitten, Durnford "regarded slaves with respect for their humanity, treating their bondage more as a state of being than a measure of human quality."

Yet during his lifetime, Durnford emancipated only four slaves. When he died, he owned seventy-seven slaves worth $71,550. In his will, he freed one of them, Albert, probably his son by his black mistress,

Wainy, a house servant twenty-seven years younger than he. In addition, Albert inherited $2,000 for his education.

JESSE JAMES: PUBLICITY ENEMY NO. 1

The Wild West was a tough place to make a living, but Jesse James knew a little show business couldn't hurt.

On January 31, 1874, the James gang robbed the St. Louis & Texas express train as it was passing through Gads Hill, Missouri. One gang member handed the conductor an envelope containing a brazen press release signed Ira A. Merrill. It read:

> THE MOST DARING TRAIN
> ROBBERY ON RECORD!
>
> The southbound train of the Iron Mountain Railroad was stopped here this evening by five [there were ten] heavily armed men and robbed of ——— dollars. The robbers arrived at the station a few

Jesse James *(Left)* and his public relations staff

minutes before the arrival of the train and arrested the agent and put him under guard and then threw the train on the switch. The robbers were all large men, all being slightly under six feet. After robbing the train they started in a southerly direction. They were all mounted on handsome horses.

P.S. There is a hell of an excitement in this part of the country.

The newspapers ran the press release the next day. Naturally, the James gang did not head "southerly"—it went westerly.

HO CHI MINH, *LE CHEF*

Ho Chi Minh, leader of the Vietnamese Communists from 1945 to his death in 1969, once worked for Escoffier, "the king of chefs and the chef of kings."

His path to Escoffier's kitchen at the luxurious Carlton Hotel in London began in trade school in Saigon, where Ho trained to be a sailor. He later landed a job as a kitchen boy on the ship *Latouche-Tréville* and traveled the seas, ending up in London in 1914. After working as a snow-shoveler, he found a job as a dishwasher at the Carlton. When master chef Escoffier asked Ho why he refused to throw away leftover food, he replied that it should be given to the poor. In response, Escoffier promoted him to assistant pastry cook and offered to teach him to be a chef.

But Ho Chi Minh was more interested in political reform than in cooking delicacies for the rich. Still, he never forgot the taste of great food and enjoyed a *haute cuisine* meal to the end of his days.

THE PERFECT HOSTAGE

John II of France was a washout as a king—greedy, vindictive, and inept—but as a political hostage, he was beyond compare. Captured by the English at the battle of Poitiers (1356), he was later released to raise his own ransom. Unable to produce the cash, he voluntarily returned to England to resume his captivity.

John's lot as a prisoner was hardly austere. His "jail" was London's Savoy Palace, and he enjoyed fine food, hunting, and horseback outings, and a busy social schedule. France meanwhile languished in economic and political chaos.

By 1360, France and England had agreed on a ransom of 3 million gold crowns. Incredibly, John was paroled, while three of his sons were retained in his place. Back in France, he imposed burdensome taxes and minted a new gold coin bearing his likeness. Still, he couldn't raise the required capital. When one of his sons escaped from custody, John returned to England to replace him and to honor his commitment. He died there—a hostage—in 1364.

THE BLACK SWALLOW

One of the greatest American fighter pilots of World War I never flew for the United States. All of his medals and military decorations were bestowed by the French.

Eugene Jacques Bullard, the world's first black combat pilot, was born in 1894 in Columbia, Georgia, the grandson of a slave. His childhood dream was to live in France, because he'd been told that bigotry was unknown there. So Bullard sailed to Europe as a stowaway, and in 1914 he enlisted in the French Foreign Legion. After recovering from serious wounds received at Verdun, Bullard got himself transferred to the French Flying Corps, where he earned the nickname "Black Swallow of Death."

When the United States entered the war in 1917, it was announced that all American pilots then serving France would be accepted in our air corps and commissioned as officers. Bullard was among the applicants, but his application was ignored. The United States, in fact, did not commission a black man as a flying officer until 1943.

Bullard remained in the French Flying Corps. In one dogfight, his plane was riddled with bullet holes, forcing him to land in enemy territory. Ten days and eighteen flights later, the hero who had been awarded the croix de guerre for his trench fighting at Verdun was startled to find himself permanently grounded—on charges of insubordination. Bigotry, he discovered, was *not* unknown in France. He served the rest of the war in the French infantry.

After the Armistice, Bullard worked in Paris as a bandleader, then married a French countess and ran his own nightclubs and an athletic

Eugene Jacques Bullard

club. During World War II, he joined the French underground. After being wounded at Le Blanc, he returned to the United States and worked at a succession of menial jobs. He lived his last years in a cluttered Harlem apartment, where he died in 1961. He was buried in the French War Veterans Cemetery in Flushing, New York.

THE PHANTOM FIRST LADY

For the first two years of Franklin Pierce's term as fourteenth president, his wife Jane never once appeared in public. She remained hidden in her bedroom and attended no social functions, not even the inaugural ball. Newspapers called her "the shadow in the White House."

Her peculiar behavior stemmed from a recent and tragic incident. On January 6, 1853—two months before he was to be sworn in—Pierce, Jane, and eleven-year-old Benny, their sole surviving child, were in a rail-

49

way accident. Benny was the only fatality—the back of his head was sliced off. According to a cousin's letter, Jane "saw that dreadful sight for one moment, but Mr. Pierce threw a shawl over the precious little form and drew her away . . ."

Jane's grief was intensified by feelings of guilt for neglecting Benny when he was alive. Secluded in her White House bedroom, the frail but pretty woman wrote pathetic notes in pencil to her dear son, asking forgiveness for not showing her love. She had another reason for hiding herself away. Her husband, she believed, had betrayed her by actively campaigning for president once he was nominated as a dark-horse candidate. Pierce, a handsome recovered alcoholic ("hero of many a well-fought bottle"), had promised he would stay out of politics. Jane, quiet and extremely religious, abhorred political life.

When Jane finally reappeared in public at a New Year's Day reception in 1855, she was hardly a cheerful sight. "Her woebegone face banished all animation in others," said a contemporary. For the rest of her life, she dressed in mourning clothes.

THE LIBELED PIRATE

Sir Henry Morgan, the most famous of the Caribbean buccaneers, was so incensed when called a pirate that he sued for libel—and won.

Morgan, a Welshman, came to the West Indies in 1655 as an ensign in the English army. Soon afterward, he took command of a privateer vessel. With the unofficial approval of England's anti-Spanish government, he and his shipmates killed, burned, raped, and looted their way through Spanish cities in Cuba, Panama, and Venezuela. In gratitude, King Charles II knighted Morgan and appointed him deputy-governor of Jamaica in 1674.

Morgan's reputation as a bloodthirsty pirate peaked in 1684 when *The Buccaneers of America* was printed simultaneously by two publishers in England. Written by John Esquemeling, one of his former crew members, the book gave a colorful account of Morgan's brutality. Furious, Morgan sued the publishers for libel and demanded the exorbitant sum of £10,000 from each in damages. He categorically refuted the atrocities described by Esquemeling, denied that he was a pirate, and insisted that he had acted for his government. He was successful in his defense; both publishers agreed to pay him £200 and to print apologies in future editions.

THE PUSSYCAT PIRATE

Bartholomew Roberts (1682–1722) was one of history's boldest and most successful pirates—and also one of the most humane. As far as his crew was concerned, he was a pussycat.

Roberts first went to sea legitimately—as a merchant seaman. In 1720, his ship, the *Princess*, was attacked by pirates, under the command of Howel Davis, and Roberts was pressed into service. He hated pirating at first, but quickly grew to like it, and when Davis died, Roberts succeeded him in command.

In two years, Roberts plundered more than four hundred ships, and he was feared by all seafarers. Although he spared no enemy, he treated his own men with the fatherliness of a Boy Scout troop leader. Bedtime aboard ship was eight o'clock, and gambling, fighting, and belowdecks drinking—he himself imbibed only tea—were strictly forbidden. Once Roberts urged a captured clergyman to join his crew as their chaplain, promising that his duties would be light. When the cleric turned him down, Roberts released him unharmed.

Roberts was as well known for his personal fastidiousness as for his decency. Even in battle, he was always impeccably dressed, down to his starched shirt and red damask breeches and waistcoat. According to his wishes, he was buried at sea dressed to the nines after

Captain Bartholomew Roberts

he was fatally wounded in an engagement with a British naval vessel in 1722.

MAKING AMERICA BRITISH AGAIN

Rhodes Scholarships, awarded annually for study at Oxford University, grew out of a British imperialist's insane plan for making the United States a British colony.

After amassing a huge fortune through his control of South Africa's Kimberley diamond mines, Cecil Rhodes (1853–1902) became an influential statesman and a major force in the colonization of Africa. But Rhodes, a white supremacist, looked beyond the Dark Continent in his expansionist dreams. In a series of seven wills written between 1877 and 1899, he directed that his estate be used toward bringing the entire world under British rule. In particular, he felt that the very idea of American independence was a mistake, to be corrected by "the ultimate recovery of the United States of America as an integral part of the British Empire."

In his early wills, Rhodes proposed to endow a "secret society" to carry out these ends. Later, he dropped the idea in favor of special scholarships at Oxford for male university students from British colonies and the United States, and even for students from Germany who spoke English, who would work to unite all English-speaking peoples within the empire. Fortunately, since Rhodes's death in 1902, the trustees of his estate have ignored his crackbrained notions and awarded the scholarships bearing his name solely on the basis of academic achievement and professional promise. In 1975, even the all-male restriction was dropped. Such well-known Americans as U.S. Supreme Court Justice Byron White and singer/actor Kris Kristofferson have won Rhodes Scholarships to Oxford.

FATHER OF MODERN EMBALMING?

Thomas H. Holmes said he was the father of modern embalming, yet he refused to be embalmed.

Born in New York City in 1817, young Holmes first dabbled in embalming while in medical school—from which he was expelled for swiping a cadaver and carelessly leaving it on a professor's desk. Holmes later moved to Brooklyn, where he practiced medicine (without a license) and established himself as one of the nation's first professional embalmers. As a sideline, he developed what he touted as the first effective embalming fluid. It may well have been, but Holmes never applied for a patent, and his right to the title "father of modern embalming" remains in question.

During the Civil War, Holmes won a government contract to embalm the bodies of dead Union soldiers. He restricted his clientele to officers, figuring their families would be wealthy enough to afford his $100 fee. By war's end, Holmes had collected on 4,028 embalmings.

Back in Brooklyn after the war, Holmes continued plying his craft and refining his embalming formula. Specimens of his work filled his home—bodies in hall closets and under the basement floor, preserved heads displayed on living room tables. In the window of his pharmacy, bottles of his Innominata embalming fluid ($3 a gallon) and his homemade "Great Root Beer" were ghoulishly stacked side by side.

In his declining years, Holmes got into several scrapes with others who claimed leadership of the new profession. He gave instructions that upon his own death, which came in 1900, he *not* be embalmed. He trusted no embalmer's work but his own.

THE KING WHO DIED IN AMERICA

King Peter II of Yugoslavia is the only European monarch to be buried in the United States.

Technically, Peter became king in 1934 when his father, Alexander I, was assassinated in Marseilles. Since he was only eleven years old, his father's cousin, Prince Paul, ruled Yugoslavia as regent. However, when Paul signed an agreement with Hitler and Mussolini in March 1941, he was overthrown and young Peter was crowned king. Ten days later, the Nazis invaded Yugoslavia, and Peter fled to Great Britain. He set up a government in exile and joined the Royal Air Force. When the British government backed Tito as leader of postwar Yugoslavia, Peter became a king without a country.

Living most of his life in Paris, Monte Carlo, and the United States,

Peter worked in public relations in New York before taking a job with a savings and loan association in California.

Peter died in Denver, Colorado, on November 4, 1970, and was laid to rest at the Serbian Church monastery in Libertyville, Illinois.

THE JINX

Robert Todd Lincoln, eldest son of Abraham Lincoln, earned the tragic distinction of being nearby when three different U.S. presidents were shot to death by assassins. After the third murder, he carefully avoided the next chief executive, saying: ". . . there is a certain fatality about presidential functions when I am present."

Away at Harvard during his father's White House years, Robert spent the last few months of the war as a captain on General Grant's staff. After witnessing Confederate General Lee's surrender at Appomattox, Robert arrived in Washington for a visit on April 14, 1865—the

Robert Todd Lincoln

last full day of his father's life. That night Lincoln was shot while watching a play. Robert rushed to his side, staying until the president died the next morning.

After the funeral, Robert went with his mother to live in Chicago. He studied law and prospered as an attorney. Always an introverted man, Robert resented any intrusions on his privacy. Those who looked for resemblances between father and son found few, and many observed that he was proud and oversensitive, like his mother. But the Lincoln name kept Robert in the political spotlight, even though he shied away from the glare. To him, politics meant sacrifice, not glory. And so when President James Garfield named him secretary of war in 1881, he accepted it as a duty. One hot July morning later that year, Robert arrived at the train depot in Washington just in time to see the president gunned down. Looking gray and weak, Garfield took Robert's hand and seemed to revive, but within three months he was dead.

By 1897 Robert had become a millionaire as president of the Pullman Company. The son of the Great Emancipator was now a rich industrialist.

In September 1901 he took his family to Buffalo, New York—they were to meet President William McKinley. No sooner had the Lincolns arrived than they heard the news: the president had just been shot. Robert was able to see McKinley once before he died a week later.

Four U.S. presidents have been assassinated while in office, and Robert Todd Lincoln was close to three of them at the hour of their death. The fourth—John F. Kennedy, who was nine years old when Robert died in 1926—now lies buried in Arlington National Cemetery, only 100 yards from Robert Todd Lincoln's own grave.

THE CAPTAIN OF KÖPENICK

In Prussia in 1906, an out-of-work cobbler pulled off the zaniest military impersonation and hoax ever.

A penniless ex-convict who'd spent years in prison for various petty offenses, Wilhelm Voigt could find no employer willing to hire him. In frustration, the old man donned a Prussian officer's uniform he'd bought at a secondhand store. Then he installed himself as commander of a military detachment.

Though only semiliterate, Voigt was blessed with a bold streak and a talent for mimicking the speech and mannerisms of Prussian officers.

With all the aplomb of a career man, he ordered his troops aboard a bus bound for Köpenick, a suburb of Berlin. Once there, he marched the men to the town hall and placed several officials, including the mayor, under armed guard while he pocketed 4,000 marks from the public coffers. No one seemed to notice the shabbiness of his uniform or his upside-down cap badge.

The ruse did not last. Ten days later, police arrested Voigt in his garret. He was sentenced to four years in jail.

By then, Voigt's escapade had made him an international hero, and newsmen and cartoonists called him "the Captain of Köpenick." Kaiser Wilhelm was also amused, and he issued a pardon. Voigt retired to Luxembourg on a generous pension from a wealthy Berlin dowager who had been impressed by his unmitigated chutzpah.

In 1928, playwright Carl Zuckmayer presented a three-act dramatization of the story, which he likened to a "modern fairy tale." His play, *Der Hauptmann von Köpenick*, later inspired a German film of the same title in 1931.

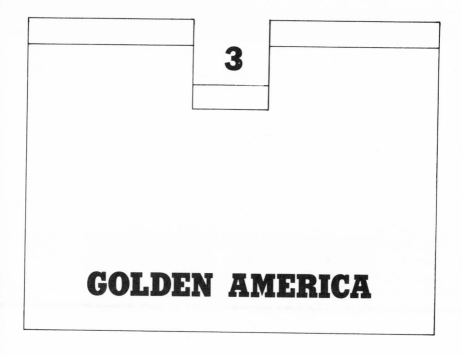

3

GOLDEN AMERICA

A GOOD-WEATHER TOUR OF THE U.S.

What city has the most pleasant climate in the United States?

The National Oceanic and Atmospheric Administration released a study of how much energy is required each day of the year to raise or lower the temperature of homes in various U.S. cities to a basic, optimum level of 65 degrees F. Using these figures, we learned that San Diego, California, has the mildest climate in the country, while Barrow, Alaska, has the harshest.

If you wanted to spend a year following the best weather around the United States, you would start out, not surprisingly, by moving to Miami for the month of January. February would find you in Hilo, Hawaii, and March in Yuma, Arizona, which happens to receive more sunshine than any other city in the country.

During the month of April, you would live in Charleston, South Carolina. May is best in San Diego. For June, you could choose between Hartford, Connecticut, and Block Island, Rhode Island. Then you could really unpack your bags, because July, August, and September would all be spent in the same place—Oakland, California. Yes, that's right. Oakland has the most even temperatures during the summer months.

Then it's back to San Diego for October and November, before returning to Florida for the December holiday season, this time in West Palm Beach.

DID BLACKS DISCOVER AMERICA?

A great number of historians now agree that Columbus was not the first explorer to set foot in America. Historians say that the New World was port of call to many ancient mariners—including blacks from western Africa—centuries before the time of Columbus.

Between the years 1000 B.C. and 500 B.C. a new culture sprang up in Central America. The people known as the Olmecs were far more skillful at metallurgy and agriculture than other Indian groups of the area. It is believed that they taught their neighbors a kind of hieroglyphics and the use of the calendar. Could the Olmecs have learned these skills from visitors who came from what Europeans once derisively called the "Dark Continent"? It seems likely. Surviving Olmec artifacts show black people with distinctive African features working and fighting alongside Indian allies.

When Columbus arrived in the New World, he heard stories of these black men, and he collected golden spearheads identical in workmanship to those used by West Africans. The Indians referred to the spearheads as *guanin,* which means gold in several African languages.

Was it possible for western or northern Africans, who were known as excellent mariners, to make the trip to the New World? The distance from the West African coast to the Caribbean area is only about half the distance Columbus had to traverse from Spain.

Furthermore, a north equatorial current could have taken sailors from Africa to the New World in a relatively short trip, estimated at thirty days under sail—a voyage Columbus and his crew would have envied.

FLAGGING DOWN BETSY ROSS

Betsy Ross did not sew the first American flag, nor did she live in the historic Flag House in Philadelphia. That story is a myth.

This historic scene probably never happened

In 1870, Betsy's grandson, William Canby—claiming to have heard the whole story from his grandmother—delivered a talk to the Historical Society of Pennsylvania. He described how, in 1776, George Washington, Robert Morris, and George Ross—members of the congressional flag committee—visited Betsy's shop in Philadelphia and asked her to make the first Stars and Stripes. She redesigned their rough sketch to include a symmetrical arrangement of five-pointed stars. And thus, said Canby, the first American flag was made by a simple seamstress. All untrue.

By 1885, Betsy Ross was a textbook heroine, and the legend has persisted since then. In fact, however, no record exists of a 1776 flag committee or of any Betsy Ross connection with the first U.S. flag. It was not until August 1777 that the Second Continental Congress set the design of the Stars and Stripes and passed a resolution making it our official flag. The first American flags, moreover, often had stars with six or eight points. And no one knows who made them.

SICILY: THE FORTY-NINTH STATE?

If a group of Sicilian nationalists had succeeded in their efforts, Sicily—not Alaska—would have become our forty-ninth state.

Following World War II, a separatist party in Sicily drew support from wealthy landowners and mafiosi, who saw secession as a means of beating out the Communists for control of that southern Italian island. The separatists also attracted many young idealists who resented Rome's shabby treatment of Sicily. They all wanted Sicily to be part of the United States.

Among those drafted into the movement was the bandit Salvatore Giuliano. A common gangster to some and a folk hero to others, Giuliano wrote to President Harry S Truman in 1947, asking his help in liberating Sicily and making it "the forty-ninth American star." Annexation to the United States, said Giuliano, would protect Sicily from Soviet expansionism in the Mediterranean, as well as rescue the island from the poor-sister status it suffered at the hands of Italy. With the letter to Truman, Giuliano enclosed a copy of a handbill that had been widely circulated throughout Sicily. It featured a drawing of Giuliano severing a chain that linked Sicily to Italy while another man stood astride North America and chained Sicily to the United States.

The separatist cause was ultimately done in by squabbles among its leaders, as well as by a 1946 law that granted a good deal of political autonomy to Sicily. By the early 1950s, the island's dream of American statehood was a thing of the past.

U.S. CITY BOMBED DURING
A RACE RIOT

In 1921, Tulsa, Oklahoma, became the first U.S. city to be subjected to aerial bombing during a race riot. Over seventy-five people, mostly blacks, were killed during all the fighting. Two square miles of property, including more than 1,100 homes, were destroyed.

Before the riot, Tulsa blacks were so highly successful that the black business district of the segregated city was known as "The Negro's Wall Street." Envious white hatred of the black population of 10,000—in a city of 100,000—was running high.

Then on May 30, 1921, a white female elevator operator accused a nineteen-year-old black, Dick Rowland, who worked at a shoeshine stand, of attacking her. Though Rowland denied the charge, he was jailed. The next day, the *Tulsa Tribune* carried a sensational account of the incident, and less than an hour after it hit the stands, a white lynch mob gathered at the jail. Armed blacks, seeking to protect Rowland, also showed up. Someone shot a gun. The riot was on.

Whites invaded the black part of town, burning, looting, and killing. Among the dozens of casualties were a brilliant black surgeon and an elderly couple on their way home from church. The $85,000 Mount Zion Church was destroyed. Overhead, police fired guns and bombed the area by dropping dynamite from private planes which they had commandeered. Eventually, the National Guard was called in and martial law declared.

The police arrested over 4,000 blacks and interned them in three camps. All blacks were forced to carry green identification cards. And when the city was zoned for a new railroad station, the tracks were routed through the black business district, thus destroying it.

PATRICK HENRY'S DARING PROPOSAL

In 1784, Patrick Henry proposed a daring solution to the problem of hostility between Indians and whites—government-sponsored intermarriage. Only he, known for the famous statement, "Give me liberty or give me death," could have got away with it.

The super-orator eloquently introduced the bill in the Virginia Assembly. It stipulated that when free white male or female Virginians married Indians, the couples would receive £10 immediately and £5 more at the birth of each child. They would also be given tax breaks and free education for their male children up to age twenty-one.

Due to Henry's persuasiveness, the bill passed its first and second readings. But by the time the third reading came up, Henry had been elected governor. Without his support at the assembly, the bill failed its final test.

In a letter written that December to James Monroe, John Marshall, later chief justice of the United States, said: "We have rejected some [bills] which in my conception would have been advantageous to this country. Among these I rank the bill for encouraging intermarriages with the Indians. Our prejudices, however, oppose themselves to our interests, and operate too powerfully for them."

GEORGE WASHINGTON'S FIRST ELECTION

The first election George Washington won was *not* for president of a new United States. It was for membership in the Virginia House of Burgesses under British colonial rule—and he won by getting many of the voters drunk.

The House of Burgesses, the first elective assembly Great Britain established in its overseas possessions, was controlled by the governor's veto power. Only freeholders—those owning real estate—were allowed to vote.

Washington first decided to run for burgess in 1755. He was unpopular because, as commander in chief of Virginia forces protecting the frontier, he had seen fit to bolster his troops by seizing horses and wagons from the people. He also had conducted a campaign against the saloons where his soldiers became "unfit for service." But after losing two elections (in 1755 and 1757), Washington developed more political savvy and a higher tolerance for alcohol. Though it was illegal, he gave way to the custom of offering liquid "ticklers" to voters. In 1758, he arranged to have his campaign manager provide the freeholders of Frederick County with 160 gallons of various liquors. He received 310 votes ("a general applause and huzzahing for Colonel Washington"), beating out three opponents. Thanking his manager, Washington wrote, "My only fear is that you spent with too sparing a hand." Washington was just twenty-six years old.

In 1761, Washington was reelected by the Frederick County voters. Thereafter, from 1765 to 1774, he represented the voters of Fairfax as one of their two burgesses. Each time he ran, he entertained his constituency—often with a supper and ball, complete with fiddler.

U.S. INDEPENDENCE FIRST ANNOUNCED IN
GERMAN

Although drafted and signed by English-speaking colonists, the adoption of the Declaration of Independence was first reported in German.

Philadelphia publisher Henry Miller scooped the English-language newspapers by reporting the approval on Friday, July 5, 1776—the day after it happened. Miller simply was lucky enough to run the only newspaper in town with a Friday edition. His *Der Wöchentliche Philadel-*

phische Staatsbote carried a brief notice about the Declaration that Friday and ran a complete German translation of the document the following Tuesday (English-language readers first saw the complete Declaration on Monday, July 8).

The *Staatsbote* was outspokenly anti-British, and the account of the adoption had a headline set in an especially bold typeface. Needless to say, the British took a dim view of Miller's politics and later confiscated his press and type. He got them back, but the *Staatsbote* ceased publication in 1779, when Miller retired.

OFFBEAT MUSEUMS

If you're vacationing in Las Vegas, Nevada, Elm Creek, Nebraska, or Washington, D.C., this year and you run out of things to do, here are three unusual museums that might be worth a visit.

The Liberace Museum in Las Vegas houses some of the prized pos-

Eleanor Valentine of
The Red Light Museum

sessions of the flashy pianist known as "Mr. Showmanship." Visitors sign the register at a piano-shaped reception desk and pay a small fee that goes toward performing-arts scholarships. On display are a fleet of classic, customized cars; togs from Liberace's wardrobe, including a $60,000 replica of George V's coronation robe; and, of course, a collection of pianos, the highlight of which is a gem-encrusted miniature presented to Liberace by the Queen of England.

If you are one of the vanishing breed still dedicated to the American automobile, Mont Hollertz Chevyland U.S.A. in Elm Creek, Nebraska, will appeal to you. Some eighty Chevrolets are exhibited, tracing the evolution of the car. All are in running condition and have been meticulously restored. Among the models on view are: a 1914 Royal Mail Roadster (one of ten known to exist), a 1927 Roadster, a 1955 Nomad, and samples of every Corvette ever made.

Should your taste run to fast women instead of fast cars, the Red Light Museum in Washington, D.C., supplies a documentation of the world's oldest profession. In the museum's red-draped rooms, which are situated over a striptease bar, you'll see a Victorian-era erotic slide show; daguerreotypes, lithographs, and photographs of prostitutes; a nineteenth-century sex manual; and erotic French postcards from the mid-1800s.

THE SMALLEST TOWN

Missouri once boasted the smallest town in the world that human beings could walk through. This miniature community, every building one-twelfth the size of a normal building, was known as Tiny Town. Founded in 1925, it occupied nearly six acres of a public park in Springfield, Missouri. And it was designed, built, and run by students.

Tiny Town began as a manual training project for the public school children of Springfield. For two months, during school hours and on their own time, the youths meticulously laid out streets and constructed more than 400 Tom Thumb buildings, including a courthouse, schools, gas stations, a barbershop, and a YMCA. The homes were of many different architectural styles. They even ran off a small-scale newspaper, the *Tiny Town Times*, and peddled it for two cents a copy.

The students adopted the city manager form of government and conducted elections among themselves. Gordon Cummings, sixteen, was elected city manager; Hazel Wilhoit, a fourteen-year-old orphan, mayor.

These two mini-municipal officials junketed to Washington and called on President Calvin Coolidge. Eighteen other children, as duly elected town commissioners, enacted ordinances, which were strictly enforced by the juvenile police department.

Tiny Town was a popular tourist attraction during its public exhibition, May 15–June 13, 1925. Today, it no longer exists.

NIAGARA FALLS MOVING TO LAKE ERIE?

Majestic Niagara Falls, once a mecca for honeymooners and daredevil tightrope walkers, still hosts 5 million tourists annually—but it may not be around for our descendants to enjoy, at least not in its present form.

As millions of gallons of water rush over the falls every minute, the underlying rock is being worn away, causing the falls to recede at the rate of one to two feet per year. Since their formation some 12,000 years ago, the falls already have withdrawn seven miles upstream. At the present rate, they would meet up with Lake Erie about twenty miles from their present site within the next 35,000 years or so.

Some geologists believe that the falls will shrink as they recede, becoming a small waterfall near the mouth of Lake Erie. Events, natural or man-made, could slow the process. In fact, before the Niagara River was used to generate hydroelectric power the rate of recession was two or three times what it is today. Diverting more water from the falls to meet our energy needs would reduce the rate even further.

WHEN DRUMS WERE OUTLAWED

In parts of the antebellum South, black slaves were barred from banging drums—slowly or otherwise.

"Whatsoever master or overseer shall permit his slaves . . . to beat drums, blow horns or other loud instruments," a 1755 Georgia colonial law decreed, "shall forfeit 30 shillings sterling for every such offense." There were similar statutes elsewhere in the South.

Of course, the prohibition had nothing to do with noise pollution. In the United States as in their native Africa, blacks beat out long-distance messages to one another on drums, and often these messages were calls to revolt. Indeed, state militia units were sometimes able to quash rebellions in the making after receiving advance warning from the telltale drum calls.

To be sure, African drum music was an effective means of long-distance communication. For one thing, it was far more complex in its rhythms and structures than Western music and thus difficult for whites to understand. For another, drums could approximate the tones and pitch of human speech, so slaves actually were able to "talk" to each other and thus convey intricate messages—not just codelike signals.

The drum statutes were not easy to enforce, nor did they keep blacks from communicating musically in other ways—such as clapping or stamping their feet. Along with most slave laws, the drum statutes were repealed during the Reconstruction era.

THE CORSET THAT SAVED LINNVILLE

The residents of Linnville, Texas, were saved from an Indian massacre because of a whalebone corset. In August 1840, a band of Comanches raided the customs office outside the tiny port town on Lavaca Bay. After killing and scalping the customs officer, Major Watts, they prepared to rape his wife. Her outer clothes came off easily enough—but not her sturdy corset. The Indians struggled mightily to undo it but finally gave up and took the half-dressed woman prisoner.

The delay in the assault gave the townsfolk time to pile into their boats and escape to the far side of the bay. When the Indians finally rode into Linnville, it was deserted. They looted and burned the town, then tied Mrs. Watts to a tree, shot an arrow into her breast, and left her to die.

She didn't. The same corset that had saved her townspeople, that had saved her virtue, also had blunted the arrow and saved her life. When the Texas militia found Mrs. Watts, she had only a bad sunburn and a minor wound.

THE LAZIEST PRESIDENT

Calvin Coolidge's most-quoted dictum was, "The chief business of America is business," but his most urgent priority was apparently sleep. Throughout his term of office (1923–29), the thirtieth president averaged ten hours of sleep a day, and ten hours of loafing but barely four hours of work. Despite his Vermont Congregationalist roots, many historians consider him the laziest chief executive in the nation's history—a president with a unique "genius for inactivity."

Rising around six o'clock, Coolidge rarely settled down to work before 9:00 A.M. He broke for lunch and a two-hour nap at 12:30, then resumed the duties of state in the late afternoon. Seldom did he work past six or retire after ten. Groucho Marx spotted him at a theater one evening and quipped, "Isn't it past your bedtime, Calvin?"

Coolidge was also the most vacation-minded president. Each summer he would knock off for two to three months and hole up in one of a number of favorite havens—the Black Hills of South Dakota, White Pine Camp, New York, Swampscott, Massachusetts. These were isolated places, for the most part, not easily reached by road or well served by telephones. Scholar Dr. Mortimer Adler told us recently that Coolidge once went to New England for a vacation and would not allow a tele-

Calvin Coolidge fishes during one of the many escapes from his office

phone to be installed where he was staying. He ran the country without a telephone for three months.

STATEHOOD AT LAST FOR BUCKEYES

Ohio did not officially become a state until 1953.

In February 1803, the U.S. Congress approved Ohio's official boundaries. Its first delegation of senators and representatives was seated in Washington, D.C., soon thereafter. But somehow Congress never got around to voting on a formal resolution to admit Ohio into the Union, and it remained part of the Northwest Territory.

Yet, for 150 years—when they were not legally allowed to do so—Ohio's congressmen voted on such momentous measures as the declarations of war that plunged the United States into the War of 1812, the Mexican War, the Civil War, the Spanish-American War, and World Wars I and II, as well as the amendments to the U.S. Constitution that abolished slavery, instituted and repealed Prohibition, and granted women's suffrage.

In 1953, while Ohioans proudly celebrated what they rightly felt was the 150th anniversary of Buckeye statehood, a bill was introduced in Congress by Ohio Rep. George H. Bender to rectify the situation. "The State Constitutional Convention presented the Constitution of Ohio to Congress on February 19, 1803," Bender said, "and Congress chose to ignore it."

The resolution passed both houses and was signed into law by President Eisenhower on August 7, 1953. It recognized Ohio as the nation's seventeenth state—a century and a half behind schedule.

THE LOST STATE OF FRANKLIN

The state named Franklin, once a part of the United States, no longer exists, and most Americans have never heard of it. But, for four years, it was a reality.

In 1784, to satisfy a debt, North Carolina ceded a huge section of its Over-Mountain Territory to the United States. It took thirty days for news of the cession to reach the remote wilderness territory that North Carolina had so high-handedly given away. Unhappy about it, the frontier settlers called a convention in the county seat of Jonesboro and established themselves as a state, named for Ben Franklin.

North Carolina repealed the cession in November 1784, but the Franklanders, as they called themselves, went on with their plans for statehood. Their first governor was John Sevier, a dashing frontiersman and Indian fighter. Although Congress would not accept a Franklander representative and North Carolina Gov. Josiah Martin declared the new state in revolt, Sevier set up the state's legal and military machinery in his log-cabin capitol building, and made treaties with the Cherokees. The state's population was a paltry 25,000. Salaries usually were paid in linen, furs, liquor, or tobacco.

Since North Carolina had never given up its claim to the region, taxation was double for residents, and the law had to operate through two court systems. Indian troubles, feuding, and allegations that Sevier was involved in shady deals in real estate and with the Spanish exacerbated the problems of keeping Franklin afloat. In 1788, Franklin lost its fragile hold on statehood. Today, it is part of Tennessee.

STATEHOOD FOR AMERICAN INDIANS

During the Civil War, American Indians were so important to the Confederate cause that they were promised their own state if the South won.

In 1861, just after war broke out, an Arkansas lawyer named Albert Pike was dispatched to the Indian Territory to woo the Five Civilized Tribes—the Cherokees, Choctaws, Chickasaws, Creeks, and Seminoles—over to the Confederate side. Only the Cherokees balked at first, and even they came round after the other four tribes aligned themselves with the South. The alliance made sense since many Indians were slaveholders and thus had a vested interest in the Southern cause. Later in the war, the North also recruited Indians—including Senecas, Delawares, and Osages—as well as some pro-Union Cherokees and Creeks. But it was the South that held out the most tempting inducements, including guaranteed representation in the Confederate Congress and an all-Indian state—to be established more or less on what is now present-day Oklahoma.

In all, some 5,500 Indians fought on the side of the South, and 4,000 fought for the North. Most served with valor. Indeed, the last Confederate commander to surrender was a Cherokee chief, Brig. Gen. Stand Watie. It wasn't until June 23, 1865—more than two months after Robert E. Lee surrendered to Ulysses S. Grant at Appomattox—that he threw in the towel.

U.S. INDIANS IN HIGH PLACES

Virtually all of New York City's skyline has been built by American Indians. Mohawks, to be precise.

Native to New York State, Mohawks are famed for their catlike agility, tightrope walker's balance, and indifference to heights. For nearly a century, these strengths have earned thousands of Mohawks high-level positions as riveters on skyscraper projects in New York and other North American cities.

Evidently, the Mohawks' low anxiety level at high altitudes is inborn. As early as 1714, an English traveler wrote of it. But it wasn't until 1886 that the Mohawks made their high-steel debut, in the construction of a bridge spanning Canada's St. Lawrence River.

Offered jobs by the Dominion Bridge Company in exchange for permission to build on their land, Mohawks from the Caughnawaga reservation astounded their employers by scampering along the structure. Soon there were Mohawk riveting crews working on bridges and buildings throughout the region.

But it was in New York City, during the Manhattan building boom of the 1920s and 1930s, that they reached the height of their fame. Commuting by subway from their small settlement in nearby Brooklyn, Mohawks played a major role in the construction of the Empire State Building, Rockefeller Center, and other landmarks. Today, despite the ups and downs of the economy, Mohawks entering the construction trade waste little time rising straight to the top.

WHAT HAPPENED TO MAUCH CHUNK, PENNSYLVANIA?

In 1954, the citizens of Mauch Chunk (Indian for Bear Mountain) and East Mauch Chunk voted to rename their neck of the woods Jim Thorpe, after the invincible Indian star of track, field, football, and baseball, who four years earlier had been elected the greatest male athlete of the twentieth century by the Associated Press. To change the town's name, the residents were offered fame and fortune: a sporting goods manufacturing plant, a Professional Football Hall of Fame, a research hospital. Said the late Jack Huber, a borough councilman: "All we saw were dollar signs, but all we got was a dead Indian." Huber was referring to Thorpe's remains, donated by his widow, Patricia Thorpe, in exchange for a promise to build a mausoleum in his honor.

Most of the residents' dreams of commercial glory did not come true, and some frustrated locals once tried to change their city's name *back* to Mauch Chunk. The attempt failed.

Eventually a mausoleum in honor of Thorpe was built. Its inscrip-

tion reads: SIR, YOU ARE THE GREATEST ATHLETE IN THE WORLD. KING GUSTAVE, STOCKHOLM, SWEDEN, 1912 OLYMPICS.

Today, the sign at the city limits reads WELCOME TO JIM THORPE, and, in smaller letters, FORMERLY MAUCH CHUNK. The town's citizens are probably not the only ones to have to bear endless tourists' questions about their locale's unusual name. Here are a few of America's many personalized towns: Casanova, Virginia; Princess Anne, Maryland; Geronimo, Oklahoma; Tecumseh, Kansas, Michigan, Nebraska, and Oklahoma; Pocahontas, Virginia; Jenny Lind, California; Gene Autry, Oklahoma; and George, Washington.

THE CONTROVERSIAL PILGRIM

More than 360 years after the landing at Plymouth Rock, there is a controversy raging over the identity of one of the Pilgrims.

Among those early settlers in what is now Massachusetts may have been a black man. His name was Abraham Pearce, and he signed on in 1623 to go to the new Plymouth Colony as an indentured servant. When his passage was paid off, he became a full-fledged freeholder, voter, and landowner. The only possible reference to his color— "blackamoor"—appears below his name on a 1643 roster of men available for the Plymouth militia.

The controversy flared up in June 1981, when a black actor was cast as Pearce at Plimouth Plantation, where the settlement has been recreated for tourists. The actor left after two months, and the plantation declared that more research was needed to determine if Pearce had, indeed, been black.

In December, Plimouth Plantation fired its director of programs, Robert Marten, who had worked there for seventeen years. Marten was in favor of retaining the black actor and had said publicly that the departure of the actor was prompted by objections from white descendants of Pearce and other Pilgrims. After his firing, Marten commented, "I believe I have the right to say what I said" and urged that the Pearce matter "be brought into open debate and not sat upon or controlled by any institution."

AN ALL-BLACK BROOKLYN

Population shifts have resulted in many mostly black towns in the United States. But Brooklyn, Illinois, located near St. Louis, Missouri, was created all-black from the start and remains that way to this day.

Founded by runaway slaves in 1858, Brooklyn—also known as Lovejoy after the martyred abolitionist editor Elijah Lovejoy—was incorporated as a town in 1873 and grew steadily thereafter. As its early leaders saw it, the key to prosperity and happiness was steering clear of whites. Apparently they were on to something: by the turn of the century, black Brooklyn boasted a thriving business district, safe streets, and an efficient and honest municipal government. To be sure, there were a handful of whites among the general population of 1,900, and while they were permitted to vote, they rarely ran for public office. Nor were there any white doctors or police officers. The school system was segregated at the insistence of the black majority, and operated under the separate-but-equal principle.

These days, Brooklyn is no longer a showcase of middle-class stability. The population is 2,000, the housing is substandard, and the residents are poor. But Brooklyn remains all-black and largely immune to the racial tensions that often plague conventional towns.

THE PALISADE MASSACRES

Easterners bound for the Wild West on the Central Pacific Railroad in the 1870s didn't mind the empty stretches of desert scenery, since there was a good chance they might see a real-life shootout once they stopped at the infamous town of Palisade, Nevada. According to historian Gerald B. Higgs in his book *Lost Legends of the Silver State,* big-city newspapers reported horrifying stories of bloodshed in Palisade, and their blazing editorials called it the toughest town west of Chicago.

It all started when passengers alighting from the train nearly got their heads blown off during a street brawl between two gunfighters. As the shots rang out, the passengers screamed and ran for cover. For the next three years, fascinated and appalled travelers continued to witness bank robberies, battles with Indians, and shootouts in Palisade. The press demanded that something be done.

Nothing was done, and the carnage continued. But imagine the faces of those Easterners if they had known that the 290 residents of

Palisade staged all of it. Even the local army troops and Shoshone Indians were in on the joke, and no one gave away the sham for those three years. With just a few gallons of beef blood and a lot of blank rifle cartridges, the citizens put on quite a show. In reality, the town was so peaceful that it never bothered to elect a sheriff.

The song "Massacres at Palisade," written by George Russell, pays fitting tribute to the town. Here's an excerpt:

> *When the train pulled in, the show would begin,*
> *The fightin', the shootin', the robbin', and the dyin'*
> *And the passengers watched from the windows with fear*
> *And the town laughed as the train pulled clear.*
>
> *And everyone took part, it's true,*
> *The cowboys, the Indians, and the cavalry too,*
> *And when the shootin' was done, the battles won,*
> *The town of Palisade just hung up their guns.*

THE FANTASY THAT BECAME CALIFORNIA

California is the only state to be named for a fantastic place existing only in an early novel. That place is the black Amazon kingdom of California, introduced to the world in the sixteenth-century romantic Spanish novel *The Exploits of Esplandián* by Garcí Ordóñez de Montalvo.

In the book, Esplandián, the perfect knight, goes to "an island called California, very near to the Terrestrial Paradise, which was peopled by black women. . . . The island itself is one of the wildest in the world . . . everywhere abounds with gold and precious stones." California's Queen Calafía fights a duel with Esplandián, after which the island turns Christian.

In 1862, Edward Everett Hale, author of *The Man Without a Country*, made the connection and stated that the name California must have been given to the territory by an explorer who knew Montalvo's book, perhaps Spaniard Fortún Jiménez, who visited Baja California in 1533–34 and thought it an island. The name first appeared in print in Juan Cabrillo's journal, written after he reached Alta California in 1542. He used it as though it were already familiar.

SON OF THE LEANING TOWER

How can you see the Leaning Tower of Pisa without leaving the United States? Easy. Go to Niles, Illinois.

Fifty years ago, a Chicago millionaire, industrialist Robert A. Ilg, head of the Ilg Electric Ventilating Company, visited the Italian town of Pisa and fell in love with the Leaning Tower. The original 177-foot marble tower sank seven feet below the ground, became a tilted landmark, and was the site of some of Galileo's greatest experiments. Ilg decided to build a half-scale replica of the Leaning Tower in Niles. The cement replica was 96 feet tall and was designed to lean. Ilg even added imported Italian bells like those used to counterbalance the massive Pisa original. In 1960, he gave his tilted tower to the YMCA and moved to the San Francisco Bay area where he lived until his death. Ilg Tower can be viewed only from the grounds. Although it is structurally sound, it has been closed to the public for several years.

The Leaning Tower of Ilg Park

THE YEAR WITHOUT A SUMMER

In 1816, there was no summer. Across northern Europe and the eastern United States, daytime temperatures rarely reached 50 degrees F. A June 6 blizzard dumped ten inches of snow on parts of New England. And it was all because of a volcano on the other side of the world.

On April 5, 1815, one of history's greatest volcanic eruptions rocked Sumbawa, in what is now Indonesia. The uppermost 4,000 feet of Mount Tambora—about eighty cubic kilometers of matter—exploded, ripping a seven-mile-wide crater in the peak and killing 12,000 people. Another 80,000 people died of starvation when a layer of ash blanketed farmlands. The blast was eighty times stronger than the Mount St. Helens eruption, and was heard on Sumatra, 931 miles away.

A massive cloud of volcanic dust worked its way around the world, and by the following summer lay suspended over the Northern Hemisphere, deflecting the sun's radiation. At night, the mercury often dipped below freezing. On July 4, the high temperature in normally sultry Savannah, Georgia, was 46 degrees F. Frost, snow, sleet, and ice caused crop failures as far west as Illinois, and many people died of wintertime illnesses. It was one summer when the living was hardly easy.

THE RED GHOST OF ARIZONA

In 1883, a huge red monster mounted by a ghostly rider killed a woman in the southeastern corner of the Arizona Territory. The beast left behind cloven footprints and long, red hairs. Nicknamed the Red Ghost, it inspired many scary tales. One rancher, however, identified the creature for what it was: a camel with a man—perhaps a dead man—on its back.

Camels were not uncommon then in the West. Jefferson Davis, who was secretary of war under President Franklin Pierce, persuaded Congress to allocate $30,000 for the purchase of camels to be used in the army's exploration of the Southwest deserts. The U.S. Army First Camel Corps was organized in 1855, and by the following year thirty-three camels had been bought—for about $250 apiece—from markets in the eastern Mediterranean. The army planned to import as many as 1,000 additional camels, but the Civil War erupted, and by 1863 the camel program was officially abandoned. Some of the beasts were sold at auction, but many of them were simply turned loose in the deserts of Texas, Arizona, and California.

Who was the Red Ghost's rider? That the man was dead was verified when five miners came across the camel and shot at it, dislodging the skull from a human skeleton on its back.

The camel attacked several other people, but there were no more reports of the Red Ghost after 1884. In 1893, a rancher named Mizoo Hastings shot and killed a camel in his turnip patch, and it turned out to be the Red Ghost. The camel's body was covered with a network of knotted rawhide strips. It became clear that the skeleton had been tied to the camel's back. Perhaps it was a grisly joke, or perhaps a murderer had bound his victim—alive or dead—to a walking coffin.

FOR SALE: THE LIBERTY BELL

The Liberty Bell was once bartered as scrap metal. Its value was appraised at $400.

The famous bell, which rang in the first public reading of the Declaration of Independence, was installed at the Pennsylvania State House in Philadelphia in 1753. It was stowed away for safekeeping during the Revolutionary War but later resumed its sonorous career, announcing state meetings and summoning local congregations. The bell and the State House fell into disuse around 1800, after the U.S. Congress had moved to Washington, D.C., and the Pennsylvania legislature had moved to Lancaster.

In 1824, the State House, now known as Independence Hall, was spruced up for the visit of Lafayette, the French general who had aided the colonies against the British. The Philadelphia city fathers decided to complete the refurbishing of the building in 1828. They contracted John Wilbank, a bellmaker from Germantown, Pennsylvania, to cast a replacement for the Liberty Bell. He agreed to knock $400 off his bill in exchange for the 2,000-pound relic. When Wilbank went to collect it, however, he decided it wasn't worth the trouble. "Drayage costs more than the bell's worth," he reportedly said. The city sued Wilbank for removal of the bell but backed off when he agreed to donate it to the city as a gift.

Wilbank no doubt was happy to be relieved of the burden, unaware that he had just bartered away what would become the most venerated symbol of American independence.

THE PLOT TO OVERTHROW THE
U.S. GOVERNMENT

Can the U.S. government be overthrown? A group tried in 1934.

Imagine the scenario: an army of 500,000 men, drawn from the ranks of the American Legion, marches to Washington and takes over the White House. The conspirators tell the world that President Franklin D. Roosevelt, because of poor health, needs help. A member of his cabinet takes over. This dictator then herds the unemployed into labor camps. All persons are registered.

It might have happened. It *was* a plot. Who was behind the plot? Why did it fail? Let's backtrack.

In July 1933, Legionnaire Gerald C. MacGuire, a former marine, backed by Grayson M.P. Murphy, a stockbroker and director of Morgan's Guaranty Trust Company, asked Maj. Gen. Smedley D. Butler to make a speech in favor of restoring the gold standard at the upcoming American Legion convention. Butler, a Republican who had campaigned for Roosevelt, refused. He also declined similar requests made by MacGuire and financier Robert S. Clark.

Then the request changed. Butler was asked more than *forty* times to lead an army of legionnaires in a coup. MacGuire said the army would be financed by "private interests" and the $1 annual dues from Legion members. Meanwhile, the American Liberty League—affiliated with antilabor, profascist, and anti-Semitic groups—was formed. In it were Murphy, Clark, and representatives of the Du Pont, Rockefeller, and Mellon interests.

An alarmed Butler finally contacted reporter Paul Comly French, who found links among the American Liberty League, Wall Street, and those plotting against FDR. French's newspaper articles exposed the plot.

In 1934, a congressional committee held hearings on the matter. Did powerful Wall Street tycoons actively back the coup, or were they merely interested in reestablishing the gold standard? Much evidence was struck from the committee's record as "hearsay." We will probably never know the whole truth.

SMALLEST U.S. "NATIONAL PARK"

Most national parks are as vast as they are beautiful. "St. Agnes National Park" is only six feet square. It is also the only park we know of conceived and built by one person.

After recuperating from a heart attack in the late 1950s, the renowned newspaper reporter and biographer Gene Fowler (1890–1960) built a rock garden behind his home in the Brentwood section of Los Angeles. It covered a six-by-six area where his wife, Agnes, often liked to sit under a beach umbrella and watch him work. After positioning the last boulder, Fowler, in his wife's honor, posted a sign: "St. Agnes National Park."

Actor Thomas Mitchell, a friend of the Fowlers, spotted the sign and mentioned it to his nephew, who happened to be Secretary of Labor James Mitchell. He in turn told Secretary of the Interior Fred A. Seaton. Together, the two Eisenhower cabinet officers journeyed to the Fowler home and ceremoniously dedicated the smallest unofficial national park in the United States.

NATION OF ROUGH AND READY

The boldest tax rebellion in California's history was not Proposition 13. In 1850—long before Jarvis and Gann—settlers in a California boomtown of 3,000 persons protested the tax on gold by proclaiming themselves the Great Republic of Rough and Ready.

A group of Wisconsin men with gold fever had come west the year before, led by Captain A. A. Townsend, who christened them "the Rough and Ready Company." In the Sierras, sixty miles north of Sacramento, they struck a healthy gold vein and monopolized it for a time. They eventually had plenty of company, however—including a taxman for the embryo state of California.

E. F. Brundage, one of the original settlers, called a town meeting on April 7, 1850, to protest the taxation. He lambasted the chaotic California legislature and, in utter seriousness, proposed establishing a separate and independent government. A majority of 100 at the gathering responded with boisterous "yeas."

The new republic died within three months due to its settlers' lack of interest in independence. (Some say it was because residents of nearby towns would not sell liquor to any "noncitizens" for the Fourth of July, which the settlers wanted to celebrate nonetheless.) But today in the town of Rough and Ready, California, residents still speak of their short-lived sovereignty.

THE SLAVE PRINCE

In 1788, a farmer in Natchez, Mississippi, named Thomas Foster, bought a slave newly arrived from Africa. The slave, who claimed to be of royal blood, was dubbed "Prince" and put to work in the fields.

Nineteen years later, Dr. John Cox, a local physician, recognized him as the man who had saved his life in Africa twenty years before. He knew the black man as Ibrahima, a scholar and military commander whose father was king of the Moslem empire of Futa Jallon in West Africa. The prince told Cox that he had been defeated in battle and sold onto a slave ship bound for America. Cox tried to purchase Ibrahima's freedom, but his owner refused to sell him for any price.

Cox thereupon began a campaign to bring public attention to Ibrahima's plight. Even President John Quincy Adams appealed for his release. But he was not freed until 1827, when he was too old to work.

Meanwhile, Ibrahima had married in America and had raised a family. The prince later toured the North to raise funds to liberate his wife and children, who were still enslaved to Foster. His campaign was sponsored by Secretary of State Henry Clay and the American Colonization Society, whose goal was the settlement of freed slaves in Liberia. Eventually, Ibrahima raised enough money to buy back his family. They sailed to Liberia in 1829. That winter, Ibrahima made plans to return to his homeland. But before he could realize his dream, the sixty-seven-year-old prince fell ill and died.

MEN WITHOUT A COUNTRY

Confederate President Jefferson Davis and Confederate General Robert E. Lee both died as men without a country. The Southern leaders were denied U.S. citizenship after the end of the Civil War and did not regain it until more than 100 years later.

Neither Davis nor Lee was eligible for the general amnesty that was declared by President Abraham Lincoln in December 1863. After the war, President Andrew Johnson made it still tougher to gain a pardon. Davis, however, was not interested in a pardon. Held prisoner for two years at the war's end, Davis was never brought to trial. In May 1867, he was released on bond and for the remaining twenty-two years of his life was not a citizen of any country.

Lee, on the other hand, did want to rejoin the Union and work to rebuild the defeated South. He sent President Johnson the oath of allegiance to the Constitution, which was required for a special pardon. Unfortunately, his oath was lost—or perhaps Johnson simply ignored it. Lee died, still a noncitizen, in 1870. A century later, researcher Elmer Parker discovered the misplaced oath in a cardboard box at the National Archives.

Finally, after more than 100 years of neglect, the two Confederate leaders were given back their citizenship through special resolutions of Congress. Citizenship was granted to Lee on July 22, 1975, and to Davis on October 17, 1978.

LIVE FREE OR DIE

In 1969 the state legislature of New Hampshire decided to discard its rather ordinary license plate slogan "SCENIC NEW HAMPSHIRE" and replace it with the more dramatic and idealistic "LIVE FREE OR DIE," a phrase attributed to Revolutionary War General John Stark.

Although the new slogan was a radical change, the state retained its traditional method of producing license plates. All New Hampshire plates for noncommercial vehicles are stamped "LIVE FREE OR DIE" by unfree prisoners incarcerated at the state prison in Concord.

Recently a New Hampshire husband and wife preferred to live freely without displaying that sentiment on their car's license plate. George and Maxine Maynard taped over the motto because they found it repugnant to their beliefs as Jehovah's Witnesses. George Maynard was arrested and convicted of defacing the license plate. The case of *Wooley* v. *Maynard* reached the U.S. Supreme Court, and in 1977 the court ruled in favor of Maynard, thus upholding the citizen's right to refuse to have his private property subject to use as a "mobile billboard" for the state's ideological message.

GERM WARFARE IN AMERICA

The military of major nations today have biological warfare units. But turning germs against one's enemies is hardly a new idea. It was devised more than 200 years ago as a weapon against the American Indians.

In 1763, British forces in Pennsylvania were losing ground to partisans of the Indian chief Pontiac. The British commander, Sir Jeffrey Amherst, driven by a hatred of Indians, conceived the idea of infecting them with smallpox-infested clothing and assigned an officer to carry out the plan. The disease already was rampant among the British forces, and the Indians were known to be highly susceptible to infection. Whether the plan actually came off remains uncertain. But by the following spring, smallpox had stricken several tribes in the area.

The practice of killing Indians with disease did not end with Amherst. In Brazil, greedy profiteers continued to practice genocide against the Indians of the interior. Their weapons included "gifts" of smallpox-infested clothing. As many as 6 million Indians in Brazil have been killed since the sixteenth century.

RATIFYING THE BILL OF RIGHTS

150 YEARS LATE

Although the Bill of Rights was proposed as an addition to the U.S. Constitution in 1789 and formally ratified in 1791, three of the original thirteen states waited until 1939 before ratifying it.

As originally drafted, the Bill of Rights was to consist of twelve amendments guaranteeing such rights as freedom of speech. When it came before the Massachusetts legislators, they postponed voting on the bill because they felt it didn't go far enough in guaranteeing human rights. Under their rules of procedure, any unfinished business died at the end of the legislative session, and so in 1790 the amendments went into the "miscellaneous" file of the state archives. On the 150th anniversary of the "birth" of the Bill of Rights, Gov. Leverett Saltonstall resubmitted it to the state's General Court, and it was ratified by the legislature on March 2, 1939.

Meeting in 1789, both houses of the Georgia state legislature likewise dawdled over the bill and never got around to making a decision.

On March 18, 1939, following Governor Saltonstall's example, Georgia's state senate voted for ratification.

In 1790, Connecticut's house resolved to accept ten of the proposed amendments, but the council vetoed that in favor of accepting all twelve. The lawmakers could only agree to postpone the matter. On April 19, 1939, Connecticut—which, in 1650, had been the first colony to adopt a bill of rights for itself—became the last of the thirteen original states to give its blessing to the U.S. Bill of Rights.

DISAPPEARING LIBERTY BELL

Is it possible to lose a 13,000-pound, seven-foot-tall bell? A bell fitting that description vanished in 1896.

The bell was specially cast by the Daughters of the American Revolution for the Columbian Exposition in Chicago, commemorating the 400th anniversary of the discovery of America. It was made of donated metal objects associated with the fight for liberty throughout the world. Among them were silver spoons, thimbles, wedding rings, 250,000 pennies, the flintlock from Thomas Jefferson's rifle, and Simón Bólivar's watch chain.

After the Chicago exposition, the bell went on tour; in October 1895 it was displayed at the Cotton States Exposition in Atlanta, Georgia. Then, in 1896, it was shipped to Chicago for storage. That was the last time anyone saw it. After its disappearance, many people speculated that it had been smuggled to another country, perhaps Russia; that it was hidden for unknown reasons in an old building; or that it was melted down. Whoever heisted the 13,000 pounds of metal never gave it back.

ARGENTINE FLAG IN CALIFORNIA

Long before its trouble over the Falkland Islands in 1982, Argentina captured what is now Monterey, California.

After declaring its independence in 1816, Argentina cast about for other Spanish-American colonies to join its campaign against Spanish imperialism. On November 20, 1818, two captains of Argentine ships—French privateer Hippolyte de Bouchard of the 38-gun *Argen-*

tina and Englishman Peter Corney of the smaller *Santa Rosa*—dropped anchor opposite the Spanish garrison at Monterey. There they commanded the Spanish colonial governor, Pablo Vicente de Solá, to surrender. With barely 100 men, eight small field guns, and little ammunition, the governor couldn't match the Argentine forces, numbering 360. After a brief engagement, he abandoned the garrison.

The foreign invaders soon hoisted the Argentine colors, looted the town, set it aflame, and departed, never to return.

Historians agree that the invaders' main purpose was not to loot the town or expand Argentina's territorial holdings, but to liberate the province of Alta California from Spain.

A CORPSE FOR CONGRESS

Thaddeus Stevens, a fiery Civil War congressional leader from Pennsylvania, won his last election to public office 2½ months after his death at age seventy-six.

Stevens died on August 11, 1868, in Washington, D.C., and his body lay in state in the Capitol rotunda. An unforgiving foe of slavery and

Thaddeus Stevens in 1850, when still an upright member of the House

Southern secessionism and a leader in the attempt to impeach President Andrew Johnson, Stevens had made many enemies. The *New Orleans Bee* had once been moved to call him a "malignant old man." But as many as 6,000 devotees came to the rotunda to pay their final respects, and 15,000 turned out a week later for his funeral in Lancaster, Pennsylvania.

Soon after his burial, the Lancaster County Republican Party met to form a running slate for the November election. As a "fitting tribute to the memory of our most able and distinguished champion of freedom and justice," a party spokesman said, the Republicans nominated Stevens for the U.S. House of Representatives. Provisions for filling the vacant seat with a more active representative were ignored for the moment.

The Democrats openly ridiculed the gesture, and the party's newspaper in Lancaster thumbed its nose at the notion of voting for a "Corpse for Congress." But a lot of Pennsylvanians thought otherwise. They elected the dead man by a vast majority.

The voters of Texas found themselves in a similar situation in 1982. State Senator John Wilson had died almost two months before election day, but his name remained on the ballot for legal reasons. Much to the surprise of his Republican—and living—opponent, the deceased Wilson was reelected with 66 percent of the vote.

HOW IDAHO GOT ITS NAME

Many states take their names from Indian words. "Idaho," for example, is Shoshonean for "Gem of the Mountains."

Or so the story goes. There are other stories about the origin of the state's name. But, according to the Idaho State Historical Society, just one version is correct. They claim that "Idaho" doesn't actually mean anything in any language. The word is a fake. A mining lobbyist coined it—and its spurious translation—in 1860 and offered it to Congress as the perfect name for a new territory in the Pikes Peak mining country. Congress liked the suggestion, but at the last minute caught on to the trick. Instead, the territory was named Colorado.

Meanwhile, the word "Idaho" was cropping up in the Pacific Northwest. A steamboat was christened *Idaho* and, starting in 1860, carried gold prospectors up and down the Columbia River. The passengers themselves took to talking about the "Idaho" mines, and it seemed only natural that the name be proposed to Congress again in 1863. Ironically, the very senator who had scotched the idea two years earlier was now all for it. Congress, apparently suffering from amnesia, went along, and the Idaho Territory came into being.

ARIZONA NEARLY FOUGHT U.S.

Arizona once went to the brink of war with the U.S. government over rights to the Colorado River.

In 1934, the Federal Reclamation Bureau was preparing the site of the Parker Dam on the river, which borders California and Arizona. Because the dam, once completed, would divert water to southern California, many Arizonans felt their own rights had been overlooked.

When the dam-builders extended a temporary bridge across the river into Arizona, Gov. B. B. Moeur told Washington: Dismantle the bridge or sign a contract assuring the state a 50 percent share of all power generated by the dam. The government refused.

On November 10, 1934, Moeur declared martial law and then mobilized Arizona's National Guard, armed with machine guns, at the bridge site.

When Washington agreed to stop construction on the Arizona side, Moeur called off the troops but warned the bureau: "If the work is resumed, I'll send the Guard back and camp with them myself." Such action never proved necessary. After 1934, Arizona settled its water problems in court.

THE KNOW-NOTHING AMERICAN PARTY

The American Party, whose members were called Know-Nothings, was the most bigoted of all major third parties in American politics.

The party had its origin in the "native American" movement that flourished in Eastern and Southern states between 1840 and 1856. Alarmed by the large number of Catholics and other immigrants entering the United States, groups of citizens formed anti-Catholic, anti-immigrant organizations. Believing that only native-born Americans should govern, they called for the exclusion of naturalized citizens and Catholics from public office and urged a twenty-one-year residency requirement for citizenship. They stirred up such hatred and fear with their propaganda that riots occurred in several cities, resulting in numerous deaths and the destruction of Catholic churches and property. The largest of these groups, the Order of the Star-Spangled Banner, begun in 1849 as a secret society, required initiates to take an oath not to divulge any information about the association's elaborate ritual. In 1853, its members were nicknamed Know-Nothings because when asked by outsiders what they stood for, they obediently replied, "I know nothing."

The "native American" hysteria spread rapidly, and candidates supported by the Know-Nothings were elected to Congress and state legislatures. Encouraged, the Know-Nothings, now 200,000 strong, went public and officially became the American Party in 1855. A year later, the party nominated former President Millard Fillmore for president. After a humiliating defeat—carrying only Maryland—the party split up over the issue of slavery. The proslavery faction joined the Constitutional Union Party, while most of the antislavery members eventually drifted into the Republican Party. Without the votes of these new Republicans, Lincoln would not have been elected president in 1860.

HELP WANTED BY THE PRESIDENT

Unlike today's "imperial Presidents," who have a bureaucratic apparatus to handle household matters, George Washington had to put ads in the newspaper to hire servants.

On December 19, 1789, shortly after he and Martha set up housekeeping in New York, then the nation's capital, two ads ran in the *New-York Daily Gazette,* a publication composed mainly of advertising. One was for a cook "for the Family of the President" who would be "perfect in the business" and could bring "indubitable testimonials of sobriety, honesty, and attention to the duties of the station." The other was for a coachman "well recommended for his skill in driving, attention to horses . . . and good disposition." The ads ran nearly six weeks. Good help was hard to find in those days. Perhaps it was because of the salaries—the cook's job paid $15 a month.

In spite of their fancy method of travel (in a painted coach drawn by six cream-colored horses), the Washingtons said they maintained their twenty-one-servant household quite frugally. Their yearly expenses averaged about $30,000. Compare that with the Reagans' current household budget of $50 million!

GUESS WHO MAKES H-BOMBS?

The research and development, testing and production of nuclear weapons in the United States is budgeted within the seemingly inoffensive Department of Energy, not the Department of Defense.

Why? In 1946, the Atomic Energy Commission was established to take over some of the Manhattan Project's functions. Later, the commission was divided into two agencies—the Nuclear Regulatory Commission and the Energy Research and Development Administration, which was one of the agencies brought under the umbrella of the Department of Energy when it was established in 1977.

Working with the Department of Defense, the Department of Energy Defense Program is responsible for production of nuclear weapons from the research and development phase through the study of the biomedical effects of nuclear war. The funds appropriated to nuclear defense in the 1982 Department of Energy budget amounted to $4.4 billion. That figure rose to $5.2 billion in 1983, when the defense program also took on other functions including defense waste cleanup. The proposed budget request for 1984 is $6.1 billion. According to *The Budget of the United States Government, Fiscal Year 1981*, weapons activities in the Department of Energy "will continue to provide new technology to maintain a modern nuclear force, along with the design and development of new weapon systems in response to defense requirements."

4

REMARKABLE ANIMALS

GREYFRIARS BOBBY

A dog may be a man's best friend, but no one has ever had a friend—canine or otherwise—like Greyfriars Bobby.

He was a Skye terrier, a stray who was adopted by a policeman named Jock Gray in Edinburgh, Scotland, in the mid-1850s. In time, dog and man became inseparable, and three days after Gray died in 1858, Bobby showed up at Ramsay's Eating House, where he had often lunched with his master. The proprietors tossed him his usual bun, but Bobby carried it back to his master's grave before digging in. He returned to Ramsay's the next day to pick up his lunch and every day thereafter for the next fourteen years; otherwise, he never left Gray's grave site for a moment.

Nine years after Gray's death, the city of Edinburgh passed a dog-licensing law. As an unlicensed dog, Bobby was due to be captured and killed. By this time, Bobby's loyalty to his late master was a legend throughout Edinburgh, and he found himself among friends. The city officially adopted Bobby, and Lord Provost William Chambers offered to pay Bobby's license fee that year and every year. The revered pooch was also presented with a brass-plated collar that read "Greyfriars Bobby, from the Lord Provost, 1867, Licensed." He wore it proudly.

Statue of Greyfriars Bobby, Scottish stray whose loyalty made him famous

Bobby never had to worry again. The people of Edinburgh provided him with shelter in bad weather and made certain he always had enough to eat. He was granted round-the-clock access to the churchyard, where he doggedly kept up his constant vigil until his own death in 1872. He was buried, of course, near his master's grave.

BABOON WHO RAN A RAILROAD

A century ago, a baboon helped his handicapped master run a railroad switching station.

In 1877, railroad man James Wide had both legs severed in an accident near Port Elizabeth, South Africa. He was reassigned as switchman at the Uitenhage Tower, where he settled into a rundown cabin and befriended a baboon named Jack. Wide had found his man Friday.

Jack was extremely intelligent. He learned to pump water from a well, clean house, and tend Wide's garden. Every morning, he pushed his master to work in a handcart that Wide had built to run on rails. Wide trained his hairy helpmate to perform minor chores at the signal tower, and Jack soon was manning the station. He operated the levers that set signals for approaching trains and managed the tower controls that opened or closed switches on a siding.

When Jack died in 1890, he left behind a spotless record with the railroad. In the nine years he served as Wide's assistant, he never made one mistake that resulted in the loss of life or property.

SHEEP ON THE WHITE HOUSE LAWN

The image of sheep contentedly grazing on the White House grounds would be mighty incongruous today. But in 1917, a small flock was part of the war effort. President Woodrow Wilson had decided that sheep—not valuable fighting men—should trim the White House lawn. The sheep multiplied rapidly, and soon children gathered to watch the frolicking animals. A favorite was Old Ike, a tobacco-chewing ram who favored cigar stubs.

Not surprisingly, the sheep did not confine their meals to the lawn. When they ate expensive shrubbery and whole beds of perennials, they drew a flurry of criticism from those who felt the White House was being

Presidential flock perform lawn-trimming duties—
part of the war effort in 1917

defiled. Mrs. Wilson defended the animals, and she wasn't sheepish about it, pointing out that ninety-eight pounds of "White House wool" had been auctioned to collect money for the Red Cross.

Other unusual White House pets have included Calvin Coolidge's raccoon, Rebecca, which he walked on a leash; Alice Roosevelt's snake, Emily Spinach, named after her aunt; and Tad Lincoln's turkey, Jack, who was intended to be a White House dinner but was given an official reprieve by President Lincoln.

THE U.S. ARMY'S LIVING LAWN MOWERS

The U.S. Army is now recruiting kids to work at its Fort Belvoir, Virginia, ammunition dumps. Actually, these kids are goats, and their job is to keep the 100-acre tract nibbled clean of vegetation.

The army prefers goats to lawn mowers for safety reasons. Unlike human grounds keepers, the goats never get careless with cigarettes. And unlike lawn mowers, they never give off sparks.

The Fort Belvoir goats have been on duty for seventeen years. From an original group of five, they have multiplied to a present-day herd of thirty-five.

During the winter, the goats stay at their posts and live in converted water towers. They are looked after by a full-time civilian employee of the army and are checked periodically by a veterinarian.

Every year, a few of the goats finish their hitches at Fort Belvoir and are shipped to another farm or military installation. The army has a long list of bases, from Alaska to Germany, all impatiently awaiting some experienced goats.

WHEN PARENTS FIGHT, THE CHILDREN
SUFFER

Last spring, a team of observers from the U.S. Fish and Wildlife Service and the National Audubon Society watched helplessly as a pair of rare California condors (there are only about thirty in existence) produced their first egg in two years, only to destroy it in a marital dispute.

A pair of excitable
California condors

The sad episode occurred in the coastal mountains north of Los Angeles. The parents were taking turns sitting on the four-inch-long egg. All was amicable until the couple began squabbling over custody rights, each trying to jostle the other off the egg. The pushing escalated into a full-scale brawl, and the egg was accidentally pushed out of the nest and over the edge of the cliff—to the horror of the onlooking scientists.

Happily, the bickering condors mated again and produced a second egg several weeks later. This time they kept the peace, but a band of ravens began threatening their nest. The worried scientists secured permission to shoot the intruders, but before they could, one invaded the nest. In the ensuing fight between the raven and the condors, the second egg rolled off the cliff and was smashed.

In order to save the near-extinct condors, the United States government has permitted a group called the Condor Recovery Team to remove condor eggs from their nests and breed them in captivity. The first kidnapped egg was successfully hatched at the San Diego Zoo in California on March 30, 1983.

"HERE COMES PELORUS JACK!"

For twenty-four years he was world famous. A movie was made about him. His picture was featured on postcards. He inspired numerous songs. A chocolate bar was named after him. Sightseers including Mark Twain and Rudyard Kipling came great distances to see him, and when they saw him bounding toward them, someone would always shout, "Here comes Pelorus Jack!"

No, he wasn't a person. He was a fourteen-foot Risso's dolphin who for over two decades guided steamships off New Zealand through perilous waters into safe harbor. He was the first dolphin in history whose life was protected by a special government proclamation or law.

Pelorus Jack, named for Pelorus Sound, became renowned in 1888 when he expertly piloted steamships through a six-mile stretch of the rough, swirling waters of Cook Strait between New Zealand's two main islands. He gained the love of both sailors and passengers who watched him playfully leaping through the waves toward their vessel. Often, he would scratch his back against the ship's hull, and then swiftly glide out in front and pilot the steamer to the dangerous French Pass. After getting one ship safely through, the dolphin would immediately leave to wait for another vessel.

Once, from the deck of a cargo steamer, a sailor, presumably drunk, tried to shoot Pelorus Jack with a rifle. Luckily, the shot missed. As a result, in September 1904, the government of New Zealand passed a law to protect Pelorus Jack's life, fining anyone who did him harm from 5 to 100 pounds.

In 1912, Pelorus Jack disappeared. A local newspaper printed a tentative obituary, concluding, "If he is dead, more's the pity; if he has been slaughtered, more's the shame." Pelorus Jack was never seen again.

Incidentally, no one will ever know, but he may have been a she.

PIGEON THAT SAVED A BRIGADE

In Italy during World War II, the British 56th Infantry Division was trying to take the village of Colvi Vecchia, but it was strongly defended by Germans. The British radioed the nearest American air base to bomb the village off the map. Then, in the confusion, 1,000 men from a British brigade swept into Colvi Vecchia and took it over—only to realize that they would soon be smashed by the very bombs they had ordered to help them. Their radio equipment had been lost. How to stop the American bombers? Then they realized they had with them one American homing pigeon, a blue check-splashed bird named GI Joe. The British had to send the pigeon out with a message or they were doomed.

On that smoke-filled morning of October 1943, GI Joe went winging away, managed to elude gunfire, flew twenty miles in twenty minutes, and reached the American airfield just as the bombers were about to take off. The British brigade was saved. Three years later, GI Joe was brought to London to become the first non-British animal to be decorated with the Dickin Medal for Gallantry, presented to heroic animals. The bird was then retired to Fort Monmouth, New Jersey.

BARK-OFFICE SMASHES

A singing canine is a rare beast. Only one dog in a thousand has this ability, which must be carefully nurtured from the time the animal is eight weeks old. Here are the tales of some proficient pooches.

Our Gang with Pete the Pup

Benjy, whose career spanned from 1965 (he was crooning at nine weeks) until his death in 1978, specialized in "Raindrops Keep Fallin' on My Head," which he rendered on the "Tonight Show." Benjy belonged to Mrs. Betsey Marcus of Brookline, Massachusetts.

Peppy, a three-foot-high white poodle from New York, performed from 1966 to 1971. He was trained by Girl Scout troops and performed on TV. His repertoire included Christmas carols and campfire songs.

Asta, famous for his roles in the *Thin Man* movies, appeared in more than twenty MGM films. In one *Thin Man* episode, he sang "Auld Lang Syne" to Myrna Loy.

Pete the Pup appeared in *Our Gang* comedies and sang "Jeannie With the Light Brown Hair." Pete died after eating a Thanksgiving dinner.

DUCKING FOR COVER

In the city park in Freiburg, West Germany, stands a three-foot marble monument to a duck. During World War II, many of the townspeople escaped death in a bombing raid by heeding that alert duck's warning.

On a November night in 1944, the duck, which was kept with other small animals in the city park, suddenly began squawking and flapping its wings. Those within earshot knew that its stirrings meant one thing—take cover. This was not the first time that the bird had sensed and signaled the approach of high-flying aircraft, so the Freiburgers wasted no time running for their shelters. The regular alarms failed to sound until after the first bombs hit—and there is now some question whether the attackers were Allies, or Germans who were off target.

Many died in the bombing. Among the casualties was the duck. On the base of its statue, which was unveiled on the ninth anniversary of the raid, is this inscription: "God's creature laments, accuses, and reminds!"

DONALD DUCK BANNED IN FINLAND

In 1978, the youth committee in Helsinki, Finland, sought to purge its community of a most unsavory and decadent character—Donald Duck.

The decision to cancel youth club library subscriptions to Donald Duck comic books was based partly on the grounds that Donald had been keeping company with Daisy Duck for fifty years without so much as a hint at marriage. To the committee, Donald's intentions were strictly dishonorable.

Another outrage to the youth committee was the questionable parentage of Donald's nephews Huey, Dewey, and Louie. In a 1937 comic book, the three ducklings were placed in Donald's care by a stranger identified only as "Miss Duck," who was never heard from again. However, a newspaper comic strip of the same year identified her as Donald's cousin Della. Indeed, the lack of any notarized certificate of hatching did leave the three ducklings' parentage in doubt.

However, the aspect of Donald's behavior that most upset the youth committee was his outright refusal to wear pants. (The committee perhaps believed that Helsinki schoolchildren were used to seeing the ducks in city parks waddling about in trousers?)

Fortunately, a Donald Duck fan club in Hamburg, West Germany, offered comic-book documentation that Donald didn't indulge in unsavory habits or have sex with Daisy. The comics were subsequently reinstated.

Daisy and Donald—
in *flagrante delicto*

© Walt Disney Productions

CATS ON THE POST OFFICE PAYROLL

Cats have been on the official payroll of the British Post Office for more than a century.

They're not hired to sort or deliver mail, of course, but to keep it from being eaten by mice. The problem was especially bad in London in the mid-1800s, when mice invaded the sorting rooms to gnaw at mail, money orders, and employees' sandwiches. Traps and poisons proved ineffective, and in 1868 the Secretary of the Post Office approved the hiring of three female cats at a weekly allowance of 4 pence each. But he cautioned, "If the mice be not reduced in number in six months, a further portion of the allowance must be stopped."

Within months the rodent population had shrunk dramatically, and post offices received the go-ahead to hire cats. Many did, and as the felines became more prominent in the work force, their pay improved. In 1953, the Assistant Postmaster General assured the House of Commons that female mouse-hunters received "very adequate" maternity benefits and enjoyed the same wages and employment opportunities as male cats.

Today, cats are on the payroll at three London postal sites. A tailless terror at London's Nine Elms postal garage is, at £1.80, among the top-paid mousers in the land. "Most weeks, he leaves a couple of rats on my desk as well as an array of mice," says Bill Woodford, the officer in charge. The cat's name? Kojak.

PERSECUTION OF WOODCHUCKS

New Hampshire's state legislature once passed a law offering a bounty for every woodchuck killed. The law was repealed when the number of claims by bounty hunters threatened the state treasury.

The law, which took effect on September 11, 1883, sought to eliminate the woodchuck, a notorious ravager of crop acreage and clover fields. It was passed on the strength of a stridently antiwoodchuck report submitted by the New Hampshire Legislative Woodchuck Committee. "The woodchuck is absolutely destitute of any interesting qualities," the report stated. Anyone who killed a woodchuck and presented the tail to a town selectman earned a bounty of 10 cents. No bounty was paid for woodchucks killed on a Sunday.

In 1884, only 339 bounties were paid. But in 1885, the total skyrocketed to 122,065, and State Treasurer Solon A. Carter called for the immediate repeal of the law. On August 11, 1885, the legislature obliged, though payments continued to be made as late as 1888.

UNUSUAL MAILMAN

From 1883 to 1886, a very hairy individual faithfully delivered the Christmas mail and other correspondence between the silver-mining town of Calico, California, and nearby Bismarck. His name was Dorsey, and he was a shepherd dog.

Dorsey's career began shortly after his arrival in Calico as a weary stray. Jim Stacy, the local postmaster, took the dog in and named him. When Stacy delivered the mail on foot, his new pet went along.

The black-and-white canine became a mail carrier in his own right when his master fell ill and was unable to work. Stacy fashioned a crude harness with double saddlebags for Dorsey, then sent him off to East

Maildog Dorsey:
Neither wind, rain . . .

Calico with an explanatory note tied to his collar, including a request that return mail be placed in the saddlebags. Dorsey successfully completed his rounds and, when Stacy recovered, was rewarded with his own official mail route.

When not working, Dorsey was friendly and playful. On the job, he was serious, avoiding pranksters who tried to divert him from his duties.

Dorsey became famous. When Stacy took him to San Francisco, crowds greeted them and bought photos of Dorsey. In 1973, his story was told in "Go West, Young Dog" on TV's "Wonderful World of Disney." In 1980, Dorsey was installed in the Character Hall of Fame at Calico.

VICIOUS FISHES

For sheer bloodthirsty viciousness, no fish can match a razor-toothed demon called the piranha that inhabits the freshwater rivers of South America and measures, incredibly, only eight to twelve inches in length.

There are actually some eighteen species of piranha, of which only four are dangerous. Piranhas attack if they smell blood. The faintest whiff—even from a mosquito bite—starts their spring-trap jaws snapping. One bite from a piranha's double row of neatly meshed triangular teeth can snap a finger or toe off an unwary bather, or gouge out a chunk of flesh with surgical precision.

A school of piranha can strip a 400-pound hog down to its skeleton in just minutes.

Indeed, piranha teeth are so sharp that the Indians of Guyana use them as arrow points. Yet piranhas are easily caught and prized as a delicacy among South American fishermen.

I'M STICKING WITH YOU

Just because the female deep-sea anglerfish is ugly and up to fifteen times larger than her mate doesn't mean he's not *very* attached to her. He really has little choice.

Of more than 125 species of deep-sea anglers, many live at such great depths in the ocean that there is no light at all. Young males cannot rely on chance encounters in the dark, so as soon as a young suitor detects a female, he fastens onto her. It doesn't seem to matter that he will never grow much longer than a few inches, while she may be nearly four feet in length.

Biting into her head or side, the male attaches his mouth so securely into the female's flesh that they fuse together and their bloodstreams become one. From that time on, he is totally dependent on his hostess for nourishment and life itself. The female angler—now able to have her eggs fertilized at any time by her parasitic mate—is, in effect, a hermaphrodite.

BUTTERFLIES ARE FIERCE

If you think dainty butterflies are lily-livered weaklings, think again. Most male butterflies are gutsy and aggressive within their own habitat and will pick a fight at the slightest provocation.

This trait is often seen when the male is on the prowl for a mate. The European grayling butterfly, for example, will perch on a twig or leaf to wait for Ms. Right. When he scents a female virgin of his own species, he will begin an elaborate courtship dance and emit his own identifying scent. But he will rough up almost anyone else who ventures into his territory, whether it's another butterfly twice his size, a dragonfly or a small bird. He'll even lunge at his own shadow. Black swallowtail butterflies, an especially aggressive species, have been known to chase after terrified birds for as long as half a minute.

When vying for the favors of the same female, two male butterflies will repeatedly ram each other in midair until one surrenders and flees.

THE BUG ROOM

Thousands of tiny carrion beetles live in a basement room of Yale University's Peabody Museum of Natural History. The beetles are not part of a display—they're employees.

Their job is to strip the flesh from gutted and dried animal skeletons.

A flying squirrel after a
night in the Bug Room

The "Bug Room" was established at Yale about twenty years ago,
though the method dates to the 1930s, when zoologists found that the
ravenous beetles did a better job of cleaning small, delicate carcasses
than did humans. The room's current residents are descendants of Yale's
original beetles.

The Bug Room population is regulated in accordance with the work
load. The beetles can strip a small carcass clean in a few hours, larger
ones in a few days. Later, the skeletons are soaked in ammonia to remove grease and clinging bugs, then rinsed in water. The
four-by-eight-foot room has a good supply of cotton mattress tick-
ing—an ideal medium for the beetles' egg-laying.

While they are not picky eaters, the beetles do seem to prefer marine animals and to dislike snakes.

DOCTOR ANTS

Next time you're stocking your first-aid kit or medicine cabinet, don't
forget to throw in a jar of ants.

Doctor ants, that is. Indigenous to the forests of South America,
doctor ants (of the genus *Atta*) are endowed with sharp, viselike jaws.
Brazilian Indians have used them to perform surgery that would otherwise require sutures. The edges of a wound are pressed together, then

doctor ants are applied along the seam. Once the ants have bitten the wound closed, the ants' bodies are snapped off and the jaws hold fast until the wound is healed.

Doctor ants are also known as leaf-cutter and parasol ants because they descend on trees and tear off bits of leaves, which they carry above their heads—like parasols—on the way to their nests. The leaves are deposited in the nests and serve as a growing ground for a fungus on which they feed. Fruit growers dread the ants, for they can strip an entire citrus grove overnight.

TINY GLUTTON

The smallest mammal in the world—the shrew—holds the record for gluttony, eating nearly its own weight in food every day. In order to equal this feat, a 150-pound human would have to consume about 113 pounds of food a day.

The shrew is only obeying a law of nature: the smaller the mammal, the more (proportionately) it must eat to stay alive. And the shrew, a relative of the mole, is small indeed. The smallest shrew measures about 2½ inches from head to tail, weighs less than a dime, and travels through earthworm tunnels. The biggest is the size of a small rat.

Shrews are not particularly fussy about what they eat. On occasion, they consume larvae from manure piles, their relatives, even their own feces. Ferocious little beasts, some have poisonous saliva that stuns or kills their prey, which often are larger than they.

The shrew is a marvelous species. The American water shrew can walk on water with its air-pocketed feet. The money mouse shrew jingles. The six-inch-long hero shrew has a fortified backbone that can withstand the weight of a 160-pound man. But no matter what their peculiar characteristics, all of the nocturnal mammals have mammoth appetites.

THE LONG-EARED POLITICIAN

In 1938, Boston Curtis was the surprise victor in a race for the position of Republican precinct committeeman from Milton, Washington. Why was it a surprise? Boston Curtis happened to be a mule.

Boston's hoofprints had been imprinted on the filing notice, and the legal witness at the filing was none other than Milton's mayor, Kenneth Simmons. But it was all a gag planned by Simmons—a Democrat, of course—to prove his contention that voters are often careless.

LIFESAVER PIGEONS

Between 1978 and 1982, the U.S. Coast Guard was engaged in Project Sea Hunt, a training program for an air-sea rescue team composed of pigeons.

The pigeons, who possess an extremely wide field of vision, were stationed on the underside of a helicopter in an observation chamber. Each of the three pigeons in a team surveyed a swath of the ocean surface, looking for anything "international orange" in color—such as life jackets and life rafts. On seeing the color, a pigeon lookout pecked at a response key, and the pilot circled the area. If an object was found, the pigeon was rewarded with food.

During training sessions in 1978, the first observation birds spotted a surfboard, a crate, and some fishing float-flags—all orange. Unfortunately, those birds were killed in 1979 when their helicopter made a forced landing during a futile search for five missing fishermen. But more pigeons were quickly trained to take their places. These pigeons flunked the test in actual search-and-rescue missions performed over a six-month period in 1982, and so the project was dropped.

THE PIED PIPER OF CALIFORNIA

California has long had its problems controlling pests like the medfly. Back in 1927, when 100 million mice invaded Kern County, the government resorted to calling in a real "Pied Piper."

For years, residents of this farming and oil-producing region had waged an all-out war on skunks, weasels, snakes, badgers, coyotes, and other critters that made rural life risky for children and pets. In time, the extermination program succeeded in drastically reducing the predator population in the county.

Meanwhile, a bumper crop of corn and barley in the area's 25,000-acre Buena Vista Lake basin resulted in a bumper crop of mice. Unharassed by their natural enemies, they casually fed on the grain, grew fat, and multiplied. Soon mice were everywhere, infesting barns, granaries, and houses. Roads and highways became slick with crushed mice. People would awaken at night, their bedcovers alive with the rodents. Every day, mice were killed by the thousands—yet it seemed that for every one exterminated, dozens took its place.

Finally, a poison specialist from the U.S. Biological Survey was summoned. His name was Stanley E. Piper—a "Pied Piper" who worked his magic not with a flute but with 40 tons of strychnine-laced alfalfa. Within a month, the mouse population had plummeted, and human beings had once more subdued the animal kingdom.

GOOD-BYE, DODO

Of all the animals that have disappeared from the face of the earth, nine out of ten have been birds. And of these extinct species, the most famous and most incredible bird was the ridiculous dodo.

The dodo was first found on the volcanic isle of Mauritius in the Indian Ocean. A member of the dove family, the dodo resembled a bloated and misshapen dove, the size of an overgrown turkey. It was generally three feet tall, fat, and heavy-footed, and its belly scraped the ground when it waddled. Although definitely a bird, it could not fly. Neither could it run or climb trees. It was defenseless except for a usually ineffectual hooked beak. Not many dodos existed, because the female laid only one egg a year.

In 1598, a Dutch admiral named Van Neck, exploring Mauritius, told the world about the dodo. He took two of them home to Holland, kept one and presented the other to the emperor of Germany. The Dutch dodo posed for fourteen portraits. Although the admiral had found the dodo "unpalatable" to eat, Dutch colonists on Mauritius and visiting sailors without gourmet tastes found them acceptable as food. Thus, they consumed the dodo population, while local dogs, cats, and pigs gobbled up the handful of dodo eggs. Meanwhile, the dozen dodos in Europe also had died. By 1681, the last dodo had either expired or been killed, and the species was extinct. One dodo, which had been a sideshow attraction in London, was stuffed upon its death, displayed at Oxford, and finally thrown out.

A hundred years later, people believed there had never been such a creature as the dodo, that it had been merely a legend like the unicorn. But in 1863, a persistent native of Mauritius, George Clark, realizing the island's volcanic soil was too hard to hold fossils, decided that some dodo bones might have been washed up by rains on the muddy delta near the town of Mahebourg. He led an excavation that yielded a great quantity of dodo bones, which were assembled into complete skeletons and sent to the museums of the world. Joy! The dodo lived again.

THE LIVING FOSSIL

There is one prehistoric animal alive today that is 125 million years older than the dinosaur. This is the coelacanth.

In 1938, fishermen off the coast of South Africa caught a vicious, strange-looking fish. About five feet long, it weighed 127 pounds, had bright blue scales, and possessed unusual fins. When marine biologist J.L.B. Smith was called in to identify the animal, he felt for a moment that he was "quite off the rails." He recognized the creature as a coelacanth, a member of a group of fishes that existed as early as 350 million years ago—nearly 125 million years before the dinosaur age. They were thought to have become extinct about 70 million years ago. Yet here was proof that this line of fish had survived—a real coelacanth that, according to Smith, was the product of 30 million generations. Upon closer examination, the biologist concluded that although larger than most of its fossilized forebears, the coelacanth differed little from them.

The discovery of this ancient form of life in our modern world sparked much scientific excitement. Coelacanths were related to the group of fishes that evolved into the first land vertebrates and ultimately into human beings.

Since 1938, only twenty specimens have been caught in the waters off the Comoro Islands northwest of Madagascar, where the fishes make their home. So few coelacanths have been found because they probably live among rocks that impede fishing trawls.

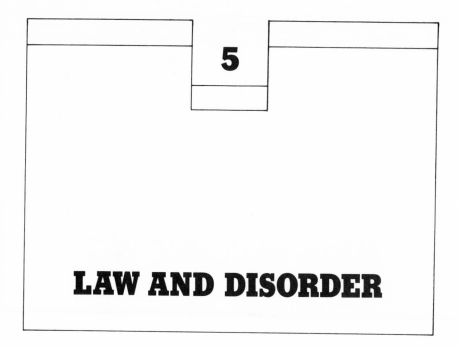

5

LAW AND DISORDER

MEN ARRESTED FOR TOPLESS BATHING

As recently as 1936, it was illegal for men to wear topless bathing suits in New York.

American men won topless rights after a decade of controversy. In the 1930s, male bathers began discarding the shoulders-to-thighs tank suits for new swimming trunks.

In 1934, eight men were fined $1 each for topless bathing at Coney Island. "All of you fellows may be Adonises," said the presiding magistrate, a woman, "but there are many people who object to seeing so much of the human body exposed." A year later, a mass arrest of forty-two topless males in Atlantic City, New Jersey, fattened the municipal coffers by $84. The city fathers declared: "We'll have no gorillas on our beaches."

Gradually, the guardians of national decency relented, and local ordinances were revised to allow topless bathing for men. In 1936, it was economy rather than morality that finally induced the Westchester, New York, County Park Commission to allow swimming trunks. The commission, which purchased suits for rental at county beaches and pools, found that the trunks were substantially cheaper.

MINISKIRTS ONCE OUTLAWED

Short skirts were once illegal on the streets of Greece.

After his faction seized control of the Greek government in 1925, Gen. Theodore Pangalos wasted little time in declaring himself dictator. He suspended the constitution, cracked down on opposition newspapers, exiled his political rivals, and publicly hanged corrupt bureaucrats.

But what drew the most attention in the European press was his decree that no woman could publicly wear a dress with a hemline more than fourteen inches above the ground. Police armed with tape measures stopped women on the streets of Athens for spot checks. Any female over the age of twelve who didn't measure up was forced to change her ways or hustled off to jail.

The miniskirt ban was consistent with Pangalos's notorious puritanism. But there may have been another motive for his actions: his wife, some said, was bowlegged.

CRAZY JUSTICE

Two justices of the U.S. Supreme Court served on the bench although they were insane.

This was possible because Supreme Court justices are appointed for life. They cannot be removed except by impeachment for "bribery, treason, or other high crimes." They can be ill, senile, incompetent, or even insane, and still cannot be forced to resign.

John Rutledge of South Carolina, a lawyer at age twenty-one and governor of his state at forty, was appointed associate justice of the Supreme Court in 1789 by President George Washington. After a year, Rutledge resigned, but later asked Washington to put him back on the U.S. Supreme Court as chief justice. Washington agreed and nominated him. Then Rutledge, infuriated by a treaty that discriminated against the Southern states, made a public speech which insulted Washington and the Senate. Awaiting his confirmation, Rutledge served as chief justice of the Supreme Court for an entire term, until the Senate refused to ratify his appointment 14 to 10. Rutledge tried and failed to commit suicide by drowning. During his term, a friend reported, "His mind was frequently so much deranged as to be in a great measure deprived of his sense."

Henry Baldwin, a lawyer and congressman from Pennsylvania, was nominated for the U.S. Supreme Court by President Andrew Jackson in 1830. An obsessive night worker, he neglected his private affairs and he was almost bankrupt. A court historian wrote: "Towards the close of his life his intellect became deranged, and he was violent and ungovernable in his conduct upon the bench." He was removed from the bench only by death in 1844. He was so impoverished that his friends had to raise money to bury him.

PAUL REVERE ON TRIAL

Paul Revere, the Revolutionary War patriot immortalized in Henry Wadsworth Longfellow's poem, "The Midnight Ride of Paul Revere," underwent, at his own request, a court-martial on charges of disobedience and cowardice.

In 1779, Lieutenant Colonel Revere was ordered to take 100 men and join 2,000 others in attacking the British on Penobscot Bay in Maine. But the American naval forces failed to play their part, and Revere's men were routed. During the confusion of the retreat, soldiers and commanders were separated. It took the forty-four-year-old Revere five days to find his men at Fort Western.

Capt. Thomas Jenness Carnes made accusations of unsoldierly behavior against Revere, who then was relieved of his command. For three years, Revere demanded a court-martial to clear his name, and he finally got one in February 1782. Revere was tried and acquitted on two specific charges: refusal to obey a general's orders pertaining to use of a boat, and leaving the battlefield without orders from his commander.

THE GHOST HAS HER DAY IN COURT

Can a man be convicted of murder based on the testimony of his victim's ghost? It happened in a sleepy West Virginia village, Greenbrier Valley, in 1897.

No one witnessed the death of young Zona Heaster Shue, a bride of only two months. Her new husband, Erasmus "Trout" Shue, a blacksmith, said he had come home and found Zona's body at the bottom of the stairs. Bystanders noticed that he allowed no one near the corpse. Zona's mother, Mary Heaster, doubted it had been an accident, and when the girl's ghost appeared to her and described the murder four nights in a row, she went to the authorities.

They exhumed Zona's body and found her neck had been broken. Trout was charged with murder. At the trial, Mary Heaster testified: ". . . she came back and told me that he was mad that she didn't have no meat cooked for supper . . . the second night she told me that her neck was squeezed off at the first joint."

Shue was his own worst witness. He contradicted previous testimony, gave irrelevant details about his alibi, and repeatedly protested his innocence. The jury was impressed with the ghost story, though it was admitted only as circumstantial evidence. After an hour and ten minutes of deliberation, the jury returned a verdict against Shue: guilty of murder in the first degree. He was sentenced to life imprisonment.

CAPTAIN BLIGH'S THREE MUTINIES

For two centuries, Captain William Bligh has been infamous as the sadist who provoked a mutiny on the H.M.S. *Bounty*—probably the most notorious mutiny in history. Little known is the fact that Bligh actually was involved in *three* mutinies.

In 1789, Master's Mate Fletcher Christian, revolting against Bligh's cruelty and stern discipline, wrested command of the *Bounty* near the Friendly Islands in the southwest Pacific and set Captain Bligh adrift in an open boat with eighteen others. While the mutineers sought their own version of tropical paradise on remote Pitcairn Island, Bligh and his small crew spent six weeks sailing 3,618 miles in their small boat before miraculously reaching land in the East Indies.

In 1797, Bligh was in command of the H.M.S. *Director* and became caught up in a chain-reaction mutiny involving the entire fleet at The Nore, England. The mutineers were demanding more pay, stronger grog (which had been watered down to reduce drunkenness), and the dismissal of abusive captains. Ironically, Bligh was not on that hit list, but he was nonetheless relieved of command and put ashore.

As governor of New South Wales, Australia, in 1808, Bligh came down hard on insobriety and curtailed the sale of alcohol. His actions set off the Rum Rebellion, and he was removed from office and held in custody.

Captain Bligh, in shirt-sleeves, bids an angry adieu
to the crew members who cast him and eighteen others
from the H.M.S. *Bounty* in the famous mutiny

Afterward, Bligh returned to England, ultimately rising to the office of vice admiral. But he never lived down his reputation as "that *Bounty* bastard."

COMIC OPERA BOMBING

An aerial bombing occurred inside the United States on November 12, 1926, in Williamson County, Illinois. It was not a foreign power that initiated the raid, but a bootlegging gang of farmboys led by Carl, Earl, and Bernie Shelton. Their air strike was against a rival gang headed by Charlie Birger.

Originally, the two gangs had worked together, but once they quarreled over protection money, the war was on.

The target of the Sheltons' outrageous air raid was Birger's stronghold, Shady Rest, a roadhouse built of foot-thick logs. For $1,000 and a stolen car, they hired a World War I biplane and a barnstormer pilot. Blackie Armes of the Shelton gang climbed aboard with three dynamite bombs, and the pilot took off. While the plane made a pass over Shady

Rest, Blackie desperately tried to light the fuses, finally succeeded, then threw the bombs over the side. Two were duds. The third exploded beside a cockfighting pit. It destroyed some bleachers and killed a bulldog and a caged eagle.

The pilot flew Blackie back to the field and landed. When he saw the armed and angry Shelton gang waiting, he forced Blackie out of the plane with a .38 pistol, then roared off.

To retaliate for the failed attack, a Birger gang member drove to the nearest landing field and shot up what he thought was the offending plane, then set it on fire. It was the wrong plane.

LAW WITH NO BITE

Illinois is one of three states in the United States where, by law, dentures must have the owner's Social Security number marked on them. (The others are Montana and Minnesota.)

A prime mover behind Public Act 82-366 was Dr. Edward Pavlik, an orthodontist in Olympia Fields, Illinois. Pavlik, who serves as consultant to the Cook County Medical Examiner's Office, headed the dental team that investigated America's worst air disaster, the 1979 DC-10 crash in Chicago in which 274 persons died. Of the 244 victims identified, 90 percent were named through dental records.

The new law, says Pavlik, "will facilitate quick and proper identification of persons who die in accidents." It also will help elderly people, especially those in nursing homes, find their own dentures at lunch or dinner time.

There's one loophole in the legislation: no penalty exists for dentists who fail to mark a patient's Social Security number or name inside the false teeth. "There are simply no teeth in the denture law," Pavlik unhappily admits.

THE JUVENILE EXECUTIONER

Jean-Baptiste Sanson was appointed official executioner of France in 1726 when he was seven years old.

His grandfather had been the first member of the Sanson family to be the nation's executioner. In 184 years, six Sanson men, one inheriting the job from the other, were in the business of separating heads from the bodies of criminals in Paris.

When little Jean-Baptiste inherited the bloody job, he was too young to aim a blade at any condemned person's neck. But as official executioner, the youth had to be present on the platform while his deputy, Francois Prud'homme, carried out the grim task. For eleven years, Jean-Baptiste observed each beheading, until he reached his majority at eighteen, when he was allowed to use an ax (for commoners) or a sword (for aristocrats) to carry out the beheadings.

After he had grown up and married, he had seven sons of his own, and the eldest inherited the job from him. This eldest son, Charles-Henri, became the most prolific of the Sanson line. He was chief executioner when the French Revolution came and the guillotine was introduced, and he and seven assistants beheaded 2,700 persons—the family record.

WHEN CAPITAL PUNISHMENT WOULD NOT

WORK

The debate over capital punishment often centers around whether it works as a deterrent to crime. The case of John Lee was one in which capital punishment didn't work, period.

In November 1884, Emma Anne Keyse of Babbacome, England, was found with her throat slashed. Her footman, John Lee, was convicted and sentenced to death. Lee protested his innocence, then told a warden, "They won't hang me." But they did try.

On February 23, 1885, James Berry, the public hangman, placed a bag over Lee's head, adjusted the noose, stepped back, and pulled the bolt that should have released the trapdoor. But it didn't. Berry stamped on the trapdoor. Other people stamped too, but nothing happened. Finally, Berry moved Lee aside and tested the mechanism. It worked. Lee was put back in position, the bolt was pulled—and again the trapdoor stuck.

Lee was taken back to his cell while Berry and some assistants worked on the trapdoor. It seemed to be in order, and so Lee was brought out again. Once more, the trapdoor would not open to receive its victim. After a half hour of this torture, Lee's captors gave up trying to hang him. His sentence was commuted to life in prison, but he was paroled in 1907. He died of natural causes in 1911.

SENTENCED TO LAS VEGAS

It was a gambler's dream come true. Convicted of illegal betting in 1978 in San Antonio, Texas, Tony Salinas was fined $10,000—and sentenced to five years on probation in Las Vegas.

It was the start of a new life for the forty-two-year-old Texan and the end of his anonymity as an illicit professional gambler. A former junior high math teacher and football coach, Salinas pulled off some betting coups soon after starting his "sentence" in Nevada. He picked 61 percent of the winners during the pro football season, wagering a mini-

Tony Salinas—
earning the wages of sin

mum of $20,000 per game. His fame spread quickly, and soon he was making his picks on the radio. More recently, he was named World Champion Football Handicapper by the Castaways Hotel, winning $85,000. He quickly bet the entire amount on a Monday Night Football game—and won.

Salinas doesn't rely on luck. He keeps careful records of player injuries, trades, and anything else that might influence a team's chances. Whenever possible, he bets on the underdog. "Nobody wants to be an underdog," he explains, "and the players will try harder to prove they are not."

Salinas's probationary term expired in 1983, leaving him free to leave Las Vegas.

PRISONERS: BEHIND BARS AND AT LARGE

The number of people in prisons in the United States is larger than the population of Tucson, Arizona, Charlotte, North Carolina, or Albuquerque, New Mexico. It is also larger than fourteen different nations that are members of the United Nations.

Citizens of North Dakota and New Hampshire are least likely to be incarcerated, while the states with the highest per capita prison populations are South Carolina, Florida, North Carolina, Delaware, and Georgia. Leading all the states, however, is the District of Columbia, where 1 out of every 233 people lives in a prison cell. In fact, the nation's capital has five times as many prisoners as it does legislators.

In 1978, the latest year for which complete figures are available, 1 of every 43 prisoners in the United States managed to escape from prison. However, 94 percent were recaptured. Although there were no escapes in Oregon and North Dakota, fifty-six convicts (1 out of 10) in Vermont broke out of confinement.

CONVICTED OF KILLING THEMSELVES

Suicide is illegal in some states, but offenders are rarely prosecuted. After all, what would be an appropriate punishment? Still, a few offenders have been sentenced. Dr. John Duffy, a history professor at the University of Maryland, has researched two such cases.

In 1765, the superior council of the colony of Louisiana passed a harsh sentence on the body of Jean Baptiste, a suicide. His corpse was tied to the back of a cart and dragged to the public square, where it was hung upside down from a scaffold for twenty-four hours.

André Sauvinien, who killed himself in Louisiana in 1752, was sentenced by the colony's attorney general. His memory and good name were to be "tarnished and sullied forever," and all his property was to be seized. Fortunately for Sauvinien's family, the ruling was overturned by the superior council on the grounds that he was insane when he killed himself.

NATION WITHOUT GUNS

In these days of controversy over handguns, it may be surprising to learn that one technologically advanced nation voluntarily gave up guns for more than 200 years. That nation was Japan.

When primitive guns were first introduced to Japan in 1543, master craftsmen immediately improved upon the weapon. Soon Japan had better—and more—guns than any country in Europe. Why then did Japan reject the gun and turn back to the sword?

The reason was a cultural one.

Before guns, battles were filled with pomp and ceremony. As their feudal lords watched, champion warriors (samurai) from opposing sides stepped forward, introduced themselves and boasted of their past heroic feats. Then, using magnificent fighting swords, they went into combat. The gun, however, destroyed the noble rituals of battle; the machinery outshined the man. As Noel Perrin writes in his book *Giving Up the Gun:* "It was a shock to everyone to find out that a farmer with a gun could kill the toughest samurai so readily."

Abandoning the gun was a slow process. There was some confiscation, but Japanese rulers reduced the number of guns mainly by restricting manufacture of the weapon. The last major battle of that period using guns occurred in 1637.

In 1853, the "civilized" West came to Japan in the form of Matthew Perry of the U.S. Navy. He opened trade with the isolationist country and convinced its leaders to modernize their defenses—namely, to bring back the gun.

THE GREAT ONE-MAN MANHUNT

In 1919, fifty-five-year-old J. Frank Norfleet, a Texas rancher, went to Dallas on business. Checking into the St. George Hotel, Norfleet was introduced by Reno Hamlin, a livestock dealer, to four of his friends—W. B. Spencer, Joe Furey, E. J. Ward, and Charles Gerber—all involved in the stock market. They had a tip on a stock that could make them all rich and convinced Norfleet to invest with them. He laid out $45,000 for his share, stipulating that the money had to be returned the next day. The next day, the money and the five men had disappeared. Norfleet had been swindled.

Displeased with the efforts of the Dallas police and Pinkerton private detectives, Norfleet took the law into his own hands. Abandoning everything else in his life, he delved into the backgrounds of the swindlers, obtained leads from other con men, bought himself a gun, and set out to get his revenge.

Like police inspector Javert pursuing Jean Valjean in Victor Hugo's *Les Miserables*, Norfleet chased leads on his five swindlers across the United States. In less than a year, he found two of them, Ward and Gerber, in a San Bernardino, California, jail, convicted of another con game. Then Norfleet's findings led to the capture of Hamlin in Fort Worth, Texas. That made it three down and two to go. Sifting through postal and telephone records, Norfleet found that Furey had been wiring money from Jacksonville, Florida, to his wife in California. Norfleet cornered Furey in a café, forced him at gunpoint into a train, and had him arrested in Fort Worth. Furey was sentenced to twenty years. That left Spencer. Still obsessed, Norfleet obtained a police photo of him in Omaha, Nebraska, circulated it, and trailed him to Salt Lake City, Utah. Exhausted, Spencer was caught and landed in Leavenworth Prison.

The five-year manhunt was ended. All five culprits were behind bars or dead. Norfleet made the pursuit of con men his profession for the next twenty-five years, then retired to his Texas ranch.

THE CAMPAIGN OF CONVICT NO. 9653

In 1920, Eugene V. Debs ran for president of the United States and collected nearly a million votes—though he campaigned entirely from a jail cell.

A tall, fiery labor agitator, Debs, then sixty-five, was serving a ten-year sentence in the federal penitentiary in Atlanta, Georgia, for violating the World War I Espionage Act, prohibiting antigovernment talk.

Debs had run for president—and lost—four times before, each time as a candidate for the Socialist Party, whose precursor, the Social Democratic Party, he'd founded in 1898. Creator of the first industry-wide union, he was beloved by workers, who cheered his electrifying speeches. But in the 1920 campaign, Debs could make no speeches, although he was allowed to issue weekly bulletins to the voting public from his cell. His "Last Call to the Voters in 1920" contained bitter words: "The people can have anything they want. The trouble is, they do not want anything. At least they vote that way on election day." That year, the people chose Republican Warren Harding over Democrat James M. Cox and Eugene Debs. Debs received only 6 percent of the vote.

Eugene V. Debs—the presidential candidate leaves jail

On Harding's order, Debs was released from jail early. Debs said, "It is the government that should ask *me* for a pardon."

ARRESTING THE PRESIDENT

Next time you get ticketed for speeding, don't be too hard on yourself. A U. S. president was arrested for the same offense while in office.

William West, a Washington, D.C., police officer, was on patrol in the northwest part of the city one day when he spotted a horse and buggy tearing west on "M" Street, greatly in excess of the speed limit. Seizing the horse's bridle, West was dragged half a block before he could stop the animal. He was about to arrest the driver when he saw it was none other than President Ulysses S. Grant.

Embarrassed, West apologized profusely. But the president was not one to cop a plea. "Officer," he reportedly said, "do your duty." While Grant continued home on foot, West impounded the presidential rig; later it was returned to the White House.

To be sure, West needn't have been shocked to find the president at the reins. By the time he took office in 1869, Grant already had two speeding arrests under his belt. Each carried a $5 fine.

Once again, a few years after his presidency, Grant broke a law. On a fishing trip in McKean County, Pennsylvania, Grant discovered that he was fishing out of season. Without hesitation he turned himself in to the nearest justice of the peace, who was understandably reluctant to apply the law to the august offender. Grant insisted on paying the full fine, however, and reprimanded the officer for his lack of zeal in enforcing the law.

THUG POWER

Over a period of 500 years, a secret religious sect in India called the Thugs ritually murdered a total of about 12 million victims.

Originally, the term "thug," which today means "cutthroat or ruffian," was Hindi for "swindler." Beginning in the thirteenth century, the

---

119

Thugs traveled about India in bands, preying on travelers. With great cunning they would ambush their mark or lure him to an isolated spot, then throttle him. The murder weapon never varied: a length of silk weighted at one end, which was whipped around the victim's neck and pulled tight. The killers would then strip the victim of cash and jewels, hack his body to pieces with a pickax, and bury him. All witnesses, even dogs, were likewise dispatched. One Thug named Buhram reportedly took a record 931 lives during his forty-year career, although *he* claimed that he stopped counting after 1,000.

Being a Thug was a hereditary occupation. The membership included both Hindus and Muslims, united in their fanatical devotion to Kali, the Hindu goddess of the destructive aspect of nature. For the Muslim members of the sect, their Thug practices had nothing to do with Islam.

The most common victims were transients, seamen on leave, or money bearers, who were not likely to be known or missed by local folk. The Thugs never laid a finger on women, carpenters, stonecutters, washermen, lepers, metalworkers, musicians, cowherds, and others thought to be either descendants of Kali or sacred to her.

A major general in the Bengal army spearheaded the campaign to rid India of the Thugs in the 1830s. Hardworking and idealistic, Sir William Henry Sleeman at first found his British compeers skeptical of his assessment of the Thugs and reluctant to join him in the hunt. But Sleeman persisted, mobilizing police and military contingents throughout the Indian subcontinent. By the time they had finished, Sleeman's forces had slain hundreds of Thugs in battle, hanged 412, and jailed nearly 3,000. All other suspects and their families were required to register with the government and were kept under close police scrutiny. While no Thug activity was reported after the 1840s, the registration law remained in effect until India gained its independence from Great Britain in 1947.

A HAIRLINE DECISION

More than 150 years before hippies and the Vietnam protests, a U.S. Army colonel was court-martialed for refusing to get a haircut.

In 1803, Colonel Thomas Butler was stationed in Tennessee when his commander, General James Wilkinson, ordered that officers might no longer wear their hair in the traditional queue, or ponytail. Most officers obediently took shears in hand, but not Butler. A career man with a distinguished record dating to the Revolution, he was not, at fifty-five, about to surrender his cherished locks so easily. For disobeying orders, he was arrested on charges of insubordination and neglect of duty.

The matter became a cause célèbre, as Butler's friends rallied to his defense. Among them was Andrew Jackson. Petitioning President Jefferson on Butler's behalf, he wrote: "The removal of such an officer for . . . his well-known attachment to his locks . . . opens a door for the greatest tyranny."

But Jefferson stood by Wilkinson. On July 10, 1805, a court-martial found Butler guilty of mutinous conduct and sentenced him to a year's suspension without pay. Shortly thereafter, he died, but not before leaving specific instructions regarding his hair: "Bore a hole through the bottom of my coffin, right under my head, and let my queue hang through it, that the d--d old rascal may see that, even when dead, I refuse to obey his orders." Butler's last request was granted.

THE AMAZING CASE OF MYRA CLARK GAINES

In one of the longest and strangest civil suits ever, Myra Clark Gaines spent nearly fifty years, $600,000 in lawyers' fees, and $250,000 in court costs to prove she was the sole heir to her father's fortune. At least thirty lawyers, including Daniel Webster and Francis Scott Key, argued her case. She won in the end—yet she died penniless.

Her father was Daniel Clark, a prominent New Orleans merchant and politician. When he died in 1813, he left a fortune of $35 million and, allegedly, a will giving it all to Myra. But the document was nowhere to be found, and the courts were skeptical when she first pressed her claim in 1836. They also doubted her assertion that her parents had been wed. Under Louisiana law, a child born out of wedlock had no claim to the father's estate, no matter what the will said. Myra's parents had, in fact, been wed in secret. Unfortunately, she could not produce the marriage certificate.

Myra got nowhere with the state courts, so she appealed to the federal courts and finally to the U.S. Supreme Court, which ruled in her favor in 1861—twenty-five years after she'd begun her suit. The decision was invalidated, however, when Louisiana seceded from the Union and tossed out all judgments issued by federal courts. Finally, in 1883, a circuit judge ordered the city of New Orleans to pay Myra $1,925,667.83, plus interest. But the city was in no hurry to pay, and Myra—exhausted

Myra Clark Gaines

by her long struggle—fell ill and died in a New Orleans boardinghouse on January 9, 1885, before she had collected a penny.

Her family picked up where she left off, however, taking the case back to the Supreme Court three more times before New Orleans finally came up with the cash in 1891. The city was spared paying the full amount, however, because some portions of the claim were denied. The grand total was $567,707.92.

Myra's heirs barely escaped a more prolonged ordeal. It was only on her deathbed that Myra had agreed, albeit reluctantly, to make out a formal will of her own.

THE CHASTITY POLICE

Although TV programmers may fear the vigilance of the Moral Majority, today's self-appointed guardians of decency have nothing on the Chastity Police. Established by Queen Maria Theresa of Austria (1717–80) to counter her husband's infidelities, the Chastity Police were not concerned simply with purging sex from the stage and literature. They wanted it out of the bedroom too.

With the queen's crack troops hiding under beds and peering through keyholes, no adulterer was safe from arrest. Eagle-eyed policemen were also stationed at theaters and opera houses to monitor performers for bare ankles and exposed midriffs; offenders were hauled off to jail. Meanwhile, border patrols rifled mailbags for smutty pictures and books. Prostitution, of course, was the ultimate offense, and *any* woman walking unescorted through the streets of Vienna risked deportation to a rehabilitation commune in southern Hungary. The more clever prostitutes took to walking in pairs and kept a string of rosary beads handy in case they were spotted by an officer.

Even Casanova, the most famous of all lovers, fell afoul of the Chastity Police. They stormed the Vienna hotel room where he was closeted with his mistress, whom he maintained was his sister.

The two were breakfasting at the time.

THE DAY BEFORE ADULTHOOD

You say tomorrow's your birthday, and you become an "adult"? Actually, you can take your first legal drink today. And vote, and sign a legal document. Whether the age of majority in your state is eighteen or twenty-one, common law holds that you may enjoy the "privileges of adulthood" beginning on the day *before* your birthday.

The oldest known court case testing this principle, *Nichols* v. *Ramsel*, occurred in 1677 in England. A man had signed his will and died on the day before his twenty-first birthday. The court determined that he had reached legal age and that the will was valid. The court computed the man's age by including the day of his birth, saying that, under the law, there is no such thing as a fraction of a day. And so, from the day before his birthday, he was an adult. This legal precedent has held ever since and is the rule most commonly followed in the United States.

Those born on February 29 reach adulthood on the 27th (the law regards leap-year births as occurring on the 28th).

A PECULIAR PRISON SUICIDE

William Kogut, San Quentin convict No. 1651, committed suicide with a deck of playing cards.

Sentenced to be hanged in 1930 for killing a woman with a pocket-knife, he vowed to the judge that he would never be executed. Consequently, the warden was careful to have all tools for a potential suicide or escape kept away from Kogut. He wasn't careful enough.

As the date of his execution approached, Kogut's intentions were unreadable. He busied himself playing cards in his cell. Pretending to concentrate on solitaire, he tore the red spots out of the red cards, knowing they contained explosive ingredients—nitrate and cellulose. A hollow iron leg from his bunk served as the container for the spots, which he had soaked in water. After sealing the ends, he had a primitive pipe bomb.

On the night of October 9, 1930, Kogut put the bomb on the hot oil heater in his cell, laid his head on the pipe, and waited. The explosion rocked the prison. One version of the event has it that a prison doctor picked the ace of hearts out of Kogut's skull during the autopsy.

In any case, Kogut succeeded in being the agent of his own death, taking the satisfaction from someone else—though one wonders if it was worth it.

CRIME FIGURES: GOOD AND BAD

There are fifty-nine murders a day in the United States, and the rape rate has doubled in the last ten years.

In 1979 (the most recent year for which complete figures are available), fourteen children aged ten or younger were arrested for murder or nonnegligent manslaughter, six for forcible rape, and eight for embezzlement.

The U.S. city with the highest murder rate is East St. Louis, Illinois (1 of 1,418 people murdered each year). In second place is the appropriately named Kilgore, Texas, followed by Compton, California. The big-city murder leader is Atlanta, Georgia, followed by Gary, Indiana, and St. Louis, Missouri.

East St. Louis is also the city with the worst rape rate (1 of 187 women raped in 1979). Next in line are Highland Park and Benton Harbor, Michigan, and Jacksonville Beach, Florida.

Atlanta and Gary have the worst big-city rape rates, with Newark, New Jersey, in third place.

Now the good news:

The largest city without a murder in 1979 was Boulder, Colorado (pop. 81,086), followed closely by Greece, New York (pop. 81,008). The largest town without a rape was West Hartford, Connecticut (pop. 65,963), and the largest without a robbery was Fairfield Township, Ohio (pop. 33,470).

Citizens of Vermont are least likely to be murdered, and the women of North Dakota are least likely to be raped.

The largest university campus without a violent crime was Iowa State (enrollment 21,881).

THE HANGINGEST JUDGE

"I sentence you to be hanged by the neck until you are dead, dead, dead!" roared Isaac C. Parker one morning in May 1875. After the murderer was led out of the "Court of the Damned," Judge Parker wept briefly,

Isaac C. Parker sent seventy-nine men to the gallows

then called the next case. This scenario was repeated 160 times while Parker served as federal judge of the district court for western Arkansas at Fort Smith. His district, the nation's largest, covered 74,000 square miles of "semicivilized country filled with the worst of criminals" and included the Indian territory that became Oklahoma.

As a judge who passionately believed that "the certainty of punishment . . . halts crime," Parker thrived on his work. He convened court at 8:00 A.M., didn't adjourn until dark, and frequently held night sessions. He dispensed frontier justice six days every week for twenty-one years. Parker admitted that his juries knew the verdict he wanted: "I tell you, a jury should be led! . . . If they are guided, they will render justice, which is the greatest pillar of society."

The "Hanging Judge" tried 13,490 cases, convicted 9,454 defendants, and sentenced 155 men and 5 women to hang. Eighty-one, including all of the women, eluded the noose through such tactics as Supreme Court appeals and presidential commutations. From his chambers, Parker watched the other seventy-nine hang. His reputation must have preyed on Parker's mind. Shortly before his death in 1896, he explained, "I never hanged a man. The law hanged them. I was only its instrument."

THE HABEAS CORPUS PRANK

The most fundamental guarantee of personal liberty was passed into law because of a prank.

The principle of habeas corpus insures that no one can be imprisoned without a specific charge and a proper trial. The Latin words *habeas corpus* mean "you should have the body," and in issuing a writ of habeas corpus, a judge directs that the prisoner be physically brought to court to hear the charges against him.

When England's House of Lords met to vote on this principle in 1679, chances of passage were scant until one mischievous vote-tallier counted the "yea" of a very fat peer as ten votes. No one noticed the joke or called for a recount, and the Act of Habeas Corpus passed into law. A century later, it was incorporated into the U.S. Constitution as well. Today, while dissidents in totalitarian countries still can be detained on vague charges and languish in jail for years without a trial, Americans are protected against such outrages—thanks to a bit of sophomoric humor and faulty arithmetic.

U.S. MUTINEER

Only one U.S. Navy officer has been hanged for mutiny. He was Philip Spencer. Piracy was his dream.

In 1841, young Spencer joined the navy and a year later signed on board the *Somers*, a training ship. He was one of only thirteen officers; most of the crew of 120 were teenaged apprentices. The other officers snubbed Spencer, suspecting that he had gained the post through the influence of his father, John Canfield Spencer, President John Tyler's secretary of war. Spencer compensated by being overly friendly with the enlisted men, a habit abhorred by the ship's commander, Alexander Slidell Mackenzie.

The ship was returning from Africa, when Lieutenant Guert Gansevoort, second in command, informed Mackenzie of a rumored plot: Spencer had instigated a wild plan to murder most of the officers, throw the "small fry" overboard or make them walk the plank, then turn the ship into a pirate vessel.

Spencer said it was all a joke, but he was put in double irons anyway. In his razor case, searchers found a paper with names of the crew written in Greek and designated "certain" or "doubtful." Boatswain Samuel Cromwell and Seaman Elisha Small were arrested on this evidence.

Fearing that the mutiny might take place even with the accused ringleaders in custody, and on the advice of his officers, Mackenzie decided to hang the three men. On December 1, 1842, the deed was done and the bodies were thrown overboard.

Despite adverse opinion, a court-martial absolved Mackenzie.

ZEKE PROCTOR'S ONE-MAN PEACE TREATY

An intimidated U.S. government once signed a "peace treaty" with a solitary Cherokee Indian. His name was Zeke Proctor.

Proctor, former high sheriff of Going Snake District (in present-day Adair County, Oklahoma) and a veteran of the Union army, was a dangerous man. He had a bad temper and had killed at least one person (but was believed to have killed many more).

On April 15, 1872, he was on trial for the shooting death of a woman named Polly Hilderbrand. Like everyone else in the Cherokee Territorial Court, Zeke was heavily armed. Inevitably, gunfire broke out. When the smoke cleared, the dead included nine courtroom spectators and two U.S.

marshals. The next day, the court reconvened and hastily found Zeke not guilty. However, fearing that he would have to face the white man's law for the courtroom deaths, Zeke fled into the hills with fifty armed Cherokee supporters.

The U.S. government decided that Polly Hilderbrand's murder had been a matter between the Cherokees and therefore under the jurisdiction of an Indian court. Rather than pursue Zeke and worsen relations with the Cherokees, President Ulysses S. Grant chose to overlook the courtroom massacre and awarded Zeke total amnesty.

Zeke himself became a deputy U.S. marshall in 1891 and was reported to have rigorously respected his one-man "treaty" with the U.S. government. He died, a model citizen, of pneumonia in 1907.

BOMB BLAST COVERUP

Five former air force men are suing for damages inflicted on March 1, 1954, by BRAVO, the test of an H-bomb on the Pacific island of Bikini. They say the United States and its contractors knew that east winds would carry the bomb's fallout to the Marshall Islands but gave the go-ahead for the test and later attempted a coverup. Federal officials insist the contamination of twenty-eight servicemen and hundreds of Marshallese was accidental.

Late on the morning of the blast, say witnesses, radioactive ash settled "like a snowstorm" on Rongerik Atoll in the Marshalls, 125 miles away, where the servicemen lived. The radiation dose was fifteen times the level now allowed nuclear workers for a whole year. Military doctors pronounced the men in good health on May 16, 1954; since then, the United States has refused to provide medical care for them.

The five former airmen say they have developed cancer and other serious conditions, including reproductive problems. Therefore, they have filed claims of $10 million each for punitive damages plus medical costs against contractors who worked with the government on BRAVO. (According to precedent, servicemen cannot sue the government for service-related injuries.) Why did they wait so long to sue? Gene Curbow, one of the five, says it was "a mixture of patriotism and ignorance." The government admits that the men were exposed to large doses of radiation but denies that their injuries are related.

Servicemen who believe their health has been affected by BRAVO may write to attorney Gordon A. Stemple, 2020 Avenue of the Stars, Suite 440, Century City, California 90067. Former members of the U.S. armed forces who fear that they may have been exposed to excessive radiation as a result of other atomic tests should write to: National Association of Atomic Veterans (NAAV), 1109 Franklin Street, Burlington, Iowa 52601.

THE PRICE OF CRIME

Members of a notorious nineteenth-century New York City street gang not only hired out as paid killers—they even printed an itemized price list for their services, ranging from a simple punching to murder.

The Whyos, as they were called, terrorized lower Manhattan in the late 1800s. Five hundred strong at their peak, the Whyos warred savagely with other gangs, fought among themselves, and advertised their services through printed handbills distributed openly on city street corners. When one of their kingpins, Piker Ryan, was arrested in 1884, police went through his pockets and found the following price list:

Punching	$ 2
Both eyes blacked	$ 4
Nose and jaw broke	$ 10
Jacked out [knocked out with a blackjack]	$ 15
Ear chawed off	$ 15
Leg or arm broke	$ 19
Shot in leg	$ 25
Stab	$ 25
Doing the big job [murder]	$100 and up

The Whyos disappeared around the turn of the century, supplanted by more politically powerful and devious gangs.

BIG BROTHER *IS* WATCHING

The biggest government security agency in the United States today screens and then destroys nearly forty tons of recorded phone calls and other messages a day. The CIA? The FBI? Wrong on both counts. It's the NSA—the National Security Agency—and chances are you've never heard of it.

Few people have. While its budget is *twice* that of the CIA, and its headquarters, in Fort Meade, Maryland, are nearly as vast as the Pentagon, the NSA operates in total secrecy. It has no official spokesmen and issues no press releases; indeed, its 24,000 employees are forbidden to tell anyone where they work. Five years after it was created by President Truman in 1952 as a Cold War measure, its existence was finally made public.

The NSA collects foreign intelligence information, and eavesdropping is a big part of the agency's daily work. Every international phone call and telegram to and from the United States is electronically recorded and then analyzed by computers which check for calls or messages placed by subjects under NSA surveillance. (Most turn out to be innocuous and irrelevant, and the agency winds up destroying tons of classified documents a day.) Between 1962 and 1973, the FBI and other government agencies persuaded the NSA to monitor the international communications of hundreds of U.S. racketeers, drug traffickers, and antiwar activists—even though these Americans had nothing to do with

Big Brother was watching in the film *1984*—the NSA is listening in 1983

foreign intelligence. In 1973, when antiwar activity was intense, the NSA listened in on more than 24 million communications.

If all this sounds illegal, it is. "That all this is 100 percent against the law, that it violates every provision of the Bill of Rights, bothers the NSA, its parent, the Defense Department, and successive U.S. presidents not a whit," writes journalist Harrison E. Salisbury. But in 1978, Congress acted to restrict such domestic spying. It did nothing, however, to protect those U.S. citizens living outside the country—the agency is still free to record their messages to and from the United States.

So, next time you leave the United States and phone home—or wire your friendly neighborhood arms supplier—mind your words. Big Brother really may be listening.

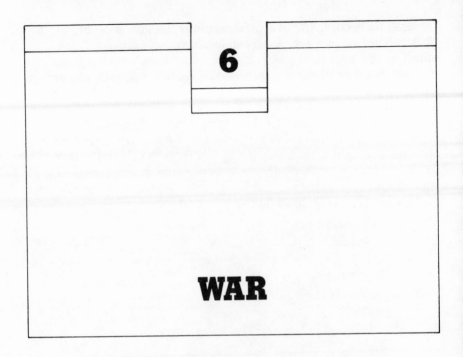

6

WAR

THE TRAVEL AGENCY THAT BOOKED
AN ARMY

Thomas Cook and Son is probably the world's top travel agency. It even books space on the first commercial trip to the moon—whenever that might be. But Cook's strangest booking was in 1884, when it became the only travel agency ever to organize and take an army to war.

That year, General Charles Gordon, based in the Sudan, was under attack by partisans of the Mahdi, a local religious leader. To bail Gordon out, the British War Office hired the firm most familiar with the Sudan: Cook's. (The agency had been founded forty-three years before when Thomas Cook, an ex-missionary, put together a half-fare railway outing to a beach near Liverpool.)

For a fee of $15 million, Cook's assembled a fleet of 27 steamships, 28 ocean liners, 650 sailboats, and 800 whaleboats to carry 18,000 relief troops and 130,000 tons of ammunition and provisions 2,000 miles up the Nile to the besieged garrison at Khartoum. Rough waters rocked the boats, and the North African heat wore the soldiers to a frazzle. But most frightening was a violent waterfall that had to be negotiated. Several men were killed and more than 100 ships severely damaged.

Still, the flotilla reached Khartoum exactly on schedule—but too late to save Gordon. Three days before, he and most of his men had been killed.

THE WILD WEST SHOW GOES TO WAR

Kaiser Wilhelm's German army may have patterned its logistics after Buffalo Bill's Wild West Show.

In 1891, the show toured Europe, delighting audiences with dazzling feats of horsemanship. Certain members of the German audiences were especially entranced—Prussian army officers, who were fascinated by the speed with which trainloads of tents, horses, costumes, and people were coordinated and transported.

Kaiser Wilhelm II himself saw the show in Berlin, and in city after city his officers attended local performances—not for the entertainment but for the military intelligence they gathered. The efficiency of this small army of cowboys and Indians was astounding. Said Annie Oakley, star sharpshooter of the show, "We never moved without at least forty officers of the Prussian guard . . . taking down every detail."

Behind this organizational wizardry was James A. Bailey, of Barnum and Bailey Circus fame. He also streamlined that once-cumbersome production into a model of precision. In 1900, when the circus toured Germany, the Prussians were still taking notes. They watched the beautifully orchestrated loading and unloading and the precision ballet of hundreds of roustabouts as they raised the tent city or took it down in a matter of hours. Everything, including a cookhouse that could seat 1,000, seemed to appear and disappear like magic.

The German officers took notes as the tents came down and the circus was loaded onto sixty-seven railroad cars. Army engineers even traveled with the circus to complete their study. The techniques they observed later were adapted to the movement and operations of German field kitchens, heavy artillery, and troops during World War I. And so it was that the circus—created for children's happiness—may have aided a war machine.

WHEN THE U.S. INVADED RUSSIA

The Cold War did not begin in the 1950s but in 1918, when U.S. troops invaded Russia with the aim of unseating the Communists. Actually, it wasn't a cold war. It became quite heated.

Early that year—with the end of World War I still months off—several of the Allied nations sent troops into Russia. Britain and France's principal motive was to pressure Moscow back into the war against Germany, with whom the Soviets had just established a separate peace. Japan took part in the invasion out of territorial greed. And the

Yanks in the war against the Bolsheviks

United States went in to keep an eye on Japan, to protect vital ammunition and supply depots, and to secure northern Soviet ports against the German forces. Or so the United States maintained.

Just before the invasion, civil war had broken out in Russia between the ruling Bolsheviks, or "Reds," and the counterrevolutionary "Whites." Although the Whites failed to capture Moscow, they did secure much of the country. The real reason for America's intervention was to help the Whites topple the Communists.

In August and September, 1918, the United States landed 4,500 troops at Archangel, on the White Sea, and 8,000 at Vladivostok, in eastern Siberia. After Germany surrendered in November 1918, there was no longer a valid reason for the Allies to remain in the USSR, but they were in no hurry to decamp. American troops engaged the Bolsheviks in battle and backed the Whites in their ultimately thwarted campaign. It wasn't until April 1920 that the last U.S. soldiers returned home.

THE AMERICAN WAR WITH LIBYA

The United States tangled with the hitmen of Libya once before.

From 1784 to 1815, the U.S. government paid tribute (or bribes) to the Barbary States—Algiers, Tunis, and Tripoli, now a part of Libya—as protection against the Barbary pirates who were seizing ships and holding the crews for ransom. When the Americans said "no" to Tripoli's increased demands, Yusuf Karamanli, the Qaddafi of his day, arrogantly declared war on the United States on May 14, 1801.

The United States tried to blockade Tripoli in the Mediterranean, but Admiral Murad Reis, a Scot married to the pasha's daughter, captured the U.S. ship *Philadelphia* and its crew of 300. The pasha demanded $3 million.

Then, on February 16, 1804, in a dramatic undercover action, Lieutenant Stephen Decatur recaptured the *Philadelphia* right below the pasha's castle walls. Decatur, last to seek safety, leaped onto the rigging of his ship, the *Intrepid*, as it sailed away from the *Philadelphia* after setting it afire. The pasha's price for peace suddenly fell to $500,000.

Meanwhile, Captain William Eaton and Lieutenant Presley O'Bannon, with only 500 U.S. Marines and Greek mercenaries, crossed the barren desert and stormed Derna, on Tripoli's coast. From this daring offensive of April 27, 1805, comes the line in the Marine hymn "to the shores of Tripoli."

Tripoli made peace, but it still cost the United States $60,000 to ransom its prisoners. The United States continued to pay tribute to the other Barbary States for ten years.

THE FIRST KOREAN WAR

The first conflict involving the United States and Korea did not begin in 1950. The initial Korean War took place almost eighty years before Communist North Korean forces battled with UN troops, most of whom were American.

In the 1860s, American traders were considering Korea as a potential source of trade, and the U.S. government hoped to establish a commercial, political, and religious beachhead in Korea. But the Koreans viewed Westerners as barbarians.

Frederick Low, the U.S. minister to China, was dispatched to Korea in May 1871 with the aim of breaking through its isolationist policies. A few months earlier, news had reached Washington of an American-owned merchant ship that had been destroyed in Korean waters by suspicious natives. Accompanied by the "Asiatic Squadron"—a flotilla of five run-down boats manned by 1,500 sailors and marines under the command of Admiral John Rodgers—Low set out to convince Korea of the good intentions of the United States.

While Low's diplomatic mission failed, Rodgers led two of his ships on a reconnaissance mission up the Han River. When the Koreans fired on the ships, the Americans retaliated, killing several Koreans. The U.S. forces then easily defeated the Koreans in the conflict. Three Americans died in the skirmish, and ten were wounded. There were nearly 350 Korean casualties. The undeclared four-day war was not reported by the U.S. press until a month after the fighting, when the *New York Herald* ran the headline: "Our Little War with the Heathen."

The "little war" solved nothing. Korea remained up for grabs, with China and Japan both trying to gain the upper hand. China forced Korea into a treaty of friendship and trade with the United States, but in 1894 Japan invaded and conquered Korea. By 1905 Korea was officially a Japanese protectorate. Koreans would not know independence again until 1945, when the Japanese surrendered at the end of World War II.

THE OTHER "BAY OF PIGS"

More than a century before the Bay of Pigs incident in 1961, another group of Cuban exiles with U.S. military backing failed in an attempt to conquer Cuba.

The exiles' leader, Narciso López, launched two attacks from the United States. Many Americans were in favor of taking Cuba from Spain, and the U.S. government did little to stop López.

López offered the leadership of one expedition to Robert E. Lee and Jefferson Davis, but both turned it down. So López himself led the invaders, mostly Americans.

In 1850, he landed in Cuba with 600 men but was driven off. A year later, he tried again with 400 men, hoping to aid the revolution led by the lawyer-patriot Joaquin de Agüero. A group under W. L. Crittenden, nephew of the U.S. attorney general, was captured first. The fifty prisoners were shot in a public square, and their fingers and skull pieces were nailed up as warnings to others.

López and his men were captured in 1851. López was strangled with a sharp metal collar tightened by a screw. Cuba did not win its independence from Spain until 1902.

CUBAN AID

Cubans gave $6 million to the American Revolutionary War effort.

It is well known that, because of their antagonism toward the British, the French provided the American colonists with troops and ships. In 1781, George Washington met with the French General Jean Baptiste de Rochambeau, who then sent a message to the French Admiral François de Grasse at Santo Domingo, requesting military and financial help for the Americans. De Grasse had the military help—twenty-nine ships and 3,300 men at his disposal—but not the money. He tried to raise funds in Santo Domingo and Haiti, to no avail. So he went to Cuba, which was dominated at the time by Spain.

Spain tolerated the Americans only because it hated Britain more. But many Cuban Creoles—cattle ranchers, planters, and professionals—also chafed under unfair taxation and sympathized with the colonists. The Creoles dug into their pocketbooks to come up with the surprising sum of $6 million—most of which came from the women of

Havana, who donated their diamond jewelry—for General Washington. Those funds helped finance the crucial Yorktown campaign.

SANDINISTAS—INSPIRED BY U.S.

Had it not been for the United States, the anti-U.S. Sandinista party, which rules Nicaragua today, might never have come to be.

Since 1909, U.S. Marines had been periodically sent to Nicaragua to restore order and protect "American lives and property" from eruptions of violence and political instability. Installed as a Conservative Nicaraguan president in 1911, Adolfo Diaz called in the U.S. Marines in 1912 to keep Liberal rebels quiet. New revolts in 1926 brought the marines back, and by that winter, U.S. intervention became greater: about 2,000 marines occupied Nicaragua. President Calvin Coolidge also sent statesman Henry Stimson to make peace between the rebels and President Diaz.

But a guerrilla leader, Augusto Sandino, and his 200 followers retreated to the hills and continued to wage war against the U.S.-backed government and the marines. While U.S. officials viewed Sandino as a terrorist, thousands of Americans opposed U.S. intervention in Central America and hailed him as a hero. One ardent anti-interventionist was Senator William E. Borah of Idaho, who said, "The people of Nicaragua are being exploited in shameless fashion by American corporations protected by U.S. Marines."

Finally, in February 1933, a month after the last marines departed, Sandino made peace with the new president, Juan Sacasa, a liberal. Anastasio Somoza Garcia, the powerful leader of the U.S.-trained national guard, bitterly opposed Sandino and was angered when Sacasa granted amnesty to the rebels.

On February 21, 1934, after dining with Sacasa, Sandino and two aides were ambushed by Somoza's henchmen and shot. For legions of supporters in Nicaragua and the United States, Sandino became a martyr in the war against "Yankee Imperialism." Somoza himself illegally seized the presidency three years later, thus beginning his family's long stranglehold on Nicaragua. But the Sandinistas, named for their fallen hero, never gave up. They overthrew the last Somoza ruler, Anastasio Somoza Debayle, in 1979.

CIVILIZED WARFARE

American Plains Indians, known as great warriors, practiced one of the most civilized methods of assessing bravery in battle. Instead of killing an enemy, they merely touched or hit him. The ritual of recording these usually bloodless victories was called "counting coup."

Warriors of some tribes carried into battle a pole called a coup stick (from the French word *coup*, meaning a "blow"). It was bound with skin or fur and decorated with feathers. If the warrior was able to touch an enemy with it, he gained credits.

The Indians designed elaborate point systems to keep track of their triumphs. The highest number of points usually went to the first person in a battle who touched an enemy. A warrior who killed an enemy usually received the fewest points. In some tribes, a warrior who saved his friend's life in battle could paint a cross on his clothing. A black feather torn down the middle was sometimes given to the man who sighted the enemy.

Indians often recited their coups out loud. Each time he earned a new coup, a warrior was entitled to recite his complete coup history. Bragging was accepted, but not lying or excessive exaggeration.

COURT OF A PEEL

A U.S. Army private was once court-martialed for peeling potatoes improperly.

While assigned to kitchen duty at Fort Meyer, Virginia, Pfc. Andrew God, Jr., was accused of hacking the eyes off potatoes instead of carefully digging them out with the point of his knife, and of peeling the spuds too thick. It was a wasteful practice, claimed his captain and the mess sergeant, and God was taken to court on charges of having "willfully suffered potatoes of some value, the military property of the United States, to be destroyed by improper peeling."

At the 1959 trial, God pleaded not guilty. "You can't jab a potato with a knife and dig into it," he said. "If the knife slips, you've got it in your hand." Moreover, his lawyer showed that a month's worth of God's accumulated potato peelings—saved in a large pan—actually weighed less than the mess sergeant's.

In the end, the court ruled that the case against God was half-baked, and the charges—though not the potatoes—were "repealed."

JUST DESERTS

Desertions and defections have always hampered U.S. military operations, but never so seriously as during the Mexican War (1846–48). Throughout the fighting, so many Americans switched over to the enemy that they formed their own Mexican-American brigade.

In the spring of 1846, as opposition to the U.S. annexation of Texas was growing, many U.S. enlisted men had their own bones to pick with the army over arbitrary and unduly harsh discipline and treatment. Thus, Mexican General Pedro de Ampudia had little trouble luring hundreds of U.S. soldiers over to his side with promises of generous land grants, Mexican citizenship, and guaranteed quick military promotions.

At first, the Americans fought as replacements for felled Mexicans. Later, they were grouped into the San Patricio Brigade, consisting of three artillery companies. The San Patricios, whose ranks eventually swelled to several hundred, fought hard and inflicted many casualties against their former platoon mates. After the American forces defeated the Mexicans and San Patricios at Churubusco in 1847, captured defectors were court-martialed on charges of desertion and treason. Many were hanged; others were subjected to a gauntlet of indignities, including hard-labor prison sentences, head-shaving, and having the letter "D" branded into their cheeks with a hot iron. The executions outraged the Mexicans, who valued the San Patricios as brave comrades. (In 1982, a proposal to build a monument in honor of the brigade was under study in Mexico City.)

The Mexicans continued to solicit deserters and the San Patricio Brigade was not disbanded until a treaty of peace was signed by the United States and Mexico in May 1848.

HARD CHEESE FOR ARGENTINA

The Uruguayan navy once fought a sea battle using cheeses as cannonballs.

It happened in the 1840s. The aggressive Argentine dictator Juan Manuel de Rosas, in an attempt to annex Uruguay, ordered his navy to blockade Montevideo, the capital. The besieged Uruguayans held their own in the battle until they ran out of conventional ammunition. In desperation, they raided the galleys of their ships and loaded their cannons with very old, hard Edam cheeses and fired them at the enemy.

Contemporary chronicles record that the Uruguayans won the skirmish.

NO WATERLOO BATTLE

The great battle of Waterloo did not take place at Waterloo. To be accurate, we should say of someone in defeat, "He met his La Belle-Alliance." For it was there, not at Waterloo, that Napoleon Bonaparte's French forces were beaten on June 18, 1815, by the Allies, led by the Duke of Wellington and Prussian General von Blücher. Waterloo, a suburb of Brussels, Belgium, is seven miles north of the battlefield.

Delayed by rain, the battle began at 11:30 A.M. Wellington's troops were ranged along a ridge at the town of Mont-Saint-Jean; four miles to the south were Napoleon's forces on a facing ridge at La Belle-Alliance. In between was a valley of death where, for more than eight hours, thousands of men fought and died in the blood-soaked mud. At the end of the battle, more than one third of Napoleon's men were wounded or dead. Napoleon wept, wishing he too had died.

Victor Hugo, an authority on the Napoleonic Wars, later wrote: ". . . and Waterloo, which had no share in the battle, has all the honor. A dubious honor, as attested to by the battle-scarred little towns on the battlefield, including La Belle-Alliance."

U.S. INVADED THE FALKLANDS

More than 150 years ago, the U.S. Navy invaded the Falkland Islands and took prisoners.

In 1831, Louis Vernet, Argentine governor of the islands, seized three American fishing schooners in retaliation for U.S. noncompliance with Argentine fishing regulations and nonpayment of duties. Ordered to investigate, Captain Sylas Duncan of the U.S.S. *Lexington* demanded that Argentina arrest Vernet as a pirate.

When the Argentines refused, Duncan sailed to the Falklands. A party from his ship landed at Port Louis, looted houses, arrested the inhabitants as pirates, and took seven of them away in handcuffs. In a letter discovered in 1982 in the National Archives in Washington, D.C., Duncan wrote that the prisoners "appeared greatly rejoiced at the opportunity . . . of removing with their families from a desolate region."

Diplomatic relations were suspended. In 1833, the British took over the Falklands, reestablishing a prior claim. When the Americans and Argentines started speaking again in 1841, the United States refused a request for reparations for Duncan's raid on the grounds that ownership of the islands was still in dispute. The United States never did pay up.

BIZARRE PLAN TO AVERT THE CIVIL WAR

Shortly before the U.S. Civil War began on April 12, 1861, Secretary of State William H. Seward presented to President Abraham Lincoln a clever plan to avert the coming catastrophe: provoke war with a foreign power.

On April 1, Seward wrote a memo to Lincoln titled "Some thoughts for the President's Consideration." He advised that the United States should demand "explanations" from Spain and France for their intervention in the Caribbean; if Spain and France did not respond, the United States should declare war. In short, pick a fight. Lincoln gracefully but firmly turned down Seward's proposal.

Why had Seward devised such a scheme? War would unite the states, he said. If Spain could be provoked to fight, the South would quickly join forces with the North, eager to claim the Spanish colonies of Puerto Rico and Cuba as slave territories. In any case, the United States might obtain some island bases.

THE GRAYBEARD REGIMENT

During the U.S. Civil War, one Union regiment—the 37th Iowa Volunteer Infantry—was largely, and deliberately, composed of old men. It was nicknamed the Graybeard Regiment.

In 1862, the U.S. War Department authorized the formation of the 37th Infantry to show that men past draft age were willing and able to go to war. The unit of 914 men was assembled that December at Camp

Colonel George
Washington Kincaid,
commander of the
37th Infantry

Strong, near Muscatine, Iowa. The oldest man was eighty-year-old Pvt. Curtis King. Six men were in their seventies, including a seventy-two-year-old drummer, Nicholas Ramey. Another 136 men were in their sixties. Nearly all of the members of the regiment were over forty-five.

Required to hike in the mud and sleep in the rain like other soldiers, the Graybeards were spared none of the rigors of daily army life. They were, however, exempted from combat duty, serving instead as guards of military prisons, railroads, and arsenals in Missouri, Tennessee, Illinois, Indiana, and Ohio. Only three were killed in action, but 145 died of disease and 364 were discharged because of physical disabilities.

By war's end, more than 1,300 of the sons and grandsons of Graybeard members had enlisted. So the regiment accomplished its major purpose—to serve as a grand propaganda tool for recruiting.

HOST TO THE CIVIL WAR

The actual fighting in the U.S. Civil War began in one man's kitchen and four years later ended in the same man's parlor. The man who hosted the start and finish of the Civil War was a prosperous Virginia merchant named Wilmer McLean.

McLean owned an estate near Manassas Junction called Yorkshire. In July 1861, his house became the local Confederate headquarters and came under fire during the first major land battle opening the war. Union forces even managed to put a shell down McLean's chimney, landing in a kettle of stew simmering for General P.G.T. Beauregard's lunch.

Prompted by the Second Battle of Bull Run a year later, McLean moved to a remote southern Virginia village called Appomattox Court House. There, at the war's end in April 1865, he was approached by an officer seeking a site for Lee's surrender to Grant. The courthouse itself was locked for the weekend, and other quarters proved unacceptable. Reluctantly, McLean offered his parlor.

Souvenir mongers, including some Union generals, carried off his parlor furniture, and the unhappy McLean soon went bankrupt trying to market a lithograph of the historic ceremony. His Appomattox house was dismantled by an entrepreneur who planned to display the house in Washington, D.C. The businessman failed to raise enough money for the move, and the house was left in ruins until the National Park Service reconstructed it after World War II.

THE YOUNGEST GENERAL

When Galusha Pennypacker, U.S. Civil War hero, was awarded the rank of major general, he was too young even to vote.

Pennypacker first joined the army as a quartermaster-sergeant with the 9th Pennsylvania Volunteers in 1861 at age sixteen. That August, he was elected captain in the 97th Pennsylvania Volunteers. The tall boy-soldier was a colonel by 1864. His men loved him. At Fort Gilmer he led troops across a mile of brush in full view of the enemy. Though his horse was killed and he was wounded, he kept on fighting. His twentieth birthday was spent convalescing from three wounds sustained at Green Plains, Virginia, but he was soon back in the action.

On January 15, 1865, at Fort Fisher, North Carolina, he led a brigade across enemy defenses and was the first to reach the top of the third protective earthen wall where he triumphantly planted a regiment flag. Standing in plain sight of the enemy, he watched as a Confederate soldier took aim and shot him, badly wounding him in the side and hip. A month later, by brevet, the twenty-year-old was appointed brigadier general of the Volunteers. He was the youngest soldier to achieve that rank on either side of the Civil War. In March 1865, he was breveted a major general, and he was still not yet twenty-one.

Pennypacker remained in the army through the Reconstruction period, refused an opportunity to run for governor of Pennsylvania, and lived out a lonely retirement in Philadelphia, where he died on October 1, 1916.

LAST-DITCH DITCH

An effort was once made to change the course of the Mississippi River. During the U.S. Civil War, the river's course was a hazard for the North because it looped past Confederate Vicksburg right under bluffs bristling with guns that gave the South command over seventeen miles of water. Boats passing beneath could not raise their guns high enough to train them on the fortifications above. A linchpin, Vicksburg was an important prize because it linked Arkansas, Louisiana, and Texas with the rest of the South.

In the summer of 1862, Northern General Thomas Williams tried to build a canal to reroute the Mississippi to bypass Vicksburg in order to protect his boats, but rising waters foiled him. Then, at President Lincoln's request, Ulysses S. Grant, in the opening months of 1863, tried to widen Williams's canal to make it usable. Four thousand men were put to work with dredges and picks and shovels. Grant called this "a series of experiments to consume time, and to divert the attention of the enemy, of my troops, and of the public generally . . ." That was all the canal accomplished, for the effort was unsuccessful. On July 4, 1863, Grant finally took Vicksburg by more conventional means.

Years later, in 1876, heavy rains did cause the Mississippi to change its course, bypassing Vicksburg. By then, of course, it was too late.

THE ENGLISH CHANNEL CIVIL WAR BATTLE

An important U.S. Civil War sea battle was fought in the English Channel.

The *Alabama*, a Confederate steamship with sail power built and largely manned by the British, had bagged sixty-eight Yankee merchant ships in two years and paralyzed shipping. On June 11, 1864, it steamed victoriously into the harbor at Cherbourg, France, with its Yankee prisoners. Shortly, the chain-plated Union ship *Kearsarge* also sailed into the port. Its commander, John A. Winslow, demanded the prisoners. Raphael Semmes—who had once been Winslow's roommate and was now captain of the *Alabama*—challenged the *Kearsarge* to a battle.

On June 19, seven miles off the French coast, the two ships engaged. Watching from rooftops, towers, and cliffs were crowds of French people. The Impressionist artist Edouard Manet sketched the scene from a boat. The battle lasted only ninety minutes. When the *Alabama* started to sink, Semmes and his crew abandoned ship. In all, twenty-two men died.

In 1872, an international commission ruled that Great Britain had been responsible for the *Alabama*'s destructive actions. The penalty was $15 million, to be paid to the United States.

RANSOMING THE TOWN OF FREDERICK

On July 9, 1864, the citizens of Frederick, Maryland, paid $200,000 ransom to Confederate General Jubal A. Early when he and his troops passed through the town en route to Washington, D.C. Maryland congressmen have been trying since 1889 to get the federal government to reimburse Frederick for supporting the Union cause. The most recent attempt was made by Sen. Charles Mathias, who reintroduced the compensation bill to Congress in October 1981. With interest, the debt now amounts to about $4 million.

When General Early arrived in Frederick, the town was unprotected—Union forces were stationed farther up the Monocacy River. The town's arsenals held more than $1 million worth of Union supplies; to protect them, the city fathers quickly paid the Confederates the ransom that they demanded. They borrowed $200,000 from five local banks and carried it in baskets to the Confederates.

While Early's troops were delayed in Frederick, Union reinforcements reached the Monocacy, and the battle there gave the Union officers in Washington time to amass enough troops to foil the Confederate invasion.

It took until 1951 for the city of Frederick to repay the banks. Then its aldermen asked the federal government for compensation. They're still waiting.

CAISSONS STOP, BUT PENSIONS GO
ROLLING ALONG

Old soldiers may die, but their dependents don't necessarily fade away. In fact, widows of U.S. Civil War veterans are still receiving pension checks from the Veterans Administration.

As of February 1983, there were forty-one Civil War widows, each collecting a monthly benefit of about $70. The fourteen Confederate ladies have received benefits only since 1958, when Congress forgivingly declared them eligible.

The Civil War ended in 1865. Between 1890, when the pension program was inaugurated, and 1905, when a cutoff was declared on eligibility, many teenage girls married aging Union vets to take advantage of the pension. Of the forty-one surviving widows, most are in their nineties.

The VA also is still paying out pensions to widows from the Indian wars, the Spanish-American War, and even the Boxer Rebellion and the Philippine Insurrection. In some instances, the costs of these benefits have surpassed the costs of the war in which they were earned.

A MEDAL FOR DISOBEDIENCE

For an action during the decisive battle of Gettysburg in the U.S. Civil War, Union Army Captain William E. Miller earned the U.S. Congressional Medal of Honor despite disobeying army orders.

On July 3, 1863, the third day of the battle of Gettysburg, the final outcome was still uncertain. Both sides fully realized, however, that a Confederate win could mean a Southern victory in the Civil War. On the

Captain William E. Miller

fringe of the battlefield, Captain Miller held his Pennsylvania cavalry troops in reserve, having been ordered not to attack. But when he saw Confederate soldiers penetrating a vulnerable Union flank, he deliberately disobeyed orders and led his men in a bloody charge. Although his troops suffered heavy casualties, Miller's attack made it possible for the Union to win the battle—and ultimately the war.

For his decisive action and bravery at Gettysburg, Miller was awarded the Medal of Honor. Although he had violated orders in charging the Confederates—he was honored for his independence and initiative.

ADVICE FROM THE ENEMY

During the U.S. Civil War, a novice Union commander crossed the battle lines to ask the enemy whether he should surrender.

In September 1862, at the battle of Munfordville, Kentucky, Colonel John T. Wilder found himself surrounded and outnumbered six-to-one by General Braxton Bragg's Confederate forces. Although Wilder's brigade was the first fighting force in history to be fully equipped with repeating rifles (which his men had paid for themselves), Colonel Wilder, an Indiana industrialist and hydraulic engineer, lacked the combat experience and confidence to decide between fighting or surrendering. What he needed was professional advice—even if it had to come from the enemy.

Waving a white flag, Wilder entered the Confederates' camp and approached Major General Simon Bolivar Buckner, respected for his integrity. Buckner demurred when asked what to do. Instead, he referred the Union officer to General Bragg, who invited Wilder to count the number of cannon trained on his forces. Wilder stopped counting at forty-six. "I believe I'll surrender," he said.

Wilder promptly turned over 4,267 soldiers to Bragg—along with 10 guns, 5,000 rifles, and other supplies. Buckner said later, "I would not have deceived that man under those circumstances for anything."

NEVER SAY DIE

Who was the most indestructible man in U.S. history? A leading candidate would be Jacques Rollinger of Company B, 47th New York Volunteers, who emerged from the Civil War looking like mincemeat. He appeared before a pension board in 1865 with the following account of his mishaps.

In 1862, he was cut by a saber on his left thigh and right forearm. Shortly afterward, he was shot in the right thigh. In 1863, he suffered a sword cut that severed his spinal muscles. Next, he was captured in Missouri by outlaws who lacerated his chest with burning sticks. Rollinger escaped to Florida, where he was hit in the right leg by a shell fragment. While collapsing from the blow, he was shot just below the heart. Then he was bayoneted accidentally by a comrade, piercing his liver. Finally, he was shot through the neck. During his long convalescence, Rollinger liked to entertain friends by blowing jets of water through the holes in his neck.

Rollinger's main complaint before the pension board, however, was of a stiff knee. He also said he was on his way to join freedom fighter Giuseppe Garibaldi's army in Italy.

THE ROUGH WALKERS

Teddy Roosevelt's Rough Riders became legendary in the Spanish-American War when they fought and won the battle of San Juan Hill. Their heroic charge up Kettle Hill—the first assault on San Juan Ridge—routed the Spanish in Cuba and ended the conflict. However, the Rough Riders did not ride up the hill as everyone believed—they walked and ran up the slope. They took the heights on foot, because they had no horses—except for the few designated for the commanding officers. Roosevelt led the charge astride his horse, Texas, but his men never rode at all in the war. They fought every battle on foot.

When Assistant Secretary of the Navy Theodore Roosevelt secured congressional approval for recruiting a volunteer regiment of cavalry at the outbreak of war in 1898, he personally selected 1,000 men as his Rough Riders. Actually commanded by Colonel Leonard Wood, with Roosevelt second in command, the Rough Riders were an unlikely mix of Harvard bluebloods, horsemen, cowboys, and famous athletes. After two months of training with their steeds in Texas, the Rough Riders were ready for Cuba. But when Roosevelt's regiment embarked on the troopships, there was only enough room on board for 560 men—and absolutely no room for their 1,200 horses and pack mules.

Teddy Roosevelt and the Rough Riders on San Juan Hill

The Rough Riders soon nicknamed themselves "Wood's Weary Walkers" as they fought two months of the war entirely on foot.

THE POPGUN WAR

Three young boys armed with a toy cannon once battled the U.S. Army to a standstill.

In September 1941, several thousand soldiers, grouped into opposing Red and Blue armies, were engaged in practice war games in Louisiana. While the Blue Army's patrol scout unit was taking a break in front of a store in the Cane River town of Bermuda, Alphonse, Kenneth, and Mayo Prudhomme—fourteen, twelve, and nine respectively—played nearby with a small but very loud toy cannon that fired carbide gas. When the boys aimed a shot across the river at the advancing Blue Army convoy, the Blues opened up on them with rifles and machine guns (firing blanks). The army men assumed they'd been fired upon by their own patrol scouts, who had mistaken them for the enemy.

The boys fired back and the battle raged for nearly half an hour before the umpire signaled both sides to stop. It was only then that he discovered that the convoy—consisting of some 500 tanks, trucks, and jeeps—had been stymied by a trio of kids. "Please stop your boys from shooting that cannon," the umpire commanded Mrs. Prudhomme. "They are holding up the war and most of the Blue Army."

LIFE IN A CLOSET

During World War I, a British soldier hid from the Germans for four years in a cupboard.

Early in the war, the soldier, Patrick Fowler of the 11th Hussars, was cut off from his regiment at the battle of Le Cateau. Wandering the French countryside in a borrowed civilian coat, as he tried to evade the Germans, he met a woodcutter who took him to a house owned by the woodcutter's mother-in-law, Mme Belmont-Gobert. There Fowler was slipped inside and hidden in a cupboard less than six feet high. It became his main home. Only for a few minutes each night when all were asleep—just to stretch and eat—did he emerge from it. Luckily, though eight German soldiers were later billeted in the house and spent time drinking coffee in the room, they never bothered to open the cupboard. Once, as German surveillance of villagers stepped up, Fowler, dressed as a peasant woman, temporarily hid under a haystack. He was nearly killed when German soldiers plunged pitchforks into the hay. When Mme Belmont-Gobert moved, Fowler was transported to her new house inside the cupboard. A helpful German assisted in lifting it, apparently not noticing its weight.

In the winter of 1918, when the Germans retreated, Fowler was able to emerge from his cramped hiding place. The four years had been a nightmare and an eternity to him, yet he survived safely and well. The cupboard is now on display at the Imperial War Museum in England.

U.S. PLANES ATTACK THE SOVIET UNION

Once, in a little-known incident, planes of the U.S. Air Force attacked the USSR.

The episode took place during the early months of the Korean War, when two F-80 Shooting Stars strafed an airfield near Vladivostok.

The hedgehopping attack against the Soviet airfield at Sukhaya Rechka, sixty-two miles from the border with Korea, took place on October 8, 1950. In Korea, the drive from Inchon was under way, culminating in the capture by United Nations forces of the North Korean capital. It was a time when American hawks were urging full-scale war against Communism.

The Soviet foreign ministry vigorously protested the "provocative" attack to the U.S. minister-counselor in Moscow—who sidestepped a diplomatic confrontation by maintaining that it was a matter for the United Nations, under whose aegis U.S. forces were fighting in Korea.

The United States eventually volunteered an explanation to the UN. According to General Douglas MacArthur, commander in chief of the combined forces in Korea, the attack against Sukhaya Rechka was a mistake due to navigational error and poor judgment. The air force commander was relieved, the pilots were disciplined, and the United States offered to pay damages.

The USSR, then seeking a "breathing spell" after the massive bloodletting of World War II, according to the Soviet newspaper *Pravda*, chose not to rise to the provocation.

THE EMPTY TOMB OF THE UNKNOWN
SOLDIER

The fourth of the crypts in the Tomb of the Unknown Soldier in Virginia's Arlington National Cemetery is empty. And it may remain so.

The crypt was to contain a casualty of the Vietnam conflict. Since 1974, it has been positioned next to those holding the bodies of soldiers from World War I, World War II, and the Korean War—all of them men "known but to God." In all previous American wars, thousands of dead soldiers remained unidentified (8,526 in World War II alone). But only four of all the dead and recovered soldiers of Vietnam have not been identified. While they fulfill part of the criteria for the Unknown Soldier—they died fighting in Vietnam, Laos, or Cambodia—none meets the qualification that at least 80 percent of the body must have been recovered.

The reason for the problem lies in the sophistication of modern warfare. The Vietnam dead were recovered by helicopter and quickly flown out of the battle area. They were then identified almost immediately by using advanced technology, such as comparing pictures of their remains with X-ray photographs. So the tomb may remain empty forever.

$38 MILLION AN HOUR

President Ronald Reagan's proposed military budget will cost American taxpayers more than $38 million *an hour* over the next five years—and that's only if the United States remains at peace. Should war break out, the cost undoubtedly will be higher.

The administration's "prewar" defense budget, submitted to Congress in 1983, proposes $280.5 billion for military expenses for fiscal 1984, $330 billion for 1985, $364.8 billion for 1986, $397 billion for 1987, and $432.7 billion for 1988. That adds up to about $1.8 trillion.

If you're wondering what your share is, it works out to more than $20,000 for every taxpayer in the United States, according to the Center for Defense Information in Washington, D.C.

Pershing II
missle shoots
skyward—but
not as fast as
U.S. defense
budget

DOOMSDAY CLOCK

Beginning in 1947, the *Bulletin of the Atomic Scientists* has featured
on its cover a doomsday clock predicting the time of nuclear holocaust.
The closer to 12:00 midnight, the closer to nuclear war and the end. The
decision to move the clock hands is based on a unanimous decision by
the board of directors of the Educational Foundation for Nuclear Science. The hands have been shifted backward or forward ten times since
1947, when they read 11:53.

1949—11:57	(Soviet Union explodes its first atomic bomb.)
1953—11:58	(Hydrogen bomb developed.)
1960—11:53	(Cold War thaws.)
1963—11:48	(Partial Test Ban Treaty signed.)
1968—11:53	(Five nations possess nuclear weapons.)
1969—11:50	(Nuclear Non-Proliferation Treaty ratified.)
1972—11:48	(Strategic Arms Limitation Talks—SALT—begin.)
1974—11:51	(SALT stalled.)
1980—11:53	(Nations and groups become irrational.)
1981—11:56	(Nuclear war considered thinkable.)

The *Bulletin* and its sponsoring foundation, formed in 1945 by atomic scientists including Albert Einstein, wishes to further the cause of peace—even at the risk of scaring people to death. The objective is to push back the hands of the clock.

7

WORLD WAR II

THE U.S. ATTACK ON PEARL HARBOR

It wasn't the Japanese who first thought of launching a surprise attack on Pearl Harbor. It was the Americans.

Although U.S. Army Brigadier General Billy Mitchell, the pioneer advocate of air power, believed as early as 1924 that Pearl Harbor would some day suffer a surprise attack by the Japanese, no one took his amazingly accurate prediction seriously. Not until 1932 did a U.S. Navy admiral set out to prove the feasibility of such a sneak attack.

In that year, according to historian George Morgenstern, U.S. forces gathered in the Pacific for practice war games to see how the Hawaiian naval base might best be defended. Although the attack commander, Admiral Harry Yarnell, had many battleships, he pared his flotilla down to two aircraft destroyers and four cruisers, concentrating instead on aircraft. While the small task force crept up on its sleeping prey undetected early one Sunday morning, the attack planes zeroed in through heavy clouds to the northeast, invisible from the ground until they were practically over Oahu. The strategy worked, and Yarnell's forces "demolished" the opposition.

Japanese military officers on hand watched the simulation with interest, for Pearl Harbor was already in their gunsights. Indeed, the year before, Japanese Naval Academy students had been posed this question on their final exams: "How would you carry out a surprise attack on Pearl Harbor?" Now the answer was obvious. Following Yarnell's example with remarkable fidelity, the Japanese turned it against their teachers early on Sunday morning, December 7, 1941.

SUPERMAN WAS 4-F

When Superman tried to enlist in the U.S. Army in World War II, he was declared 4-F—unfit to serve. The Man of Steel failing an army physical? It seems impossible. But it happened, because one of his amazing powers boomeranged on him. As Clark Kent, he accidentally pierced a

George Reeves
as the original
Superman—
unfit for
military service

wall with his X-ray vision, read an eye chart in another room, and consequently flunked the test.

In actuality, Superman's creators, Jerry Siegel and Joe Shuster —afraid that soldiers would ridicule an army Superman—chose to keep him a civilian. Nonetheless, he was able to show his love for the United States. In spite of his alien status as an extraterrestrial from the planet Krypton, the government enlisted his support in the fight for "truth, justice, and the American way."

DELAYED REVENGE

The first Japanese attack on the U.S. mainland, in 1942, was triggered by cactus spines in the rear end of a Japanese naval captain.

In the late 1930s, Kozo Nishino was commander of a Japanese tanker taking on crude oil at the Ellwood oil field near Santa Barbara, California. On the way up the path from the beach to a formal ceremony welcoming him and his crew, Nishino slipped and fell into a prickly-pear cactus. Workers on a nearby oil rig broke into guffaws at the sight of the proud commander having cactus spines plucked from his posterior. Then and there, the humiliated Nishino swore to get even.

He had to wait for war between the United States and Japan, but on February 23, 1942, he got his revenge. From 7:07 to 7:45 P.M., he directed the shelling of the Ellwood oil field from his submarine, the *I-17*. Though about twenty-five shells were fired from a 5.5-inch deck gun, little damage was done. One rig needed a $500 repair job after the shelling, and one man was wounded while trying to defuse an unexploded shell.

U.S. planes gave chase to the sub, but Nishino got away. Thereafter, American coastal defenses were improved, so the mainland suffered only a few sporadic submarine attacks by the Japanese during the rest of the war, at Fort Stevens in Oregon.

NEVER SHOOT A HAWAIIAN THREE TIMES

A one-man Japanese force invaded the U.S. territory of Hawaii during the Pearl Harbor attack and captured the island of Niihau for one week.

On the afternoon of December 7, 1941, Japanese fighter pilot Shigenori Nishikaichi's bullet-riddled plane crash-landed on the tiny ranching island of Niihau, seventeen miles from Kauai. The island's few hundred residents had no radios and were unaware of the attack on Pearl Harbor.

Howard Kaleohano, a ranch hand, saw the plane crash. He raced to it, noticed the bullet holes, and suspected something was wrong. He helped the pilot out and confiscated his gun, maps, and papers. Another islander, the local beekeeper Yoshio Harada, was chosen to look after the Japanese stranger in his home. But Harada, who had dual U.S.-Japanese citizenship, was awed by the heroic young fighter and soon declared himself an ally of Nishikaichi. Together they planned to retrieve the pilot's papers and then escape. They went to the downed plane, failed to find the papers, then tried to make radio contact with the Japanese. Removing the plane's machine guns, they terrorized the Niihauans in a second attempt to find the papers.

In the confusion, Kaleohano and five other islanders got away in a lifeboat, rowing all night to Kauai to get help. Harada and Nishikaichi were so enraged by this escape that they further terrorized the villagers.

Ben Kanahele, a ranch hand, tried to disarm the pilot. He was not quick enough, and Nishikaichi shot him three times—in the chest, hip, and penis. Kanahele then picked up the pilot and slammed him into a stone wall. In a rage, the rancher drew a knife and slit the dying pilot's throat. Harada grabbed the shotgun and killed himself.

By the time Howard Kaleohano's rescue party returned, peace was restored. Ben Kanahele's bravery inspired the local proverb, "Never shoot a Hawaiian three times—he will get mad at you."

HOWARD HUGHES AND THE JAPANESE ZERO

Japan's most potent weapon in World War II—the Zero fighter plane —was perhaps inspired by U.S. millionaire aviator Howard Hughes.

In 1934, Hughes helped design and build a lightweight experimental aircraft dubbed the H-1. He proclaimed it the fastest plane in the world, and it was. On January 19, 1937, he set a transcontinental speed record, flying at 332 mph from Burbank, California, to Newark, New Jersey. Hughes became a national hero, and the H-1 captured the interest of aviation experts everywhere, including Japan.

In 1937, Hughes suggested that the U.S. Army adapt the H-1 for

Howard Hughes and his brainchild, the H-1,
after record-setting flight in 1937

production as a fighter plane. But his proposal was rejected, and the H-1 was mothballed in a California hangar. Meanwhile, the Japanese government commissioned Mitsubishi Ltd. and Jiro Horikoshi, a top aeronautical engineer, to design a superior fighter plane. He succeeded in developing a spectacularly agile aircraft, which incorporated many design features of the H-1. Thus was born the Zero—sleek, fast, and dramatically similar to Hughes's unique plane.

In 1947, Hughes testified before a Senate committee investigating his wartime defense contracts. "I am told," he said, "that the Japanese copied the Zero from this airplane [the H-1] . . . I tried to sell the airplane to the army, but they turned it down because at that time the army did not think a cantilever monoplane was proper for a pursuit ship . . ." The Japanese had quite a different opinion.

HITLER'S PLAN TO BOMB NEW YORK

During World War II, Hitler was obsessed by the idea of blitzing the Allies' chief cities—London, Moscow, and especially New York. As he figured it, even if an air attack on Manhattan did little damage, the impact on American morale would be devastating.

Three leading German aircraft companies were commissioned to produce long-range bombers. Focke-Wulf designed a six-engine aircraft with a 22,000-pound bomb load, but it never got past the drawing board. Messerschmitt's four-engine Me 264V-1 was equipped to carry a more modest 3,960-pound bomb load across the Atlantic at high altitudes, and it was test-flown in December 1942. Refined models with heavier bomb loads were later designed, but wartime supply shortages forced Messerschmitt to abandon the program.

Meanwhile, the Junkers company developed the Ju390, the largest plane then manufactured in Germany. In January 1944, the Third Reich asserted that the Ju390 had been test-flown from Bordeaux, France, to within 12½ miles of the U.S. coastline north of New York. Six months later, Allied saboteurs destroyed the Junkers project.

By 1942 the Germans were considering another angle: a rocket attack fired from underwater. They conducted experiments in submarine-launched missiles, and plans took shape in 1944 to fire V-2 rockets on New York City from a range of about 200 miles. Special U-boats were designed to accommodate the V-2s, but the war ended before such plans became reality. Wernher von Braun, director of the V-2 effort, came to the United States after the war—bringing all his underwater missile research with him. He later pioneered guided missile development for the U.S. military.

WORLD WAR II'S FALSE START

World War II officially began on September 1, 1939, when Hitler's forces invaded Poland. But the first shots actually were fired six days earlier.

Hitler had originally planned to attack on August 26, 1939. But the evening before, with sixteen combat units poised to strike, the attack was called off. Last-minute political developments—including Mussolini's sudden vow not to assist Germany in an attack on Poland—convinced Hitler that the time was not ripe for an invasion.

With great difficulty, the combat teams were radioed and summoned home. But one could not be reached. At 12:01 A.M. on August 26, a unit led by Lt. Albrecht Herzner captured the strategic Janlunkuv Pass in Poland, along with the railway station at Mosty and a small number of Polish prisoners. When Herzner telephoned central headquarters, he was told that he had jumped the gun. On orders, he released his prisoners and came home.

While this snafu should have tipped Germany's hand, the Polish government incredibly let it pass without notice. When the Nazis invaded on September 1, the Poles were taken by surprise.

THE CAVALRY'S LAST STAND

U. S. soldiers rode into battle on horseback as recently as World War II, and Ronald Reagan himself was a second lieutenant in the U.S. Cavalry reserve when that war broke out. He later dismounted to join the First Motion Picture Unit of the Army Air Force.

Although the horse cavalry in this country dates back to the American Revolution, it was already going out of style in 1914, and only four horse cavalry regiments saw service in France in World War I. After the war, the cavalry gradually replaced horses with armored tanks, which offered more mobility and firepower. Even so, the army maintained its cavalry school at Fort Riley, Kansas, through World War II.

The last mounted unit to see action was the 26th Cavalry regiment of the Philippine Scouts, which fired at invading Japanese forces in the Philippines in December 1941 and covered the American retreat to Bataan. They made their last stand against the Japanese on January 15, 1942, then retreated to Bataan, where the men were forced to slaughter their horses for food.

After the war, the army decided that horses were passé, except for use in ceremonial events. By 1953, all the cavalry horses were sold or retired. In the present-day army, "cavalry" refers to motorized transport units using tanks and trucks.

THE DUMMY D-DAY

The invasion of Normandy on June 6, 1944, owed much of its success to the most remarkable practical joke in history.

As the Allies geared up for D-Day, they knew it would be impossible to conceal their invasion plans from the Germans. But they *could* mislead them as to the time and place of the offensive. In the spring of 1944, German surveillance cameras photographed widespread "covert" military operations in southeastern England—bustling army bases half-hidden in the woods, large-scale movements of jeeps and tanks, and an oil refinery under construction at Dover, across the English Channel from Calais, France. The Germans also monitored "secret" radio transmissions concerning new troop concentrations near Dover. It all added up to a single unmistakable conclusion: the Allies would invade Europe through Calais, probably in late July.

But the Nazis were mistaken. The oil refinery was made of old sewage pipes and canvas, built by movie set designers. The combat vehicles were inflatable rubber, the military bases were dummies, the radio messages were fake—and the real invasion was planned not for Calais in late July, but for Normandy in early June.

Nor did the deception cease once the invasion was under way. While

Rubber tanks at Allied base near Dover, 1944: Hitler was duped by decoys

Allied troops were storming the beaches at Normandy, two decoy fleets accompanied by British air squadrons were crossing the Channel toward Calais. The decoy ships carried electronic devices that amplified and returned the pulses of the Germans' radar equipment, and the squadrons overhead released strips of metal foil. Both maneuvers gave the illusion on Nazi radar screens of a massive air and sea attack. Meanwhile, scores of dummy paratroopers—equipped with recordings of gunfire and soldiers' cries—were dropped on the beach south of Calais.

The elaborate ruse lured Hitler into spreading his troops dangerously thin, and the Allies got their foothold in Europe. Even after D-Day, the Führer remained convinced that the *real* invasion was still planned for late July. By the time he got it straight, Germany was on the road to defeat.

WHEN FDR WAS TORPEDOED

In one of the U.S. Navy's most embarrassing moments, the destroyer *William D. Porter* (DD 579) nearly succeeded in torpedoing the U.S. battleship *Iowa* during an Atlantic crossing in World War II. Had the *Iowa* been sunk, the casualties would have included President Franklin D. Roosevelt and his joint chiefs of staff. They were heading secretly for a Cairo conference with Winston Churchill and Chiang Kai-shek.

The bizarre mishap occurred on November 14, 1943, when the *Porter*, making a simulated torpedo attack during defensive exercises, inadvertently fired a live "fish" directly at the *Iowa*. Five minutes of pure panic ensued. The *Iowa*'s skipper desperately executed a high-speed turn, trying to get his ship out of the line of fire.

The emergency situation ended happily, however. As the torpedo entered the *Iowa*'s churning wake, it exploded, set off by the extreme turbulence of the sea. The president magnanimously forgave the destroyer's red-faced commander. The Japanese were less charitable. They sank the *Porter* off Okinawa in June 1945.

BATTLE LOST ON ROLL OF DICE

The United States won the pivotal battle of Midway in World War II thanks to a roll of the dice, according to Imperial Japanese Navy officers Captain Mitsuo Fuchida and Commander Masatake Okumiya.

Following its attack on Pearl Harbor on December 7, 1941, Japan hatched a plan to finish off the crippled U.S. Pacific Fleet. Japanese aircraft carriers would launch a massive assault on the U.S. outpost at Midway Island in the central Pacific. Japan's inevitable and overwhelming victory would intimidate the United States into negotiating a peace.

To prepare for the operation, Japan's top naval officers assembled at the combined-fleet headquarters for four days of elaborate war games, played with dice and diagrams on large sheets of paper. Masatake Okumiya, acting as umpire, threw the dice to determine the number of Japanese aircraft carriers hit by American bombers. He rolled a nine, but Rear Admiral Matome Ugaki, the presiding officer, arbitrarily reduced the number of hits to three. Ugaki's subordinates swallowed their objections, and the admiral kept up his flagrant cheating throughout the games, thus making it seem as if the battle of Midway would be a piece of cake for the Japanese.

It wasn't. By the time Japan attacked on June 4, 1942, the U.S. military had decoded Japanese communications and was ready for action. Allied observers attributed Japan's defeat in the crucial Midway battle to more than an unheeded roll of dice, however. As historian B. H. Liddell Hart said, "Japanese troubles were multiplied by a string of tactical errors. . . . Most of these faults could be traced to complacent overconfidence." With the heavy losses at Midway, Japan forfeited its edge in the war, never to regain it.

THE NAZI-ENGLISH CONNECTION

By 1938, the German nation was committed to war, but the question of strategy had not been settled. Adolf Hitler found the answer not in the works of German strategists but in the writings of a contemporary Englishman, B. H. Liddell Hart.

Liddell Hart, a military historian and philosopher, had developed a concept he called the "expanding torrent"—finding the path of least resistance and striking repeatedly through the enemy's weakest point. It was this strategy with air and ground forces that the Germans (calling

Liddell Hart

it *blitzkrieg,* or "lightning war") used to conquer France and almost bring England to its knees in 1940 in less than six weeks.

The concept was not new. Genghis Khan and the Mongols had termed it "tulughma" in the thirteenth century, and in 1864 General William Tecumseh Sherman employed such methods in his march to the sea during the Civil War. Liddell Hart was aware of Genghis Khan and Sherman, and had written about them. In 1923 he wrote, "[I] happened to watch a stream in flood and saw how aptly the water's natural process of penetrating and circumventing obstacles corresponded to my tactical concept . . ." Thus was devised the term "expanding torrent."

Hitler's dilemma was that Germany could not afford a war on two fronts. While he considered Russia his main enemy, he could not also fight a prolonged war against France. It was necessary that France be subdued quickly. Heinz Guderian, a German tank general, brought Liddell Hart's ideas to Hitler, and the problem was solved. Blitzkrieg gave promise of rapid victory.

The German general staff was opposed to the idea, but Hitler—who never trusted his generals—overrode them. In May 1940, Guderian's tanks broke into France and swept through the French defenses, as the

German general adhered strictly to blitzkrieg strategy. Ironically, the strongest point in the plan's favor may have been its English source: Hitler was an anglophile. He admired the British tradition of empire and held the notion that once Germany disposed of the "decadent" French and "subhuman" Russians, England and Germany could co-rule Europe and Asia.

Liddell Hart, like other prophets, was not honored in his own land, but rather found his greatest disciple in Guderian.

DEATH TOWN

One of the most macabre tourist sites in the world is the French town of Oradour-sur-Glane. It is a silent memorial to the 642 persons murdered there on June 10, 1944, by the SS's Das Reich Division.

At about 2:00 P.M. that day, German army trucks rolled into Oradour, and the SS sealed off the town. Their purpose? Probably to exact reprisals for local Resistance activities, though Oradour's population had played no part in them. All the townspeople were ordered into the square, including babies and the sick. The men were forced into barns and sheds and machine-gunned. The survivors were then burned to death. Five escaped.

The SS then herded the women and children into a church, detonated a smoke bomb on the altar and shot the helpless victims, riddling even baby carriages, then set the building on fire. Marguerite Rouffance, a farmer's wife, escaped through a window, then played dead in the dirt. She was the only woman survivor.

The toll of the innocents: 245 women, 207 children, 190 men. The SS looted the town and departed, singing and playing accordions.

In 1953, twenty-one men—fourteen of them Alsatians who had been conscripted into the German army—were put on trial for the crime. The sentences were light, partly because the masterminds of the murder could not be found and because Alsatians protested against harsh punishments for their countrymen.

Oradour, fifteen miles west of Limoges, is now a national monument. No one lives there. The church, its belfry destroyed, still stands. In a paneless window is a placard, "Madame Rouffance, the only survivor from the church, escaped through this window." And at a shack on the outskirts of town, one can buy souvenirs.

SNEAKING INTO AUSCHWITZ

Nearly forty years before Poland's Solidarity movement was founded, Polish inmates at Auschwitz ran a resistance movement right under the Nazis' noses.

The brains behind the operation was Witold Pilecki, a Polish army captain. In September 1940, he deliberately had himself arrested in Warsaw and sent to the Nazi death camp. There, he and five handpicked inmates organized an underground that would swell to more than 1,000.

The Union of Military Organization, as the movement called itself, aided patients in the camp hospital, stole arms from the SS storehouse, and helped prisoners to escape. Using freed inmates as couriers, Pilecki sent reports of Nazi atrocities to the exiled Polish government in London, which used them as anti-Nazi propaganda. A radio transmitter operated undetected for seven months, keeping contact with Polish secret army headquarters.

In April 1943, Pilecki escaped and went to Warsaw. He tried to persuade the Polish military to bomb the camp, where the resistance remained strong despite his absence. Pilecki then rejoined the army, fighting against the Nazis in the 1944 Warsaw uprising. He survived the war—only to be executed in 1948 for taking part in unauthorized intelligence operations in postwar Poland.

THE NAZI NATURE-LOVER

In eastern Poland stands the largest remaining patch of the primeval forest that once covered much of Europe. The placid 12,000-acre Bialowieza National Park, with its abundance of wildlife and ancient oak and spruce trees, still exists today thanks to the protection of a most unlikely conservationist—the late Nazi officer Hermann Göring.

Since the 1400s, Bialowieza had been a hunting ground for Russian czars and Polish kings. During World War I, German soldiers nearly ruined the forest and slaughtered its bison. After the war, the forest fell into further neglect.

When Germany invaded Poland again in 1939, Bialowieza found a new champion in Göring, whose titles included Master of the German Forests. Göring set about his duties in earnest, stocking the forest with game and severely limiting the number of hunting permits.

While Göring, as head of the Luftwaffe, rained death on Europe,

Nazi Field Marshal Hermann Göring *(Left)*
oversees a wolf hunt in the Bialowieza forest

he kept a sign in his Berlin office that read: "He who tortures animals wounds the feelings of the German people."

WHEN THE U.S. TRIED TO REINSTATE

A MONARCHY

During World War II, the United States created a special battalion whose mission might have resulted in the restoration of the long-defunct Austro-Hungarian Empire and the return of the Hapsburg monarchy to its throne.

The plan was the brainchild of the exiled Archduke Otto von Hapsburg, a close friend of President Franklin D. Roosevelt. Hapsburg offered to organize the battalion himself and guaranteed 5,000 volunteers. FDR backed the idea, saying it was crucial to show the world that Austria was *not* an integral part of the German empire, but a sovereign nation invaded by Hitler.

The formation of the battalion was announced on November 19, 1942, and the forces were headquartered at Camp Atterbury, Indiana. The recruits were a mix of refugees from war-torn Europe and native-born Americans of Austro-Hungarian extraction. Their training included studies in the German language and Hapsburg history.

But the battalion was doomed from the outset. The governments-in-exile of Yugoslavia and Czechoslovakia despised the Hapsburgs and the idea of monarchy, and they protested loudly to FDR. So did numerous European-American political groups. On May 3, 1943—with only 199 volunteers raised—the battalion was disbanded.

BURIAL OF A BATTLESHIP

The *Admiral Scheer,* a World War II German cruiser, came to a curious end for a ship. It was buried.

The ship was dubbed a "pocket battleship" because it had less power and protection than a standard battleship. Weighing 12,100 tons, it was armed with six 11-inch turret guns. But the *Admiral Scheer* was phenomenally successful in its hit-and-run attacks on supply vessels. For example, in one 161-day cruise, it captured four Allied ships and two tankers, destroying more than 100,000 tons of shipping.

On the night of April 9, 1945, helpless in drydock in the harbor basin at Kiel, the *Admiral Scheer* was bombed by the British Royal Air Force. Since its guns had been dismantled for repairs, it was destroyed without being able to fire a shot in protest. Later the Allies filled in the dock, burying the ship under the rubble. It was an ignominious end for a ship that was undefeated until a month before Germany surrendered.

THE BAT BOMBERS

As batty as it sounds, the U.S. Army hatched a plan to bomb Japan with live bats during World War II.

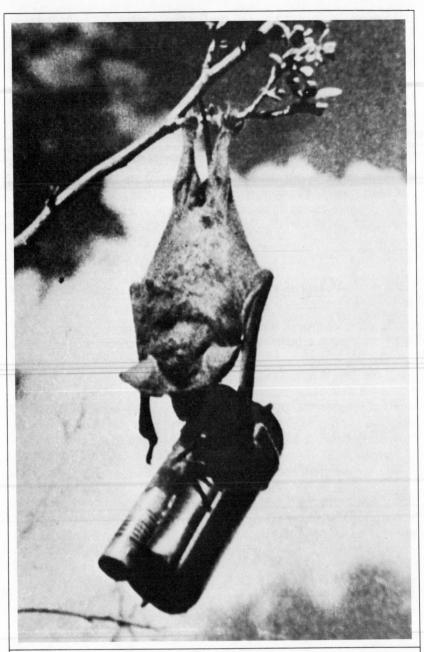

Mexican bat with explosives attached

A Pennsylvania surgeon named Lytle S. Adams envisioned it: bats carrying timed incendiary devices could be sealed into large crates (resembling egg cartons) and dropped from bombers over Japanese targets. Nearing ground level, the cannisters would spring open and the bats, partial to darkness and quiet, would head for the remotest corners of houses and buildings. The simultaneous explosion of thousands of undetected bombs would ignite the tindery wooden structures and cause an inferno.

The federal government adopted the idea early in 1942 and launched "Project X-ray." Some 2 million of the winged mammals were captured in Texas caves and stored, asleep, in giant freezers. Meanwhile, a 1-ounce bomb was designed, small enough to be clipped to a bat yet sufficiently volatile to flare for eight minutes with a 22-inch flame. When one accidentally went off at a New Mexico airfield, a large hangar and an automobile were incinerated.

The army sank $2 million into Project X-ray before mysteriously scrapping the project in the fall of 1943 without employing a single bat battalion. Some say the army had its eye on the A-bomb by then—a far more potent means of battering the enemy.

THE LETHAL PAPER BALLOON

In World War II, only six people on the U.S. mainland died from enemy action. All were killed by a bomb attached to a balloon.

Of 9,000 such balloons made, about 6,000 were launched from Japan in the winter of 1944–45 to travel 6,200 miles to North America. The hydrogen-filled balloons were 32.8 feet in diameter and constructed of handmade paper. The balloons carried several types of charges, usually an antipersonnel bomb and four incendiary bombs. A mechanism was set up to drop the bombs when the balloon was over land. The whole package was then to self-destruct, but it didn't always operate as planned.

The U.S. military found several of these balloons in late 1944. However, the first reports were censored to avoid panic. It is estimated that 1,000 reached North America, of which only 342 were sighted or found.

The program fell far short of Japanese objectives to burn forests, create panic, and kill civilians. The six victims couldn't have been more innocent. On May 5, 1945, a minister, his pregnant wife, and five Sunday school children were on a fishing trip in Oregon when one child disturbed a fallen balloon. The antipersonnel bomb exploded, killing everyone except the minister, who was some distance away. At first, the U.S. Forest Service said the explosion was "of undetermined nature." More than a month later, the grief-stricken minister, Archie Mitchell, was allowed to tell of the balloon to prevent another such tragedy.

In 1950 the Weyerhaeuser Timber Company honored those who died in the Oregon explosion by erecting a monument there. The spot is now a picnic site known as the Mitchell Recreation Area.

For the Rev. Archie Mitchell, who continued his missionary work in Indochina after the war ended, another war arose to change his life. In 1962 he was captured in South Vietnam by guerrillas and has never been seen again.

DER FÜHRER'S MAMMOTH FIASCO

In June 1942, Adolf Hitler decided to build the biggest and most destructive tank in the world. It would crush the Russian tanks. It would be invincible.

Designed by automaker Dr. Ferdinand Porsche, this Nazi King Kong of tanks was 30 feet long, weighed a bit more than 180 tons, and

Hitler's 180-ton white elephant

had steel plating 9½ inches thick. Its code name was Mammoth, and it was tested in the early months of 1944.

Lumbering through villages on its trial runs, the Mammoth crushed cobblestone streets; its vibrations buckled building foundations and shattered windows. Its bulk proved its undoing. When it left paved highways to travel dirt roads and grass, it sank deep into the earth, immobilized. Hitler built two of these monsters, both destroyed by the Germans at Kummersdorf in late 1944 before they could be seized by the advancing Allied troops.

AN UNUSUAL APOLOGY

During the heat of World War II, when the U.S. submarine *Queenfish* torpedoed and sank the Japanese cargo ship *Awa Maru*, American diplomats formally apologized and offered to replace the vessel.

Why apologize for sinking an enemy ship in wartime? The *Awa Maru* had been granted safe passage from Japan to Singapore and back by the U.S. government, even though it carried many tons of war materiels and 1,700 Japanese seamen. In exchange for the amnesty, the Japanese had agreed also to carry 2,000 tons of very special cargo—relief supplies for American soldiers in Japanese prisoner-of-war camps.

With white crosses painted on her hull, the *Awa Maru* sailed from Singapore, assured that the U.S. Navy had instructed all its submarines to let her pass unharmed. But the *Queenfish* had never received a clear version of that official order on its radio.

On the foggy night of April 1, 1945, in the Taiwan Strait, the *Queenfish*'s captain saw on his radar what he thought was a Japanese destroyer. He fired four torpedoes, each a direct hit. Only one survivor was pulled aboard the *Queenfish*, and from this lone seaman the captain learned he had just sunk the *Awa Maru*.

Afraid that the enemy would retaliate with brutality, the U.S. Navy sent no word to the Japanese until April 17, when Tokyo received an official apology along with an offer to replace the *Awa Maru* with a similar ship. Since the war ended only four months later, that offer was never made good.

KRUPP'S STRANGEST ORDER

Following World War I, in accordance with the Treaty of Versailles, Germany was forced to demilitarize. Yet the Allies ordered Germany's largest arms maker to crank up one last time to produce tons of munitions.

The bizarre policy reversal occurred in May 1920. Members of the Allied Control Commission, led by a British colonel named Leverett, arrived at the giant Krupp works in Essen, Germany, with orders to scuttle it and seize nearly a million pieces of stockpiled war materiel. But the commission was mistaken, said Krupp officials. There wasn't that much war materiel in all of Germany.

Unwilling to return empty-handed, Leverett ordered the idled plant back into full-scale operation. From its assembly lines flowed tons of new weapons, which Leverett immediately impounded and turned over to his superiors in Berlin—where the munitions were destroyed.

GENERAL MACARTHUR: "PRESENT IN SPIRIT"

Philippine law requires that the name General Douglas MacArthur be forever shouted out at parade roll calls of the Philippine Army—and that there always be an answer.

When the Japanese forced MacArthur off the islands in 1942, he made his famous vow: "I shall return." It took him and his troops two years of deadly island fighting to make good his promise, but return he did—in October 1944.

Nine months later, a grateful Philippine Congress resolved: "That in reverent appreciation of General Douglas MacArthur, his name be carried in perpetuity on the company rolls of the units of the Philippine Army and, at parade roll calls, when his name is called, the senior noncommissioned officer shall answer, 'Present in Spirit.'" Hearing this, MacArthur wept as he had not done since childhood.

In 1961, MacArthur once again returned to the Philippines. Then eighty-one, the frail soldier was greeted at Clark Field by an enthusiastic crowd. But what moved him most was when the government of the Republic of the Philippines kept its promise, as he had kept his. Again, MacArthur wept.

8

LANGUAGE AND LITERATURE

THE WORLD'S MOST BAFFLING MANUSCRIPT

The Voynich Manuscript is not the title of a new best-selling mystery, but it *is* mysterious. Indeed, it is the world's most mysterious manuscript.

Illustrated with multicolored drawings, the 204-page volume is handwritten in an unknown alphabet. In 1912 it was purchased from a Jesuit college in Italy by British book dealer Wilfrid Voynich, who gave copies to anyone wanting a crack at deciphering it.

Voynich had many takers, but none had any success until April 1921, when Professor William Romaine Newbold of the University of Pennsylvania said he had broken the code.

It was the work of Roger Bacon, the thirteenth-century English Franciscan friar and inventor, said Newbold. The manuscript, he added, indicated that Bacon had built and used microscopes and telescopes almost 400 years before they were thought to have been invented.

Newbold's findings made him an instant celebrity in scholarly circles. But within a few years of Newbold's death in 1926, his word-by-word translation and theories were disproved.

In 1960, the manuscript was acquired by a New York collector, Hans Kraus, who in turn offered it for sale at $160,000. No one snatched up

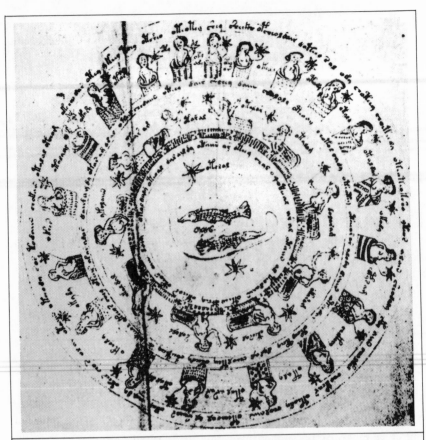
Figure it out and you'll make history

the bargain, however, and in 1969 Kraus gave it to Yale University. It remains there today—still an enigma to researchers and scholars worldwide.

CENSORED BIBLE

Noah Webster, famous for his dictionaries, also published a censored version of the Bible containing no words for sex or elimination that his contemporaries might consider vulgar.

A Calvinist, Webster wrote: "Many words are so offensive, especially for females, as to create a reluctance in young persons to attend Bible classes and schools, in which they are required to read passages which cannot be repeated without a blush; and containing words which on other occasions a child could not utter without rebuke."

His solution was to discard certain words or insert euphemisms, words and phrases "which are not very offensive to delicacy." For example, "teat" became "breast," "stones" (testicles) became "peculiar members," and a "leg" became a "limb."

Webster—who knew Latin, Greek, and Hebrew but was not a religious scholar—spent nearly sixty years annotating and editing his Bible before its publication in 1833. In addition to cleaning up the language, he also corrected grammatical errors and substituted contemporary words for obsolete ones.

By giving up his royalties, Webster was able to sell his version of the Bible for only $2. Even so, it was a failure—which hurt him deeply, since he considered it one of the greatest achievements of his life.

THE PAPER A-BOMB

Although the development of the atomic bomb was a closely guarded secret until the summer of 1945, a short story in the March 1944 issue of *Astounding Science-Fiction* magazine contained a startlingly accurate description of the real bomb. Certain there had been a leak, U.S. intelligence agents swarmed down on the magazine's editorial offices to investigate.

The fictional story, titled "Deadline," was the work of Cleve Cartmill (1908–64), a onetime journalist and radio operator.

"Deadline" is the story of Ybor, an agent of the Seilla forces, who is sent into the war-torn enemy territory of the Sixa Alliance. Ybor's mission is to dismantle the Sixa's new secret weapon—a bomb so powerful that it could destroy their whole planet. He knows that it is made of an isotope of uranium, U-235, and that one pound of the stuff would lay waste an island. "They could end the war overnight with controlled U-235 bombs," Ybor tells an underground operative he encounters while trying to carry out his mission. The underground takes Ybor to the scientist in charge of the atomic bomb, and in order to gain his confidences and get close to the weapon, Ybor must describe a U-235 explosion, the fusing device, and the mechanics of the bomb.

Ybor succeeds at his mission. But Cartmill had succeeded in writing too realistic a piece, in the eyes of the U.S. government. *Astounding*'s editor John W. Campbell, Jr., insisted to the feds that Cartmill had not been privy to classified information, nor was he an operative for the Axis powers. Cartmill had found the factual research materials for his story in public libraries and pieced it all together as fiction. Some of his sources had been publicly available as far back as 1940.

The agents took Campbell at his word and agreed that to suppress "Deadline" or the magazine might tip America's hand to its enemies. Cartmill was left free to continue writing his make-believe stories. Government agents, however, did buy up all the newsstand copies of the March 1944 *Astounding* they could get their hands on, making that particular issue extremely rare.

CHRIST IN THE NEWSROOM

What would happen if a big-city newspaper, instead of reporting the usual crime and violence, emphasized the good news and instituted a policy following the teachings of Jesus Christ? It happened once, with surprising results, when a Kansas daily took up a popular clergyman's challenge and appointed him editor in chief for one week in March 1900.

The clergyman was Dr. Charles M. Sheldon, a Congregational minister whose series of sermons was published in 1896 as a novel titled *In His Steps, or What Would Jesus Do?* The book sold as many as 30 million copies making it one of history's leading best-sellers.

It was a news event in itself when Dr. Sheldon moved into the hard-boiled city room of the *Topeka Daily Capital* to run the newspaper according to the dictates of Christ. Reporters from across the United States converged on Topeka to cover the story, and thousands of additional subscriptions were sold. Dr. Sheldon made some notable changes in company policy. He banned smoking, drinking, and profanity from the editorial offices and eliminated the paper's advertisements for patent medicines, corsets, and sporting events.

The *Topeka Daily Capital* was transformed. Signed editorials became front-page items, while crime, society events, and theatrical notices were played down. A page-one story about a famine in India included an appeal for contributions; the paper collected more than $1 million in aid to send to Bombay.

As a result of the experiment, daily circulation jumped from 15,000

Dr. Charles M. Sheldon

to 367,000. Critics of the minister's policies credited the increase to novelty and publicity. But Sheldon's supporters maintained that it proved how much people crave the inspiration of good news.

THE SHORTEST PLAY

Tristan Bernard, the French author who wrote forty plays and fifty novels—he was known as the "French Mark Twain"—wrote the shortest play in stage history.

During his long career (Bernard died at eighty-one in 1947), he was best known for his play, *The Little Café,* which launched Maurice Chevalier on his movie career, and *English As It Is Spoken,* which became a standard of the Comédie Française. But among connoisseurs of condensation, Bernard is remembered for the briefest play ever produced. This was a play called *The Exile,* written in 1932, which consisted of two characters and three sentences. Here is the entire play:

The curtain rises on the interior of a mountain cabin located near the frontier. The mountaineer is seated before his fireplace. There is a knock on the door. The exile enters.

EXILE: "Whoever you are, have pity on a hunted man. There is a price on my head."
MOUNTAINEER: "How much?"
The exile hastily leaves, as the curtain falls.

THE BOOK DOCTOR

Emanuel Haldeman-Julius believed that you *can* sell a book by its cover. In the 1920s, he became a millionaire by publishing cheap paperback reprints of classics and issuing some of them with sexy new titles.

Haldeman-Julius began his Little Blue Books line in 1919. By the time he died in 1951, his printing plant in Girard, Kansas, had turned out 500 million copies of more than 2,000 different titles. The books sold for 5 to 25 cents each. Any publication selling less than 10,000 copies a year was referred to "the hospital," a committee of editors who decided whether to drop the book outright or simply spice up the title. When Théophile Gautier's novel *Golden Fleece* was reissued as *The Quest for a Blonde Mistress,* annual sales jumped from 600 to 50,000. When Victor Hugo's play *Le Roi s'amuse* ("The King Amuses Himself") was changed to *The Lustful King Enjoys Himself,* sales increased more than fourfold.

But sex wasn't the only magic ingredient. Arthur Schopenhauer's *Art of Controversy* was retitled *How to Argue Logically* and became a self-improvement best-seller. So did Thomas De Quincey's *Essay on Conversation,* reissued as *How to Improve Your Conversation.*

Haldeman-Julius justified his flagrant doctoring of titles as a way of bringing literature to the masses. To his credit, he confined the changes to the book's covers. The title page and text were never altered.

THE PUSHY CHAPTER 29

When Henry James's novel *The Ambassadors* was first published in New York in 1903 by Harper and Brothers, Chapter 29 was accidentally printed ahead of Chapter 28. The book already had been published correctly in England. No one, including the author, noticed the mistake in the first American edition. For the second American edition, in 1907, the fussy James moved commas around, changed "had not" to "hadn't" and "engendered" to "created," etc., but didn't see the gross error. Critics praised the structure of the novel.

Finally, in 1950, Robert E. Young, a literary critic, noticed that the book's characters behaved strangely in certain chapters. They met at unusual hours, displayed mental telepathy in describing events before

A more amiable chapter in Henry James's life

they happened, and were oddly forgetful. Young wrote a paper exposing the mistake.

In 1955, Harper and Brothers proudly announced that they would be reprinting *The Ambassadors* with the chapters in the right sequence. Needless to say, Chapter 29 mysteriously preceded Chapter 28 once again. Flustered, they sent the book back to press, and at last an accurate edition was published. In 1958, Anchor paperbacks gave it a try, with another proud proclamation that the chapters would be in order. Well, you guessed it—they weren't.

As far as we know, all editions since then have been fine. But as the literary scholar Richard D. Altick wrote: "It would be a rash prophet who could assure the world that henceforth, without fail, Chapter 28 will precede Chapter 29."

THE WORLD'S LARGEST BOOK

The largest book in the world—a copy of the *Tripitaka*, the sacred Buddhist text that includes Buddha's teachings—occupies a thirteen-acre site on the grounds of the Kuthodaw pagoda in Mandalay, Burma. King Mindon of Burma decided that a special revised edition of the *Tripitaka* should be inscribed on stone in the Burmese script so that his people would have a copy lasting as long as the world did.

On Mindon's orders, fifty expert masons worked seven and a half years to engrave the book on both sides of 729 marble slabs, which represent pages. Each of the stones measures 3½ feet wide, 5 feet long, and 5 inches thick. When they were finished in 1868, the tablets were installed on individual stands in rows, and rooflike structures were built to protect them. During World War II, evacuees from Mandalay took refuge among the pages of the book and were removed with great difficulty by pagoda officials after the war was over.

Besides being the largest book, the *Tripitaka* also ranks among the world's longest. In order to read it, a person would have to spend eight hours a day for 450 days before coming to the end.

HISTORY GOES UP IN FLAMES

In the sixteenth century, the Spanish bishop Diego de Landa burned hundreds of Mayan books in Mani, Yucatán. Within hours, most written records of a great civilization were gone.

The ancient Mayans of Central America had built a complex society before the Spanish conquest. They were the only group in the hemisphere with a written language. On long strips of bark, priests inscribed glyphs (language symbols) in colors, then the strips were folded and put between covers.

The Spaniards, however, were horrified by certain Mayan rituals—such as human sacrifices—that the Mayans had assimilated from their more violent neighbors, the Toltecs. Intent on stamping out such barbarism, the Spaniards disregarded the achievements of Mayan culture, and destroyed the priceless records of astronomy, mythology, and history. De Landa said of the books he burned: "[they] contained nothing in which there was not to be seen superstition and lies of the devil . . ." Only three or four books (one may be a fake) of the Mayans remain. The writings in them have never been completely deciphered.

BOOK BURNING U.S.A.

Many countries besides Nazi Germany have burned books. The United States was one of them—when a federal agency burned the books of an author it did not like. The author was the radical psychoanalyst Wilhelm Reich, an ex-Freudian and ex-Marxist who felt he had discovered the primary energy in the universe, which he called orgone. He also advocated sexual freedom.

After escaping from Nazi Germany, Reich came to the United States and finally settled in Maine, where he made his "orgone energy accumulators," boxes inside of which people supposedly could be cured of various ailments and have their blood and tissues "energized" in order to resist disease better. In 1947, the U.S. Food and Drug Administration began a seven-year investigation of him, which ended in a court injunction requiring that all accumulators be destroyed and that all books promoting their use be withheld from distribution.

The FDA exploited the court's ruling in its favor by hounding Reich and his associates and destroying any publication that contained even the slightest mention of orgone.

Psychiatrist Wilhelm Reich being taken to jail
after the U.S. government burned his books

The biggest burning of Reichian materials took place in 1956 in New York City. Six tons of literature were loaded onto a truck under FDA supervision by orgonomist Victor M. Sobey and two assistants, then taken to Gansevoort Incinerator, where they were burned. Sobey said he "felt like people who, when they are to be executed, are made to dig their own graves first and are then shot and thrown in." Among the books burned was Reich's *The Mass Psychology of Fascism*.

On May 25, 1956, Reich was fined $10,000 and sentenced to two years in jail, where he died on November 3, 1957. Ironically, his books had also been burned by the Nazis.

A DANGEROUS BOOK

The most incendiary book in U.S. history was a 413-page, antislavery broadside titled *The Impending Crisis of the South: How to Meet It*, by Hinton Rowan Helper. Selling 13,000 copies in its first year, the book sparked at least three lynchings, several court trials, and a near-riot in the U.S. House of Representatives. It was banned by law in most of the South.

Born in North Carolina in 1829, Helper went west with the Gold Rush in 1850 and later recounted his experiences in *The Land of Gold*. But fame eluded him until the publication of *Crisis* in 1857. In it he argued that slavery was a serious drag on the South's economic and political growth and should be immediately abolished—via armed revolt by the slaves themselves, if necessary. The book, however, was not in the least sympathetic to the slaves, who Helper felt should be returned to Africa.

Helper published his book in New York, where he felt he would be safe from reproach. But it soon made its way south and caused an uproar. Most Southern states banned it outright. In Arkansas, three men were lynched simply for possessing copies, and numerous other owners

Hinton Rowan Helper

of the book were savagely beaten or jailed. Public book burnings were rife. But the most profound impact of *Crisis* was in the U.S. House of Representatives. Republican John Sherman was running for election as Speaker, but Southern Democrats attacked him for endorsing the book. A bitter two-month floor battle ensued. Although Sherman lost, the battle stirred secessionist sentiments in the South and brought the country a step closer to war.

In the late 1860s, Helper wrote three more books. All were psychotically antiblack. Their purpose, he explained, was "to write the negro out of America . . . and out of existence." More than a bit deranged, Helper would not patronize hotels or restaurants employing blacks.

A tall, gaunt man given to Prince Albert coats and addicted to cough drops, in his later years Helper tirelessly promoted the idea of building a railroad between Hudson Bay and the Strait of Magellan, fancying himself "the new Christopher Columbus." He went broke in the process and died by his own hand in a Washington fleabag in 1909.

HOW MALE CHAUVINISM GOT ITS NAME

The expression "male chauvinism" is now a part of everyday American vocabulary. But the man who was the inspiration for the word "chauvinism" had nothing in particular against women.

Nicholas Chauvin was a French soldier under Napoleon who was often badly wounded—no less than seventeen times—in his struggles for the French Republic and the First Empire. In time, he was too scarred to continue fighting and was retired. This devoted soldier received no more for his efforts than a medal, a ceremonial saber, and a pension of 200 francs (about $40).

Other men might have grown embittered, but not Chauvin. Instead, he became obsessed with Napoleon, ranting and raving constantly about the greatness of France. Even after the Little Corporal's downfall, Chauvin remained staunch. His hero worship grew so fanatical that he became a laughingstock in his village. Two French playwrights, Jean and Charles Cogniard, heard of the patriotic madman and used him as a character in a comedy. Several other playwrights followed suit, and Chauvin's name became a synonym for excessive devotion to a nation or cause.

What would the battle-bruised, faithful soldier have thought if he heard the expression "male chauvinist pig"?

WOMAN TALK ONLY

Once there was a tribe whose women had their own language, unknown to the men.

The tribe was the fierce, red-painted Caribs—originally from South America—who, at the time of Columbus's voyages, were invading the islands of the Lesser Antilles. Columbus first encountered them in 1494 on the island of Dominica. The gentle Arawaks, native to the region, were terrified of the Caribs for good reason: the invaders ate their male enemies, then wore the dead men's teeth on their bracelets, made arrowheads for their poisoned arrows from the shin bones, and arranged the skulls in trophy racks. (*Carib* is the root of *Caribbean*; the Arawak equivalent of Carib, transliterated by the Spanish, is the source of our word *cannibal*.) A double invasion by the Caribs turned the Arawak paradise into a hell. (The Caribs ate Europeans, too, but eschewed Spanish monks after one made them sick, said a French chronicler.)

The fate of Arawak women—captivity and submission to Carib males—was anathema to them. In revenge, they refused to speak Carib and instead continued to converse in Arawak, which the men considered a "female language" and would not deign to learn. Gradually, over a period of two centuries, the Arawak women were assimilated into the tribe, but they continued the practice of speaking their "secret" language, and taught it to their children.

Today about 2,800 descendants of these particular Carib Indians live on a reservation on Dominica. They are now largely Roman Catholic, play cricket, and speak one language—a form of Arawak, distinctively called Island Carib.

COULD YOU SAY THAT AGAIN IN MALTESE?

By the time Giuseppe Caspar Mezzofanti was twelve years old, he spoke at least eight languages besides his native Italian, including German, Latin, and Greek. And that was in 1786, before Berlitz. Young Giuseppe, the son of a poor carpenter from Bologna, also studied philosophy and theology. In a few years he was learned enough to be ordained as a priest, but he wasn't of age. While he waited, he studied Oriental languages and finally did become a priest. Mezzofanti's activities were so impressive that Pope Gregory XVI summoned him to Rome, where he was appointed to head the Vatican library in 1833. In five years he was made a cardinal.

This modest man became known as "the confessor of foreigners." On one occasion, he was asked to hear the confessions of two foreign criminals who were to be executed the next morning. Overnight, he learned their language and at sunrise spoke with them in their mother tongue.

When Mezzofanti died in 1849 at age seventy-five, he spoke thirty-eight languages perfectly yet had never left his native Italy. These languages included Hebrew, Arabic, Armenian (ancient and modern), Russian, Geez, Algonquin, Chinese (which took him the longest to master—four months), Hindi, Old English, Syriac, Magyari, Wallachian, Basque, and Maltese.

Mezzofanti spoke at least thirty more languages fairly well, including Serbian, Kurdish, Welsh, and Angolese, plus fifty dialects of the above-mentioned tongues. And he could understand, though not speak, twenty more, including Tibetan, Lapp, Old Icelandic, and Chippewa. Not

Cardinal
Giuseppe Mezzofanti

counting the dialects, that adds up to eighty-eight—eighty-seven more than most of us.

SPEAK UP, SING UP

Since the nineteenth century, a variety of languages have been invented to bridge international communications barriers and unite humankind. The most successful has been Esperanto, with a following today of as many as 1 million people. But the most tuneful is Solresol, based on the notes of the musical scale. It's the only language you can *hum*.

Solresol was created in 1817 by a French music teacher, Jean-Francois Sudre, and later won enthusiastic supporters throughout Europe, including Victor Hugo and Napoleon III. All its words were constructed from combinations of the notes of the scale—do, re, mi, fa, sol, la, and ti (or si). There were 7 words of one syllable, 49 of two syllables, 336 of three syllables, 2,268 of four syllables, and 9,072 of five. As the stress was shifted from one syllable to another, a single word could serve as a noun, adjective, verb, or adverb.

Despite its complex grammar and daunting vocabulary, Solresol's popularity was not surprising, for it was based on a long-established and universally recognized language: the diatonic scale. Best of all, it could be hummed, whistled, sung, or played on a piano—though as a spoken language, too, it had a uniquely musical ring. "I love you," for example, was "Dore milasi domi." None of the other world languages, including Interglossa (a mix of Latin, Greek, and Chinese), Timerio (which uses numbers instead of words), and the still-popular Esperanto has had quite the same appeal.

I'M OK, YOU'RE OK

While there are no hard statistics to prove it, it is probably OK to assume that the most widely used American word in the world is "OK." Spaniards utter it more often than "salud," and in England it is more common than "right-o." Even speakers of the Djabo dialect in Liberia say "O-ke."

Indeed, "OK" freely punctuates the conversations of people who do not know another word of English. During a World War II soccer match, a team comprised of Poles, Czechs, Danes, and Norwegians was hamstrung by their language differences until a Polish player shouted "OK!" Everyone on the team knew what *that* meant, and from then on play proceeded smoothly.

Despite its international acceptance, OK is all-American. It first saw print in 1839 in the *Boston Morning Post* as an abbreviation for "all correct" (or "oll korrect"). In 1840, while campaigning for reelection, President Martin Van Buren—born in Kinderhook, New York—was nicknamed "Old Kinderhook" by his backers. The initials of this epithet were commandeered during the campaign by New York's Democratic OK Club, and later they became a password meaning "all is right." Thus OK entered into common usage.

But all wasn't OK with the Van Buren campaign. He was soundly KO'd at the polls by William Henry Harrison.

THE AMAZING GOOGOL

Even if you flunked high school math, you probably have a good grasp of what a million or even a billion is. But what about a googol?

A googol is a number so incomprehensibly huge that it has few useful applications, even in physics and astronomy. Simply put, it is the number 1 followed by 100 zeros.

The word was coined by nine-year-old Milton Sirotta and made popular in 1940 by his uncle, mathematician Edward Kasner, in the book *Mathematics and the Imagination.* As Kasner explained it, all the words spoken since "the beginning of gabble" would not amount to one googol.

But the googol is peanuts compared to a googolplex, 10 to the googol power, or $10^{10^{100}}$. If you counted every electron in the universe, Kasner said, you wouldn't reach a googolplex.

THE ELECTION OF WORDS

Most new words enter the language through the back door, but at least two have been *voted* into it. They are "moron" and "ampere."

"Moron," from the name of the fool in a Molière play, was voted into the language by the American Association for the Study of the Feeble-Minded in 1910. The root of "moron" is the Greek *moros,* meaning foolish. The association defined the term as "an adult with a mental age of eight to twelve or an IQ under 75." It was proposed by psychologist Henry H. Goddard, who believed that mental retardation was hereditary and that its solution lay in eugenic sterilization of the feebleminded.

At the International Electric Congress in Paris in 1881, the word "ampere"—from the name of French scientist André Marie Ampère—was elected by group vote as the official term for the current that one volt can send through the resistance of one ohm. It was an appropriate choice; Ampère had made significant discoveries in the field of electromagnetism. Precedents for the coinage had been set before this meeting of the congress: "volt" was derived from the name of Italian physicist Alessandro Volta, "ohm" from German physicist Georg Simon Ohm, "watt" from Scottish inventor James Watt.

| Watt | Ampère | Volta |

HEBREW: NATIONAL LANGUAGE OF THE U.S.

During the American Revolution, a movement was launched to replace English with Hebrew as the official language of the new nation.

In 1776, anything associated with the British monarchy had a bad taste to the American rebels. Hebrew, on the other hand, was held in high regard by the former colonists, who viewed it as the mother of all languages, the key to the scriptures, and the cornerstone of a liberal education.

They had named their towns after those cited in the Bible, such as Salem and Bethlehem, and their children were named after biblical figures. Until 1817, annual commencement addresses at Harvard were delivered in Hebrew, and at Yale the language was required for freshmen. Many lower schools also stressed Hebrew.

Several members of the new Congress reportedly urged that English be banned altogether and replaced by Hebrew. Though the idea never caught on, Hebrew remained a required course at many major American universities well into the nineteenth century.

9

INVENTIONS AND SCIENCE

DONALD DUCK CREDITED WITH INVENTION

In 1964, when the freighter *Al Kuwait* capsized in the harbor of Kuwait with a cargo of 6,000 sheep, the local people feared that the rotting carcasses would poison their supply of drinking water.

Fortunately, Danish manufacturer Karl Kroyer remembered a 1949 Walt Disney comic book in which Donald Duck and his nephews, Huey, Dewey, and Louie, raised a sunken yacht by stuffing it full of Ping-Pong balls.

Putting this duck wisdom to good use, Kroyer ordered 27 billion polystyrene balls to be injected into the hull of the *Al Kuwait*. The freighter was successfully raised to an even keel, and the Kuwaiti water supply was saved. Few people who admired this great engineering feat were aware that credit for the idea belonged to four fictional ducks—and the man who drew them, cartoonist Carl Barks.

FLYSWATTER FATHER

One afternoon in 1905, Dr. Samuel J. Crumbine was attending the opening game of the Topeka, Kansas, softball season. The hardworking doctor was taking time off from his latest obsession: the extermination of flies in Kansas. Dr. Crumbine, an important member of the State Board of Health, was acutely aware of the common fly's ability to spread typhoid fever and even more aware of the public's lack of awareness of, or indifference to, this fact. Wrote Crumbine in his autobiography, "To get people to wage an unending war on flies was going to be some job." And Crumbine's steady stream of pamphlets and posters just wasn't getting the job done.

Anyway, it was the last half of the eighth inning, and the score was tied 2-2. Topeka had a man on third. The fans were going wild, some of them screaming to the batter, "Sacrifice fly! Sacrifice fly!" Others yelled, "For Pete's sake, swat it! Swat the ball!" Suddenly, it came to Crumbine . . . *swat the fly!* He never even noticed the next play.

In the following issue of the *Fly Bulletin*, SWAT THE FLY blazed prominently across the first page. The slogan caught on (a later slogan, "Bat the Rat," didn't), and schoolteacher Frank H. Rose made a fly-flattening device out of a yardstick and a wire screen. He called it a "fly bat," but Crumbine, in an immortal moment, said, "Let's call it a flyswatter." The holes in the swatter were essential because a fly can sense the air pressure of a solid object, such as a hand, approaching it.

The good Dr. Crumbine died in 1954. In his later years, during fly season, he sat at his desk writing, with a pen in one hand and a flyswatter in the other, waiting to hear the insidious buzz that would call him to the hunt.

WATER INTO GASOLINE?

Gasoline prices in the United States make more interesting the curious fact that, in the last seven decades, three mysterious strangers have come forth with a secret formula for turning water into a fuel usable in combustion engines. Such a fuel is now being tested, with some success, by scientists and tinkerers in several cities. Were these three characters in the forefront, or were they frauds?

The first man was John Andrews, a Pennsylvania inventor who, in 1916, went to the U.S. Navy Yard in Brooklyn, New York, in a Packard with a friend. They claimed to have driven from Pittsburgh in a car that was powered by a fuel developed by Andrews, and consisting principally of water. Andrews demonstrated his fuel in a navy engine the next day. He poured a half-gallon of water into the engine's tank, then added a few drops of green liquid from a vial he had taken from his vest pocket. The engine ran.

A report was made to Secretary of the Navy Josephus Daniels, who ordered more tests, but Andrews, unable to make the $2 million deal he wanted, was nowhere to be found. Rumors abounded that he had sold out to an oil company. In 1942, reporter James L. Kilgallen discovered Andrews living on a Pennsylvania farm. Andrews said he had forgotten the formula and was trying to develop synthetic rubber. In 1953 Andrews died, his secret intact.

The second man was Louis Enricht of Farmingdale, Long Island, who in 1916, at age sixty-nine, called a press conference to show how he could turn water into fuel with a green pill. William Haskell of the *Chicago Herald* said that the fuel, which tasted of bitter almonds, worked. Henry Ford talked to Enricht and sent him a car to use in experiments, but Ford did not buy the formula. Enricht's past as a railroad embezzler and promoter of shady schemes was revealed, but nonetheless he came close to getting backing for development of his formula. The chief engineer for Thomas Edison said the formula was acetylene in an acetone base, which wrecks car cylinders. Enricht ended up in Sing Sing for a fraudulent scheme to make fuel from peat. His green pill was lost forever.

In April 1973, the third man, Guido Franch, demonstrated to reporter Tom Valentine what he called "mota" (*atom* spelled backward) fuel, made from green granules and water. The fuel burned clean. However, it could not be produced commercially. Franch, who sold 3,000 percent of the rights to the process, told Valentine that the fuel was made from coal with a process he had learned when he was fifteen from a German scientist named Kraft, who had also taught Andrews the secret. In addition to synthetic fuel, Franch also marketed a used spaceship (which he said was hidden in the jungles of South America) with one billion air miles on it, flown only once by a crew of Venusians.

$50,000 REWARD FOR NEW BOMB

There has been a great deal of controversy in recent years about the proposed development of the neutron bomb, which is designed to kill as many people as possible without damaging buildings.

Meanwhile, the San Francisco Ecology Center has offered a $50,000 reward to the first person who creates the *opposite* of the neutron bomb—the vivatron bomb.

The vivatron bomb would destroy high-rise buildings and freeways but do no harm whatsoever to humans, animals, and plants. The new bomb would cause concrete, steel, and asphalt to deteriorate—but at a slow enough rate to allow people to evacuate safely.

Entries should be sent to:

VIVATRON BOMB
San Francisco Ecology Center
13 Columbus Ave.
San Francisco, Cal. 94111

THE TALK-TO-THE-DEAD MACHINE

Thomas Alva Edison, one of the greatest inventors in history, gave serious thought to creating a machine for communicating with the dead.

"I have been thinking for some time of a machine or apparatus which could be operated by personalities who have passed on to another existence or sphere," he told *Scientific American* magazine in 1920. "I believe that if we are to make any real progress in psychic investigation, we must do it with scientific apparatus and in a scientific manner."

While he was vague about the form his device would take, Edison did offer that it would be "in the nature of a valve." Once perfected and operational, the machine would greatly magnify messages or impulses from the afterworld, he said, "so as to give us whatever form of record we desire for the purpose of investigation." Edison had described his notions about a talk-to-the-dead device in an earlier interview with *American Magazine.* "I hope to be able to finish it before very many months pass," he had said.

He never did, of course. In fact, the incredible invention never left Edison's brain.

Officials at the Edison National Historic Site in West Orange, New Jersey, do not believe that Edison was serious about communicating

Edison with the phonograph he invented. He also wanted
to develop a device to speak with the departed

with the dead, scientifically or otherwise. His utterances on the subject
were made tongue in cheek, they say. Perhaps. But *Scientific American*—then, as now, one of the most respected and exacting scientific fo-
rums in the world—took him very seriously indeed.

HOW MUCH DOES YOUR SOUL WEIGH?

There is scientific evidence, claimed one scientist, that the human soul
not only exists—but that the average soul weighs approximately one
ounce.

In 1907, Dr. Duncan MacDougall, of Haverhill, Massachusetts, described a series of experiments he'd recently completed at a large hospital. MacDougall had moved the bed of a dying tuberculosis patient onto
a large, sensitively balanced platform beam scale, then kept close watch
on him throughout the final three hours and forty minutes of life. At
the precise moment of death, the beam fell and the scale showed a
¾-ounce weight loss. Five more terminal patients were similarly
weighed over the next two and a half years; at least three, and possibly
five, also lost weight suddenly at the moment of death—between ⅜ and
1½ ounces. There seemed to be no explanation other than the soul's
flight from the body. Just to be certain, MacDougall ran the same experi-

ment on fifteen dogs—all lacking souls according to traditional Judeo-Christian teachings. Not one showed any weight loss.

When MacDougall published his findings, he emphasized that he was a man of science and not a spiritualist. Yet these experiments, he believed, appeared to demonstrate scientifically the existence of the soul. Newspapers had a field day with the story, and one proposed that a convicted criminal be weighed as he was being electrocuted to test out MacDougall's findings. The ghoulish follow-up never took place, nor did anyone bother to weigh MacDougall's departing soul when he died in 1920.

THE WORLD'S BIGGEST CAMERA

If you own a camera, chances are it weighs a few pounds at most. Quite a contrast to the 1,400-pound "Mammoth," built in 1899. Measuring six feet wide, nine feet high, and twenty feet deep, it was for years the world's biggest camera.

The Mammoth was designed and built by photographer George R. Lawrence for the Chicago and Alton Railway, which used it to produce

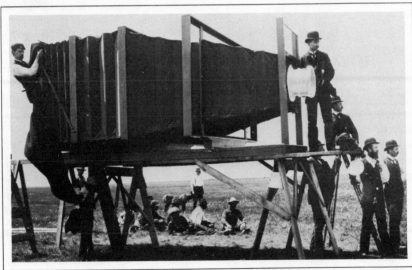

Crew of fifteen takes mammoth photos with
the Mammoth Camera for 1900 Paris Exposition

outsize photos of an ultramodern luxury train, the Alton Limited. The camera's bellows contained forty gallons of cement and its glass plate weighed 500 pounds. A crew of fifteen was required to operate the Mammoth, which took mammoth pictures—4½ by 8 feet. Developing and printing required ten gallons of chemicals for each photograph.

The pictures were displayed at the Paris Exposition of 1900. The judges were agog over the photos of the Alton Limited, but the camera vanished soon thereafter. It remained the biggest of all cameras, however, until 1959—when Rolls-Royce manufactured one that weighed 30 tons.

HEDY LAMARR'S PATENT

Hedy Lamarr—the sultry screen siren of the 1930s and 1940s who starred in such films as *Samson and Delilah, Algiers,* and *Ecstasy*— once received a patent for a radio-controlled system to steer torpedoes.

Although she was not known as an inventive actress, Miss Lamarr did have a gift for dreaming up ideas for weapons. She had acquired some knowledge in this area during her marriage to Fritz Mandel, an Austrian munitions king. At a Hollywood dinner party in 1940, she confessed to composer George Antheil that she felt guilty about living the sheltered, luxurious life of a movie queen while the war raged in Europe. Her secret wish, she told Antheil, was to leave MGM for Washington, where she would offer her services to the newly formed Inventors' Council.

Antheil dissuaded her from scuttling her film career and instead encouraged the actress to share her ideas with him. One design especially captured his imagination, and he suggested that she patent it and offer it to the U.S. government. Thus began an intense collaboration between Lamarr and Antheil, culminating in a detailed patent application. The patent—No. 2,292,387—was awarded to them jointly in 1942.

"This invention," their application reads, "relates broadly to secret communications systems involving the use of carrier waves of different frequencies, and is especially useful in the remote control of dirigible craft, such as torpedoes . . ." The document is highly technical and meticulously conceived.

Antheil was no slouch himself when it came to daring new ideas. In 1927, his *Ballet Mécanique* had its American premiere at New York's

The inventor of a secret communications system

Carnegie Hall. The orchestration included sixteen mechanical pianos, an automobile horn, a wind machine, two airplane engines, and other mechanical devices. The wind machine, however, was trained on the audience rather than above it, forcing many unhappy listeners to depart early. Antheil slipped off to Europe a few days later amid a storm of unkind reviews.

TERRIBLE TURK

The most famous automaton in history was the Terrible Turk, a robot chess player—which turned out to be no automaton at all. The secret of its inner workings was kept from a curious public for nearly sixty years.

Built in 1769 by Baron Wolfgang von Kempelen for Austria's Empress Maria Theresa, the Turk was a fantastic adult toy indeed. Larger than life, the mustachioed wooden figure sat at a chest with a built-in chessboard and wore Oriental robes and a turban. Doors could be opened to reveal brass machinery inside it.

After the baron died in 1804, the Turk was sold to Johann Nepomuk Maelzel, who owned the robot for most of its remaining working life and took it on tour. In 1809, Napoleon Bonaparte, a master strategist, so exasperated the Turk in a chess game by deliberately making false moves that the robot swept the pieces from the board in a very unmachinelike display of temper.

In 1826, Maelzel toured the United States with the Turk, a robot trumpeter, and a friend—chess champion William Schlumberger, who was suspiciously stoop-shouldered. The Turk was a big hit, with its whirring and rackety machinery, its eye-rolling and its cry of *"Echec!"* ("Check!"). Skeptics wondered why Schlumberger was so often absent when the Turk played.

The Turk was not unbeatable. In 1827, it lost to Charles Carroll, at age eighty-nine the last surviving signer of the Declaration of Independence.

In 1834, the robot's secret was given away by Jacques Mouret, a Parisian chess player who had worked for Maelzel. He revealed that once the doors were closed, a human player (usually Schlumberger) concealed himself deep inside the Turk, behind the display machinery, then slid to a spot where he could see the underside of the Turk's board and make moves with rods leading to the robot's arm.

Schlumberger and Maelzel both died in 1838. The Turk ended up in Philadelphia's Chinese Museum, where it was destroyed at age eighty-five by fire.

BEFORE KLEENEX: NOSE PAPER

When the rest of the world was still wiping its nose on its sleeve, Japan was sneezing into a paper tissue. In 1637, Englishman Peter Mundy wrote of the Japanese: "They blow their Noses with a certaine sofft and tough kind off paper which they carry about them in small peeces, which having used, they Fling away as a Fillthy thing."

In the early seventeenth century, when Hasekura Rokuemon, a Japanese envoy, visited France, he amazed Westerners by using *hanagami* ("nose paper"). In St. Tropez, the locals rushed to pick up his used handkerchiefs and even fought over them. A French account of the visit tells of Hasekura's diplomacy: "Amused at the people's freakishness, the envoy seemed to have used more paper handkerchiefs than was actually necessary so as to please the people." Kleenex, the first tissue made in the United States, did not appear until 1924.

HENRY FORD'S SOYBEAN FIXATION

Henry Ford is best known as the man who put America on wheels. But his greatest obsession was not the automobile. It was soybeans.

Actually, Ford was big on all vegetables, but he worshipped the soybean with a feeling akin to reverence. To him it was the cure for all of mankind's woes, as rich in manufacturing applications as in dietary value. In the 1930s, the Ford Motor Company built three processing plants in Michigan where soybean oil was extracted and made into automobile paint and plastic fittings for Ford cars—gear-shift knobs, horn buttons, distributor housings, and switch handles. Indeed, Ford dreamed of someday making sleek cars and beautiful furniture entirely from soybeans.

Henry Ford dreaming of his all-soybean car

At the peak of Ford's soybean mania, his company was growing more than fifty varieties of the plant on 8,000 acres and buying an additional 500,000 bushels yearly from Michigan farmers. Meanwhile, the industrialist spoke constantly about the ancient Oriental staple. No meal was served in his home without soybeans or their derivatives on the table, and a pitcher of cold soybean milk was always in the refrigerator for parched guests. Once Ford appeared at a convention dressed in a suit and matching tie woven of soy-derived fabric. At the 1934 Century of Progress Fair in Chicago, his company served a sixteen-course soybean dinner, featuring puree of soybean, soybean croquettes with green soybeans, soybean coffee, and soybean cookies.

Ford's agricultural obsessions did not end with the soybean. His researchers fiddled with cornstalks, cantaloupe seeds, and milkweed, all grown in abundance on company-owned property. But of all the fruits of nature, none drove him bananas so completely as the soybean.

AN AIRCRAFT CARRIER MADE OF ICE

During World War II, the Allies seriously considered building a gigantic aircraft carrier made of ice. The British inventor Geoffrey Pyke called his unsinkable ship *Habakkuk*, after a minor prophet in the Bible. It was to measure 2,000 feet long by 300 feet wide and weigh 2 million tons.

Pyke developed a slow-melting, impenetrable form of ice simply by adding sawdust. He called his remarkable new compound "pykrete." Once his calculations and preliminary research were finished, he sent a 232-page proposal and a sample of pykrete to his superior, Vice Admiral Lord Louis Mountbatten.

Intrigued by Pyke's wild idea, Mountbatten took data and the pykrete sample to Winston Churchill in 1942, who received him while soaking in a bubblebath. Mountbatten tossed the pykrete into the hot water. To their amazement, the ice did not melt.

When demonstrated at a Quebec conference in 1943, a .38-caliber bullet ricocheted off a block of pykrete. Pyke was authorized by the Canadian government to build a scale model of the *Habakkuk* at Patricia Lake in Alberta. The 1,000-ton ship, powered by a 1-horsepower motor, was bombed, strafed, and torpedoed, yet sustained only minor damage. Pyke's *Habakkuk* had proven itself under fire.

Still, many U.S. and British naval commanders refused to accept the icy idea. This skepticism, combined with the Allies' increasing success with conventional weapons, caused the *Habakkuk* project to be scrapped. Pyke, disillusioned, adopted the motto "Nothing must be done for the first time." He committed suicide in 1948.

ICEBERG ICE CUBES

A 100-million-ton Antarctic iceberg may soon supply some sizzling desert areas with a prime source of drinking water.

The idea has been around since the 1950s, but it received worldwide attention in 1977 when Prince Muhammad al-Faisal of Saudi Arabia set up Iceberg Transport International. Its purpose: to haul a berg to his thirsty country. The project seems not so crazy when you consider that two-thirds of the world's fresh water supply is trapped in Antarctic ice. Scientists and engineers agree that plans to move an iceberg across half the globe are feasible.

Here's how. In the Antarctic, technicians would "carve" the iceberg into a boatlike shape to avert drag, wrap it in plastic and sailcloth to prevent too much melting, then attach it to several powerful tugboats for hauling. The trip to the Arabian peninsula would take six to twelve months. At its destination, the iceberg would be beached and cut into slices for towing up inland waterways to reservoirs. There, thermal energy conversion could be used to melt the ice and produce electricity.

Another suggested method of moving the ice includes turning the berg itself into a "ship," using thermal energy conversion, air-bubble flow, or a generator, for propulsion. A fifty-foot propeller might be attached.

The cost? Less than that for water gained by desalinization. Iceberg Transport International hopes to conduct test tows by 1985.

THE FIRST LADY OF COMPUTERS

The first computer programmer was a nineteenth-century noblewoman—Lady Augusta Ada Byron Lovelace, daughter of the poet Lord Byron.

Byron left his wife and daughter when Augusta was an infant. She

Lady Lovelace

was raised by her mother and given a strict classical education at home. As a teenager, Augusta displayed astonishing prowess in mathematics. She was married in 1835 to Lord King, later the first Earl of Lovelace, a kindly man ten years her senior who supported her interest in math.

When she was eighteen, Augusta first heard of Charles Babbage's idea for an analytical engine, a calculating machine that was the forerunner of the modern computer. In 1842, she translated a paper on the engine from French to English, adding her own voluminous notes. In subsequent writings, she described the "loop" and "sub-routine" concepts—a century before their implementation in electronic digital computers.

Lady Lovelace and Babbage had a long and close friendship, and she was a dedicated partner in his work with the analytical engine. Unfortunately, she was held back by antifeminist attitudes and by her own obsession with gambling on horse races. The engine was never completed and her program never ran. Lady Lovelace died of cancer at age thirty-six. In 1982, the U.S. Department of Defense memorialized her work by naming a new Pentagon computer language "Ada."

THE VAIL CODE?

Samuel F.B. Morse may not have invented the pattern of dots and dashes known as the Morse Code. There is evidence that his associate, Alfred Lewis Vail, deserves the credit.

Morse first jotted down his ideas for the telegraph in 1832. He included notes about using dots and *spaces* as a code to represent *numbers*, not letters. Five years later, Vail wandered into a demonstration of a crude first model of the telegraph, made from a canvas stretcher, a clock, and some wire. Impressed, Vail formed a partnership with Morse to develop a more practical model. Morse set to work on a code dictionary where every English word would get a number code.

In 1838, someone created an alphabet code with an important new element—the dash. William Baxter, then an apprentice on the project, said it was Vail, but Morse later claimed credit.

Vail definitely invented the telegraph stylus and circuit breaker, but all patents were held in Morse's name.

Vail *(Left)* and Morse: who devised the dash?

THE ANCIENT CHINESE METAL DETECTOR

A Chinese emperor created a prototype of the modern airport metal detector. He was Ch'in Shih Huang Ti (259–210 B.C.), best known for unifying China and building the Great Wall as a barrier against northern invaders. He also built the Epang Palace, said to extend seventy miles and consist of 270 separate residences. Such spacious quarters were appropriate for a ruler who rarely went outside in the daylight and boasted that he governed his people without being seen or heard.

Despite his reclusiveness, Shih Huang Ti was the target of at least three assassination attempts. After one close call—his personal physician decked the intruder with his satchel, giving the emperor time to run the man through—Shih Huang Ti ordered that his palace be outfitted with a magnetic door to guard against would-be assassins. "It was the north gate of the Epang Palace," according to Tang Dynasty chronicles, written centuries later. "It was built of magnetite. When those who wore armor came to the door, they were attracted by magnetism and could not pass."

THE FATHER OF THE ATOMIC BOMB WAS NOT EINSTEIN

Albert Einstein's 1939 letter to President Franklin Roosevelt urging development of an atomic bomb—the famous document that started the nuclear age—was not written by Einstein at all. It was ghostwritten for him by a relatively less well-known Columbia University physicist named Leo Szilard.

In 1939, Szilard and Princeton scientist Eugene Wigner approached Einstein to ask a vital favor. Given his great stature, would he lend his name to the promotion of a serious study of nuclear energy's wartime applications and the design and construction of an atomic bomb?

Einstein agreed, although he confessed relative ignorance about nuclear chain reactions. Szilard wrote a draft and presented it to him for his signature on August 2. It spoke of the "vast amounts of power and large quantities of new radiumlike elements [that] would be generated" by a nuclear chain reaction set off in a large chunk of uranium.

The message finally went to Roosevelt. Later, Einstein did write and sign two follow-up messages which, together with the first, led to the

Leo Szilard

1942 formation of the Manhattan Project, which developed the atomic bomb. Szilard was one of the project's guiding forces; Einstein had nothing whatsoever to do with it. "I . . . only acted as a mailbox," Einstein later wrote. "They brought me a finished letter, and I simply mailed it."

Szilard, though, never expected that the atomic bombs would be dropped on the people of Japan, as they were in 1945. He believed Washington would demonstrate the weapon's destructive power and that the Japanese would surrender before anyone was killed. When he realized that the U.S. government was actually going to use the bombs, he wrote letters and memos in protest. After failing to stop the government, he quit physics. He spent his last years campaigning for peace and the control of nuclear arms.

EDISON AND THE ELECTRIC CHAIR

As shocking as it sounds, Thomas Edison promoted the use of the electric chair in order to turn public opinion against a rival businessman.

In the 1880s, Edison and George Westinghouse were battling for control of the new electric power industry. Edison hoped to market his direct current (DC) system, while Westinghouse championed alternating current (AC). They engaged in a bitter press dispute, with Edison declaring that AC was unreliable, unsafe, even deadly.

In 1887, the New York legislature assigned a commission to investigate alternatives to hanging as a means of execution. Edison saw an opportunity to defeat his competitor and offered the use of his West Orange, New Jersey, lab to an engineer, Harold Brown, to experiment with alternating current. Brown electrocuted more than fifty stray cats and dogs, and when the New York officials said his results with small animals might not be applicable to humans, he killed a horse and a cow. The officials were convinced.

At New York's Auburn State Prison on August 6, 1890, William Kemmler, a convicted ax murderer, became the first victim of an electric chair. Powered by alternating current, the chair proved Edison's assertion that Westinghouse's system could indeed be deadly.

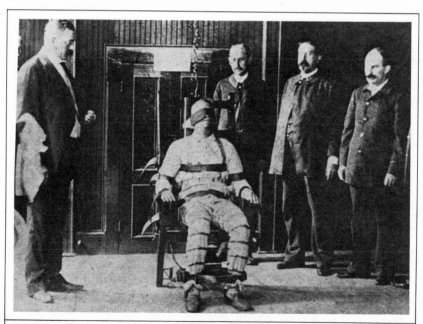

William Kemmler, the first to die in the chair

10

TRANSPORTATION ON EARTH AND IN SPACE

THE PARCEL POST KID

One of the liveliest items ever sent through the U.S. mail was a 48½-pound, four-year-old child. In 1914, May Pierstorff's parents decided to send the child to visit her grandmother in Lewiston, Idaho, 100 miles by train from their home in Grangeville, Idaho. A ticket for a child traveling alone, however, was full fare. So they elected to mail May by parcel post, then new and quite cheap.

At the post office, the postmaster looked up the rules and regulations for sending such a package. Young May fit the weight requirements—50 pounds or under. It was then illegal to mail live animals, insects, reptiles, and smelly articles, among other things. Sending baby chicks by parcel post, however, was permitted. The postmaster classified blond May as a baby chick, collected 53 cents in postage from her parents, and glued the stamps on a tag on the child's coat. After being taken into the post office workroom, May was driven to the depot and lifted into the mail baggage car. On the way to Lewiston, she was under the care of the train baggage man and upon arrival was transported to the

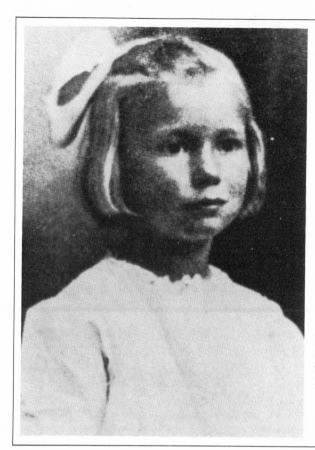

May Pierstorff was
shipped through
the mail for 53
cents

post office. Though the custom was to leave parcel post packages there
overnight, a kindly clerk took May to her grandmother.

YOU CAN'T TAKE IT WITH YOU

Greyhound recently issued its latest "Rules and Regulations." The next
time that you go Greyhound, you can take your suitcase on the bus, but
you *cannot* take along the following nine items:

> Corpses
> Snakes, live

Fuel tanks (used)
Neon signs
Animal heads
Human blood (unless packed in wet ice)
Worms, live (unless specially packed)
Automobile windshields
Bull semen (unless specially packed)

We're sorry if this inconveniences any of you.

A PRIVATE ROLLS-ROYCE FIRE ENGINE

A wealthy California banker and financier once pulled strings to have his chauffeured limousine legally reclassified as a fire truck.

In 1928, Amadeo P. Giannini presided over a vast financial empire that included what is now the Bank of America. The year before, the former fruit seller and Italian immigrant's son had put together the biggest bank merger in U.S. history; the total assets of his holdings were about $500 million.

An impatient man, Giannini felt frustrated by California's 35 mph speed limit—until he discovered it did not apply to fire and police vehicles. In November 1928, he got the state legislature to commission him an honorary fire marshal and reclassify his 1926 Rolls-Royce as a fire truck. The San Francisco Fire Department even sold him a siren and fire-alarm light, which he had welded to the hood—much to the consternation of his chauffeur, who considered such gadgetry a desecration.

Giannini now was able to race to merger meetings and takeovers at 80 mph, unhampered by speed limits. He kept the car until 1932.

IF IT'S 11:43, THIS MUST BE SAVANNAH

Baffled by the time difference as you travel from East to West? Be glad you didn't live before 1883, when there were more than eighty different time zones in the continental United States, not just four.

In those days, there was no such thing as standard time; noon was whenever the sun crossed the meridian overhead. Thus, when it was

214

noon in Washington, D.C., it was 12:24 in Boston and 11:43 in Savannah.

As the railroads expanded across America after the Civil War, making sense of rail schedules became impossibly complicated. Each company kept its own time, and consequently the confusion and missed connections reached nightmarish proportions. The Buffalo, New York, station had three large clocks with three different times—local time, New York City time (on which the New York Central ran), and Columbus, Ohio, time (for the benefit of the Michigan Southern). On a trip from Maine to California, a traveler would have had to adjust his watch about twenty times.

In 1870, New York educator Charles F. Dowd published *A System of National Time for Railroads*, in which he outlined a plan for timekeeping standardization. Using lines, or meridians, 15 degrees apart, he divided the U.S. map into four zones. Within each zone, time was uniform, and all four zones added up to a four-hour time difference across country. In 1872, Dowd revised his schedule to use Greenwich instead of Washington, D.C., as the prime meridian. The idea caught on, and in 1878 a Canadian engineer, Sandford Fleming, advocated a worldwide system of twenty-four zones. Dowd's plan was adopted by the railroads—and cities and towns throughout the United States and Canada—on November 18, 1883. Sanity was finally restored to travel, but, incredibly, standard time didn't become law until 1918.

HENRY FORD AND THE GANGSTER SEAL

OF APPROVAL

Henry Ford received unsolicited testimonials for his cars from notorious criminals Clyde Barrow and John Dillinger. Both men prized Fords for their getaway power.

Killers Bonnie and Clyde met their deaths on May 23, 1934. They drove into a police ambush in a Ford. About a month before, Barrow had written to the car manufacturer: "While I still have got breath in my lungs, I will tell you what a dandy car you make. I have drove Fords exclusively when I could get away with one . . ."

Dillinger used two stolen Fords in his April 1934 getaway from the Little Bohemia Lodge in Wisconsin after a shoot-out with the FBI. He abandoned the first Ford—stained with the blood of one of his gang members and riddled with bullet holes—not far from St. Paul, Minneso-

Said gangster Clyde Barrow: "I have drove Fords
exclusively when I could get away with one."

ta. Then he stole another. In May, he wrote to Henry Ford from Chicago
but had the letter mailed from Detroit, as a false clue for police. Here
is what he wrote:

Hello Old Pal:

> *Arrived here at 10 a.m. today. Would like to drop in and see
you.*
> *You have a wonderful car. Been driving it for three weeks.
It's a treat to drive one.*

Your slogan should be:
Drive a Ford and watch the other cars fall behind you. I can
make any other car take a Ford's dust.

Bye-Bye.
—John Dillinger

But the Ford he had abandoned played a part in Dillinger's demise. It provided a clue to police, who killed him outside Chicago's Biograph Theater on July 22, 1934.

NO SHOES, PORK CHOPS, OR GRASS

When you drive across the Golden Gate Bridge from Marin County to San Francisco, you have to stop at a toll station and pay $1 or $2, depending on the day of the week. If you don't have the money, you are allowed to leave something worth the toll or more as collateral. In the last ten years, drivers short of cash have left the following possessions in lieu of the toll: a new book, a can of motor oil, a man's wedding ring (these are left by the dozens), a rock 'n' roll cassette, a radio, a frying pan, a set of sterling silver tableware, false teeth (the owner picked them up the next day after paying his toll), and a $7,000 diamond wristwatch (the owner did not pick this up and eventually it was sold at auction for $5).

The only things the toll officers will not accept as collateral are items of clothing or uncanned food. Oh, yes, and no drugs. A young driver tried to leave a few ounces of marijuana in place of his toll. He was hauled off to jail.

STUNG BY THE BEETLE

In the 1930s, few working-class Germans could afford automobiles, a sore point with Adolf Hitler. But the Nazi leader had a solution: design a small car, underwrite its manufacture with Third Reich funds, and price it within the means of the masses. Thus was the Volkswagen born.

It seemed like a good idea at the time. But all it did was provide the

217

Nazis with a means of collecting about $68 million from 336,668 workers.

Hitler first broached the idea of a *volkswagen*, or "people's car," in 1933, and even as he turned to more pressing matters—such as the conquest of Europe and the destruction of the Jews—it remained a pet project. Designed by Ferdinand Porsche and originally named by Hitler the KdF-Wagen (Kraft-durch-Freude-Wagen, or "Strength-Through-Joy-Wagon"), the people's car was to be built at a huge auto plant constructed at Fallersleben in 1938. The manufacturer claimed it eventually would crank out 1.5 million autos a year. The German Labor Front put up 50 million marks to get the project going, but the real financing was to come from the German workers themselves through a novel installment plan. Every worker could have 5 marks—a little more than $1—drawn from his weekly paycheck and deposited in a special account. Once 750 marks had been paid, he would be assigned a number entitling him to a car as soon as it was off the assembly line. The full price was 990 marks, or just under $250.

In this manner, the Nazis raked in close to 280 million marks—$68 million—before the project was scrapped in 1941 and the plant converted to arms production. By that time, only a handful of cars had been produced, all appropriated by Nazi VIPs. None of the workers ever got a car or a refund during the Nazi regime. Not until 1961 did the German courts rule that the people were still owed cars—or their money back. Since then, Volkswagen has honored over 120,000 claims, and about 93 percent of the workers have collected a refund or a Volkswagen.

A POSTSCRIPT: After the war, the British offered the Volkswagen plant to Henry Ford II, free. He turned it down.

THE WONDER CAR

Except for a foolhardy, high-speed chase, Americans might today be driving Dymaxions—streamlined three-wheelers with the rotary maneuverability of a pirouetting dancer.

In 1927, the philosopher-scientist R. Buckminster Fuller sought to design a versatile car that could eventually be converted to an "omnimedium, wingless transport" for ground, air, and water travel. With the help of designer-engineer Starling Burgess, Fuller hired twenty-seven craftsmen and started a company to fulfill his ambition. On July 12, 1933, Dymaxion No. 1 was ready. The eleven-passenger vehicle had

Starling Burgess *(Left)* and Buckminster Fuller with the Dymaxion car

front-wheel drive, a rear-mounted 90-horsepower Ford V-8 engine, and rearview periscopes. It pivoted on its single back wheel around its 19½-foot length for easy parking, could go 120 mph, averaged 22 miles per gallon, and was adaptable for air and water transport.

Later that year, disaster struck. On a Chicago road, another car challenged the Dymaxion to a race. At 70 mph, they collided and overturned, killing the Dymaxion's driver and injuring its one passenger. The other car, owned by a Chicago politician, conveniently disappeared. Consequently, the Dymaxion developed a reputation as a dangerous "freak car." Even another Dymaxion, completed in 1934, could not counter the unfavorable publicity. An improved 1943 Dymaxion was never produced commercially.

AT THE WHEEL

The steering wheel was initially located on the right side of most American cars. The reason? Tradition. Drivers of horse-drawn vehicles were accustomed to sitting on the right side.

What was fine for buggies didn't apply to cars, as an article in the March 8, 1913, issue of *Scientific American* pointed out. For example, when passing an approaching car, it's better for the driver to be seated on the left because closeness to the center of the road promotes better judgment of passing distance. The advantages of right-hand seating for the driver are much less important—for example, it's easier to pull up at the curb. As *Scientific American* explained, curbs stand still, and parking need not be speedy.

Another explanation for left-hand drive has been advanced by historians of the Conestoga covered wagons used in pioneer days. Conestogas had a perch for the driver on the left side, and this "lazy board," as it was nicknamed, necessitated the driver using the right-hand side of the roadway to see approaching vehicles. His left-side seat, some people say, was the origin of left-hand drive in the United States.

By 1915, most American cars had left-hand drive. Now, about the problem of mailing a letter at a curbside box . . .

THE AMAZING RIDE OF DEATH VALLEY
SCOTTY

A Death Valley mining prospector came out of nowhere in 1905 to set new records for rail speed, extravagant living, and chutzpah—all in the space of forty-eight hours.

His name was Walter E. Scott, and he appeared at the Los Angeles offices of the Santa Fe Railroad in July 1905, plunked down $5,500 in cash, and asked for a three-car private train to take him to Chicago in record time. On the morning of July 9, accompanied by his wife and a yellow dog wearing a $1,000 collar, Scott arrived at LaGrande Station, where a large crowd had already gathered. Scott addressed them briefly and boarded. At precisely 1:00 P.M., the "Coyote Special" pulled out.

The train tore up the rails, once hitting 106 mph and barely stopping for engine changes. Crowds lined the tracks all along the route; inside, the Scotts dined on caviar, squab, and filet mignon. The dog ate from a silver bowl.

The Coyote Special made Chicago's Dearborn Street Station on July 11 in a record 44 hours, 54 minutes. As Scott disembarked, crowds mobbed him and tore at his clothes. Many women tried to kiss him.

The incredible ride made front pages for days. "Death Valley Scotty" was a miner, said the accounts, made rich by a secret gold mine. But in truth there was no mine. Scott's ride was bankrolled by E. Burdon Gaylord, a real estate promoter trying to publicize his mining properties. After the ride, Scotty was backed by Albert Johnson, a rich Chicago executive who gave Scotty over $200,000. Johnson's motive was merely to have some fun. In the 1920s, Scott involved Johnson in yet another grand hoax—the building of Scotty's Castle, a $2 million Hollywood-style mansion in Death Valley. Although the castle still stands and bears Scott's name, it was built with Johnson's money on Johnson's land.

LOCKHEED'S PIGEON EXPRESS

Lockheed Missiles and Space Company, the aerospace giant, uses computer terminals to transmit important technical data from one plant to another. It also uses carrier pigeons.

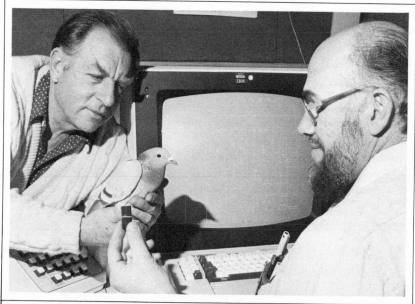

Lockheed scientists prepare micro-film capsule for feathered messenger

Since January 1982, Lockheed's Sunnyvale, California, plant has employed a fleet of fifteen trained pigeons to carry design data requiring immediate attention to the company's test base at Felton in the Santa Cruz mountains, thirty miles away. A pigeon can fly the distance in forty minutes, about half as long as it takes a car. Pigeon express is also much cheaper than hiring a courier service.

At Sunnyvale each morning, a technician transfers computer print-outs of design drawings onto microfilm, rolls the microfilm into a tiny cannister, attaches it to a pigeon's leg, and releases the bird. To date, the system has been 100 percent effective—no lost or damaged microfilms, no deliveries to a wrong address.

THE GREAT AIR MAIL FIASCO

Air mail service was officially introduced by the U.S. Post Office in 1918. It could just as easily have been introduced by "Wrong-Way" Corrigan

The first air mail—undelivered

with an assist from the Marx Brothers. Nothing went right for pilot George Boyle.

On the morning of May 15, 1918, crowds gathered at a large polo field in Washington's Potomac Park to witness the departure of America's first air mail flight. President Woodrow Wilson was on hand, along with other important government officials. At 11:00 A.M., Boyle settled into the cockpit of his 150-horsepower Curtiss "Jenny," ready to go. But the engine would not start. Mechanics sweated over the aircraft for nearly thirty minutes, while the president grew visibly irritated. Finally, someone checked the fuel tanks—they were empty.

His tanks filled, Boyle took off. But instead of flying north to Philadelphia, his first scheduled stop, he followed the wrong set of railroad tracks and flew southeast. Intending to ask directions, he touched down near Waldorf, Maryland, twenty miles from Washington, D.C. But he wrecked the propeller on landing and couldn't get off the ground again. His cargo—140 pounds of air mail—had to be delivered by truck to Philadelphia and by plane to New York.

Luckily, Boyle was only one of four pilots scheduled to fly that day. Lieutenant Torrey H. Webb, on his New York to Philadelphia run, made the first successful air mail delivery. Lieutenant James C. Edgerton (Philadelphia to Washington, D.C.) and Lieutenant Howard P. Culver (Philadelphia to New York) also helped carry the day.

The postal department, however, had one more surprise—it discovered an error in its first issue of air mail stamps. Illustrated with an engraving of a Curtiss "Jenny," a sheet of 100 stamps had been printed upside down.

OUTER-SPACE MARATHON

Valeri Ryumin of the USSR has lived longer in outer space than any other man—nearly a full year.

In the summer of 1979, two Soviet cosmonauts—Ryumin and Vladimir Lyakhov—landed near Kazakhstan, USSR, after 175 consecutive days aboard the orbital research station Salyut 6. A year later, this time joined by cosmonaut Leonid Popov, Ryumin suited up again and blasted into space. He broke his old record, with 185 days in orbit, bringing his total to 360 days.

Cosmonauts Ryumin *(Left)* and Lyakhov are bestowed with bouquets after return from record 175 days in orbit. Accustomed to weightlessness, they had trouble lifting the flowers

Both Soviet missions were aimed, in part, at studying the effects of prolonged weightlessness on humans. Upon their return in 1979, Ryumin and Lyakhov were carried in reclining chairs, like sultans, from their spacecraft. They had to learn all over again to live with gravity—how to walk properly and drink from cups, for example. They had trouble lifting the small bouquets that well-wishers gave them at the touchdown site, and they reportedly tried to swim out of bed their first few mornings back on earth.

Ryumin's sense of balance was not as far out of kilter when he disembarked on October 11, 1980, after his second trip—probably because he and Popov had exercised daily and taken care to eat properly. This time, Ryumin walked unaided from the spacecraft and, weightlessness notwithstanding, was eleven pounds heavier than when he'd left.

ASTRONAUTS CLEAR CUSTOMS

No one can enter the United States without clearing customs, except astronauts returning from space—and even they filed a declaration once.

On July 24, 1969, Apollo 11 astronauts Neil Armstrong, Buzz Aldrin, and Michael Collins splashed down from outer space after completing their historic moon landing. When they passed through Hawaii, the trio carried an assortment of lunar rocks and dust. Later, at NASA headquarters in Houston, someone half-jokingly asked if they had gone through customs. The three said no.

And so they were dutifully requested to make their declaration of lunar rocks and dust on a standard U.S. Customs form. It was signed by the three returned travelers and sent to the Honolulu district office of the U.S. Customs Service for filing.

Astronauts Neil Armstrong, Michael Collins and Buzz Aldrin *(Left to Right)*

and their customs declaration

LITTERING OUTER SPACE

Littering is not confined to our city streets. It is also a problem in outer space.

In addition to approximately 1,200 satellites now in orbit around the earth, there are nearly 3,500 pieces of orbiting space debris. These include spent rockets, fragments of wrecked satellites, miscellaneous nuts, bolts, and ceramic tiles, and bits of metallic sheeting ripped loose from spacecraft. All of it—the satellites as well as the junk—is catalogued and continually tracked by the North American Aerospace Defense Command, or NORAD.

Headquartered in a compound of fifteen steel buildings deep beneath the Colorado Rockies, NORAD houses computers that receive and process 30,000 transmissions daily from a global network of radars, telescopes, radios, and other tracking devices. NORAD's widely scattered Baker-Nunn telescopic cameras can photograph the light from an object no bigger than a basketball at a distance of 20,000 miles.

There are good reasons for monitoring the orbits of such "space trash." For one thing, even a chunk of metal as small as a grapefruit can pack a deadly wallop if it falls to earth. More frightening still, it could easily be mistaken on a radar screen for an enemy missile and precipitate an unjustified retaliation.

To be sure, the chances of real danger are slim. Of the 4,698 recorded objects now in orbit, some are in "deep space"—at least 3,000 miles up, where atmospheric drag and gravitational pull are minimal. Those should remain safely in orbit for hundreds or even thousands of years. The pieces closer to home fall out of orbit at a rate of more than one a day, but most burn up on reentry. A notable exception, of course, was Skylab, whose pieces landed on a portion of uninhabited acreage in Australia in July 1979.

NORAD admits that some bits of space junk are too small to be tracked regularly. But even these show up from time to time. Recently, a NORAD employee reportedly pinpointed an orbiting glove.

THE FLYING FRIAR

Giuseppe Desa was born in 1603 in a small town in Italy. Later known as St. Joseph of Cupertino, he became famous as the "Flying Friar."

Like Christ, Giuseppe was the son of a carpenter and was said to have been born in a stable. As a boy, he would become rigid, his mouth slightly open. Flies crawled in his mouth and on his eyeballs, but he didn't flinch. His schoolmates nicknamed him "Open Mouth." But Giuseppe, who became a priest in 1628, developed an art that left others openmouthed: he would go into a trance, then suddenly cry out and fly into the air.

Nuns who watched one of his performances feared he would hurt himself when he used an altar filled with burning candles as a runway.

St. Joseph at
cruising speed

On another occasion, the music from nearby shepherds' pipes inspired him to such ecstasy that he flew twenty yards. He once rose up into an olive tree, and—when he realized where he was—had to be rescued with a ladder. Many famous people—including Pope Urban VIII and John Frederick, Duke of Brunswick—witnessed his flights, one of which reportedly covered a distance of approximately thirty yards.

The Flying Friar became a saint in 1767, about 100 years after his death in bed from a fever.

11

HEALTH, FOOD, AND DRUGS

THE WOMAN WHO REMOVED HER BREAST

Removal of a cancerous breast (mastectomy) has become a common and relatively safe procedure in the last decade. Although traumatic and costly, this operation saves the lives of a great many women each year.

One courageous woman, back in the late 1870s, did not have enough money to pay for her breast surgery. Nancy Rogers was a widow living in Wichita, Kansas. A capable and popular practical nurse by profession, she was able to diagnose her own deadly ailment—breast cancer. Most operations were highly risky a century ago, but Mrs. Rogers had no choice. She consulted Dr. Henry Owens, whose fee for a mastectomy was $25. Though Nancy Rogers pleaded that she couldn't afford it, Dr. Owens would not lower his price.

Mrs. Rogers drove home in her wagon and packed a large basket with muslin rags, food, and a butcher knife. She cooked her sons enough food to last a week.

Telling her boys that she was going to visit a friend, she had one son drive her into town and asked him to pick her up in seven days. Nancy Rogers then rented a room for $1.50 and locked herself in. Sitting on the edge of the bed, she cut off her own breast.

How she survived the shock and pain, without anesthetic, and managed to bandage herself, we do not know. But the remarkable nurse lived on for many years.

VICTORIAN SEXUAL SURGERY

One of the most bizarre medical fads in history was female castration, or removal of the ovaries, widely practiced in late nineteenth-century America.

Some Victorians considered the ovaries the seat of the feminine personality, and prescribed their removal as a cure for everything from irritability to insanity, as well as "simple cussedness" and "eating like a plowman," according to a medical article of that era.

Pioneer of the ovariectomy (as the surgical procedure was called) in the 1870s was Dr. Robert Battey, an ambitious surgeon from Rome, Georgia, who argued that removal of the ovaries would bring a salutary change of life. His post-op patients, he reported, were "tractable, orderly, industrious, and cleanly."

Dr. Battey and his followers claimed they had excised from 1,500 to 2,000 physically normal ovaries apiece, passing them around at medical society meetings like trophies. By 1906 there were an estimated 150,000 American women whose ovaries had been removed.

Today, Dr. Battey's logic is considered unsound, but his extensive experience, using women as guinea pigs, is said to have greatly advanced abdominal surgery techniques.

Another passing fad of Victorian gynecology was the clitoridectomy (removal of the clitoris), a supposed cure for nymphomania. Currently, the hysterectomy may be reaching fad proportions in the United States where, in 1979, 640,000 hysterectomies were performed.

DOCTORS MAY BE HARMFUL

Is modern medical treatment more likely to kill than cure? Statistics gathered after "doctor strikes" indicate that today's physicians may not be living up to the first part of the Hippocratic oath, admonishing them to do no harm.

According to Dr. Robert S. Mendelsohn's *Confessions of a Medical Heretic*, there are some surprising effects of a doctors' strike. As a protest to soaring rates for malpractice insurance, doctors in Los Angeles went on strike in 1976. The result with no doctors around? An 18 percent drop in the death rate. That same year, doctors in Bogotá, Colombia, refused to provide any services except for emergency care. The result was a 35 percent drop in the death rate. When Israeli doctors drastically reduced their daily patient contact in 1973, the Jerusalem Burial Society reported that the death rate was cut in half. The only similar drop had been twenty years earlier at the time of the last doctors' strike.

SURGERY HITS AN ALL-TIME LOW

During World War II, a U.S. Navy pharmacist's mate performed a life-saving appendectomy on a crew mate in a submerged submarine—using spoons, a tea strainer, and a homemade scalpel.

The sub—the *Seadragon*—was on maneuvers in the Pacific, behind enemy lines, when Seaman Darrell Dean Rector fell ill with acute appendicitis. There were no naval medical facilities within miles; the closest thing to a doctor aboard ship was Pharmacist's Mate Wheeler B. Lipes, Jr., a lab technician by training who had witnessed one or two appendectomies.

Facing certain death if the inflammation was left untreated, Rector agreed to be operated on by Lipes. There were no surgical instruments, so Lipes improvised a scalpel from a knife blade and a hemostat handle; the cook provided a tea strainer to administer anesthesia. Spoons from the galley, bent at right angles, kept the incision open during the surgery. The instruments were sterilized with alcohol tapped from a torpedo.

The operation took place on September 11, 1942, in the officers' wardroom, with senior officers assisting the twenty-three-year-old Lipes. While he probed Rector's innards, the crew tried to hold the sub as steady as possible. Lipes located the appendix, removed it, and closed the incision, cutting the suture with a pair of fingernail scissors just as the ether ran out. Rector awoke half an hour later, and thirteen days after that he was back on duty.

Lipes's triumph was the first appendectomy ever performed aboard a submerged submarine. By war's end, another ten were performed by amateurs like Lipes, using crudely fashioned instruments. Every one was successful.

THE HUMAN TAMALE

Hard as this story may be to swallow, a Mexican leader almost became a tamale.

General Santa Anna—ingredient for a tamale

The colorful statesman Antonio López de Santa Anna, conqueror of the Alamo, was serving his third term as president of Mexico in 1844 when opposition forced him to flee the capital. Nearing the small town of Xico, his party was ambushed by local Indians. Unable to flee because of his wooden leg, Santa Anna was captured and discovered to be the hated aristocratic dictator *El Gordo* ("the fat one").

While some historians maintain that the Indians merely imprisoned their foe, there's strong evidence that they planned a more exotic revenge.

The Indians emptied their huts of chili peppers and spices, then secured an enormous pot in which Santa Anna was to be boiled whole, leaving his flesh firm and intact. Finally, he was to be wrapped in banana leaves and presented to the authorities as a giant tamale. Luckily for the prisoner, a local priest put a stop to the cookout.

Santa Anna never became the first human tamale, but he certainly must have had a corny story to tell.

THE BATTLE FOR A HEALTHY DIET

In January 1977, for the first time in history, the U.S. government offered a healthy diet to its people—and within a year took it back and issued a less healthy diet because of pressure from certain business lobbies.

When the U.S. Senate Select Committee on Nutrition and Human Needs released *Dietary Goals for the United States,* after nine years of research, the report suggested that Americans should eat more fruit, vegetables, nuts, whole grains, poultry, and fish, while cutting back consumption of meat, butter, eggs, sugar, salt, and fatty foods. It also advised substituting nonfat milk for whole milk. These seemingly modest proposals, presented by Committee Chairman George McGovern, engendered an avalanche of protests from representatives of the meat, egg, sugar, canning, and dairy industries. Even the big grain producers objected, since much of their product is used as feed for cattle and hogs.

But the harshest attack came from the American Medical Association, which issued a statement that the new diet was "radical" and potentially harmful and that it would cause a disruption of the U.S. economy.

The AMA even went so far as to say that there is no proof that diet is related to disease.

Under pressure from these powerful forces, the Senate committee held more hearings and gave in slightly. The warning to eat less meat was modified and lean meats were given the okay along with poultry and fish. Eggs were treated more favorably and their importance in the diets of children and the elderly was emphasized. Recommended restrictions on salt were also eased and the attack on sugar was limited to refined and processed sugars.

Even with these changes, the revised edition of *Dietary Goals for the United States* is still food for thought. It is true that if most Americans adopted the new diet, enormous changes would have to take place in the use of agricultural lands. But it is estimated that the diet would also cut in half the number of cases of infant mortality, diabetes, arthritis, and dental cavities, as well as reducing by 20 percent the number of people who would be stricken by cancer, blindness, heart disease, and respiratory ailments.

THE TOMATO GOES TO COURT

The U.S. Supreme Court was once in quite a stew over the tomato. Under the Tariff Act of 1883, fruits, but not vegetables, could be imported duty-free. When John Nix brought a load of tomatoes from the West Indies to New York in 1886, he was charged duty. Nix protested. The tomato was a fruit, he said; any botanist could tell you that. Finally, in 1893, Nix took the case to the Supreme Court.

Lawyers pored over the dictionary, trying to decide if the legal definition of tomato and its common definition were at odds. On May 10, 1893, Justice Gray handed down a decision: "Botanically speaking, tomatoes are the fruit of the vine, just as are cucumbers, squashes, beans, and peas. But in the common language of the people . . . all these vegetables . . . are usually served at dinner . . . and not, like fruits generally, as dessert." So the tomato, while a fruit according to nature, is a vegetable according to law.

Incidentally, at one time tomatoes were believed poisonous. But in August 1820, the courageous Colonel Robert Gibbon Johnson decided to prove to the world—or at least to the residents of Salem, New Jersey—that the tomato was not only safe but delicious. In front of the horrified townspeople, Johnson ate an entire basket of juicy red tomatoes. His doctor expected him to die; when he didn't the audience cheered.

234

Americans began eating tomatoes—but never, heaven forbid, raw. A recipe in *Godey's Lady's Book* of 1860 advised stewing them for at least three hours.

DANGEROUS SUBSTANCE

For eight decades after the invention of margarine, this artificial butter suffered restrictions as severe as those imposed on many drugs—largely because U.S. dairy interests lobbied against it.

Margarine was invented in 1869 as a butter substitute for use during shortages in the wars of Napoleon III. It was made mostly of beef fat and margaric acid.

Introduced to the United States, it ran into immediate opposition from dairy farmers. In many states it was forbidden to manufacture margarine, sell it, possess it with intent to sell, or color it yellow like butter (pink was often used). One dairy farmer said, "We want to drive the oleomargarine manufacturers out of the business." They didn't succeed—margarine was too useful and cheap.

In 1886, opposition continued as the U.S. Congress passed the Margarine Act, establishing high taxes and license fees. When vegetable oils began to be used in margarine during World War I, meat farmers, deprived of a market for waste fat, joined dairy farmers in fighting it.

In World War II, when butter was largely unavailable, civilians who couldn't afford the highly taxed yellow margarine, had to buy white margarine and color it themselves. Federal restrictions on margarine were finally lifted in 1950; then state laws were eliminated. Wisconsin, in 1967, was the last to raise the ban on coloring.

WHAT HEAVY DRINKERS DRANK

Most famous drinkers concentrated on one or two favorite beverages. We did our own research on what kept them afloat, and whiskey appeared to be the most popular libation. Blended whiskey was the choice of U.S. President Andrew Johnson, author Jack London, playwright Eugene O'Neill, and President Franklin Pierce, who was named chairman of the Massachusetts Temperance Society during a sober moment in

Gin drinker W. C. Fields enjoying a beer chaser

1843. Other political drinkers, including Sen. Joseph McCarthy and labor organizer Eugene V. Debs, voted for bourbon. Scotch whiskey was swigged by actor John Barrymore, poet Dylan Thomas, and writer Sinclair Lewis, who took it neat, a pint at a time. Playwright Brendan Behan spent days on end in the pubs of his native Ireland, where, not surprisingly, he drained many a glass of Irish whiskey. President Ulysses S. Grant slurped rye whiskey straight from the barrel during his early military career.

Author F. Scott Fitzgerald and comedian W. C. Fields both consumed gin in prodigious quantities, while champagne tickled the noses of dancer Isadora Duncan, President Grant, and heavyweight boxing champion John L. Sullivan, who would slap $100 on the bar and order bubbly for everyone. Sullivan's intestinal fortitude extended beyond the boxing ring—he could remain standing after guzzling sixty-seven gin fizzes. Apache chieftain Geronimo favored pulque and tequila, and he often rode into battle intoxicated. Fitzgerald, Barrymore, and Senator McCarthy quaffed beer when they were on their respective wagons, while Dylan Thomas chased his breakfast kipper with a pint of Guinness. Jack London was introduced to homemade brew at the age of five.

As long as some form of alcoholic beverage was available, painter Henri de Toulouse-Lautrec wasn't hard to please, but he always tucked a nutmeg into his pocket to spice his port. Those who worry about the health consequences of alcohol might be comforted by Charlie Smith's advice. On his 137th birthday, Smith attributed his longevity to vitamins—washed down with rum. A few adventurous drinkers experimented with more exotic substances when they tired of the usual liquid fare. Barrymore once sipped ethyl alcohol from his yacht's cooling system, while painter Maurice Utrillo reportedly imbibed lamp spirits, benzine, ether, and cologne.

FRENCH WINES SAVED BY TEXAS

Some of France's finest wines trace their origins back to America.

In the 1860s, a voracious insect called the phylloxera destroyed millions of acres of French vineyards. In desperation, the French government sought the help of a leading authority on the grape, Thomas Volney Munson of Denison, Texas. Munson experimented with various species of American wild grape that were resistant to phylloxera. Within a few years, he shipped the hardy rootstock to France, where local vintners grafted their blighted vines onto it. The experiment worked, and French vineyards soon were blossoming. In gratitude, the French awarded Munson the Legion of Honor medal.

In later years, Munson identified, catalogued, and classified all the wild grape species of North America. But it was his heroic rescue of the French wine industry that rates this Texan the heartiest toast from wine lovers on both sides of the Atlantic.

DROWNING IN BEER

One of history's oddest floods occurred in the London parish of St. Giles, when nine people were killed and two houses demolished by a sea of beer.

On October 17, 1814, a vat burst in a brewery, unleashing 3,500 barrels of beer. St. Giles was then a crowded slum, with whole families packed into single rooms, attics, and cellars. Indeed, "a cellar in St. Giles" then meant a wretched habitation.

The river of beer swept its victims off their feet, dashing them against walls or burying them under debris. The terrain being level, the runoff soon collected in the cellars of St. Giles, through which the rescuers waded up to their waists in brew. No drunks, however, were reported.

The only comparable disaster occurred in Boston's North End district in 1919, when twenty-one persons were killed in a flood of molasses.

COCA-COLA'S SECRET INGREDIENTS

Coca-Cola is the most popular soft drink in the world, yet fewer than ten persons alive know exactly what's in it. Each day, people in 155 countries down 250 million bottles of the soft drink, without knowing its ingredients.

More than 99 percent of Coke's recipe is identified. Coke is mostly a blend of sugar, carbonated water, caramel, phosphoric acid, caffeine, and "spent" coca leaves and cola nuts. The mystery ingredients, "Merchandise 7X," account for less than 1 percent of the syrup. Chemists and competitors have tried unsuccessfully for more than eighty years to analyze "7X."

The Coca-Cola Company declines to say how many people know the complete formula, but it is generally agreed that fewer than ten insiders have the information. If they forget the formula, they must go to the Trust Company of Georgia, where it is written down and stored in a vault. Security precautions are formidable—before the vault is opened, the Trust Company's board of directors approves an application. Then, the vault is opened only in the presence of officials, at a precisely specified time.

You may never know Coke's recipe because the Food and Drug Administration exempts cola beverage makers from having to identify certain "essential ingredients."

IT TOOK THE "OUCH" OUT OF GROUCH

The soft drink known as 7UP once contained lithium carbonate, a powerful drug now prescribed for manic-depressives.

In October 1929, just before the stock market crash, St. Louis businessman Charles L. Grigg began marketing a beverage called Bib-Label Lithiated Lemon-Lime Soda. His slogan: "Take the 'ouch' out of grouch." The drink was a huge success during the Depression, perhaps because of the calming lithium salts it contained.

The drink's unwieldy name was later changed to 7UP. The "7" stood for its 7-ounce bottle, the "UP" for "bottoms up" or for the bubbles rising from its heavy carbonation, which was later reduced. The lithium was listed on the label until the mid-1940s.

Identified chemically in 1817, lithium was prescribed for gout, uremia, kidney stones, and rheumatism, for which it does little good. Worse, it can harm heart and kidney patients.

In 1949, Australian psychiatrist Jon F.K. Cade accidentally discov-

ered lithium carbonate's effects on guinea pigs, while he was researching toxic reaction in the nervous system of manic-depressives. The little animals uncharacteristically lay on their backs in a stupor after being injected with lithium.

Though restricted by an FDA ban that was partially lifted in 1970, lithium still is taken by many Americans. It is available only by prescription.

WHEN COFFEE WAS BANNED IN SWEDEN

In the 1700s, coffee drinking was banned in Sweden. Government officials suspected that coffeehouses were dens of subversion where malcontents planned revolts. Also, coffee was imported, so its consumption drained money from Sweden's economy. And many medical men advised that coffee was bad for one's health.

Coffee consumption was skyrocketing in Sweden, so King Frederick I issued an edict in 1746 against "the misuse and excesses" of coffee drinking. This was followed by an excise tax on coffee (and tea) consumption. Those who failed to pay the tax were fined and their cups confiscated. In 1756, coffee was banned completely, but the ban failed to keep the beans out of Sweden. Coffee bootlegging became a profitable and popular profession, and government agents were kept busy conducting "coffee raids." A new, tougher law of 1766 was only slightly more effective against smuggling.

Three years later, the Swedish government conceded the battle and decided it should reap some of the profits in the coffee trade. It lifted the ban and imposed a stiff import tax.

THE HOLE TRUTH

No ones knows who invented the doughnut. But we do know who invented the doughnut hole.

He was Hanson Crockett Gregory, a ship captain born in 1832 in Maine. As a boy he often watched his mother prepare "fried cakes," marveling, as he watched, that the centers never got cooked. One day in

1847, "Hanson got a fork and poked it through the center of the fried cake," reports Fred Crockett, Hanson's great-grandnephew, "and the doughnut hole was born."

But it wasn't until October 27, 1941, that the lad's work was fully recognized. On that day, the National Dunking Association sponsored the Great Doughnut Debate. Fred Crockett was there, arguing on Hanson Gregory's behalf; opposing him was Chief High Eagle, a Wampanoag Indian who claimed that an ancestor of his had created the first doughnut hole when an arrow meant for a Pilgrim housewife went astray and pierced a fried cake she was making. "The chief's story was full of holes," says Fred Crockett. The judges agreed.

BEAN BRANDING

In parts of Madagascar, the island republic off the southeast coast of Africa, vanilla beans on the vine are such a temptation to thieves that each bean is individually branded, like cattle, for protection.

The practice of branding vanilla beans goes back to the nineteenth century, when such thievery first became widespread. Using cork and sharp pins, a grower would etch permanent identifying patterns into the beans while they were still green on the vine.

Today, vanilla is grown in Mexico, Indonesia, and elsewhere, but Madagascar remains the world's leading supplier of the treasured bean, producing approximately 1,000 tons a year. While bean-rustling is not the problem it once was, some growers still brand their beans—but with numbers rather than designs.

Vanilla beans are long, slender, and golden-green at harvest time. It is only after a four-to-five-month drying and curing process that they turn chocolate-brown in color and acquire the characteristic fragrance that makes them an ideal flavoring agent. Modern-day rustlers should be advised, however, that the going rate for cured vanilla beans is only $38–$40 per pound.

FREUD'S FASTEST ANALYSIS

During a four-hour walk around the Dutch town of Leyden, psychologist Sigmund Freud conducted an instant—and successful—psychoanalysis of Austrian composer Gustav Mahler, one of the quickest analytic cures in history.

The year was 1910, and Mahler's problem concerned a crisis in his marriage. His wife, Alma, unhappy over his impotence and neglect, had come close to having a love affair with architect Walter Gropius (whom she later married after Mahler died). On the advice of a Viennese psychoanalyst, Mahler decided to consult Freud, who was in Leyden on a rare holiday.

Mahler was good material for Freud, who traced Mahler's adult neuroses to childhood feelings. Mahler identified with his mother, Marie, rather than his brutal father—even copying her lameness in his slight limp.

When Freud asked Mahler why he had married someone with a

Gustav Mahler

name other than Marie, Mahler revealed that Alma's middle name was actually Maria and that he often called her Marie. Freud later told a colleague, ". . . we discovered his personal conditions for love, especially his Holy Mary complex [mother fixation] . . ."

It was a breakthrough for Mahler. His impotence alleviated, he and Alma lived happily until his death from heart disease a year later at age fifty-one.

THE BLUE PEOPLE OF KENTUCKY

In 1962, Luke Combs took his sick wife to the University of Kentucky Hospital. But it wasn't Mrs. Combs who attracted attention. Said Dr. Charles H. Behlen II, then a medical student and researcher at the hospital, "Luke was just as blue as Lake Louise on a cool summer day."

A team led by Dr. Madison Cawein made a medical study of Luke's condition and found that he had methemoglobinemia, a rare hereditary blood disease caused by an enzymatic deficiency that reduces the oxygen-carrying capacity of the red blood cells. Fewer than 500 cases have been found worldwide, and most of these have been in Appalachia, where intermarriage has facilitated the transmission of such genetic illnesses. The mountain people in the region are accustomed to hearing about the "blue Combses" and the "blue Fugates."

While the disease rarely causes physical problems, it does sometimes cause embarrassment. One blue person told Behlen and Cawein, "We don't go to town. People think we look funny." Some persons with the disease only "show blue" at certain times, such as when they are angry, tired, sick, or have had too much to drink. Zach "Big Man" Fugate claimed to turn blue only in the cold, or upon taking certain medicines. The color they exhibit has been variously described as that of "an oxford-cloth blue shirt," "like the skin of a damson plum," "blue as indigo," and "gunmetal."

The condition can be easily controlled by taking a medication called "methylene blue." Since the drug has the side effect of turning the patient's urine blue, physicians have explained it to the Kentuckians by saying, "You're peeing the blue out of you."

In the 1970s, a crew that was filming a documentary on the disease traveled to Troublesome Creek, Kentucky, to conduct interviews with some of the blue people. When the director found a woman with methemoglobinemia, he complained, "But she isn't blue enough!" The film crew packed up and left.

BEER AND SHOE POLISH DON'T MIX

If you polish your shoes while drinking beer, you may die, or become very ill. Nitrobenzene, found in some kinds of shoe polish, is a toxic substance which is easily absorbed into human skin. It can also be harmful or deadly when it gets into the lungs or is ingested. When it combines with alcohol in the body, it becomes deadlier faster.

Nitrobenzene, also occasionally used in dry-cleaning products, dyes, solvents, and metal polishes, is a pale yellow, oily substance. In 1978, 575 million pounds of it were produced in the United States. Its effects vary. At its worst, it can make you convulse, turn blue (develop cyanosis), go into coma, and die. One man wearing shoes freshly shined with liquid shoe polish died within a few hours of drinking beer. A factory hand who worked with nitrobenzene noticed signs of poisoning—headaches and nausea. When he thought he had recovered, he drank two glasses of beer, and fell unconscious. There have been nitrobenzene-poisoning cases involving no alcohol: babies in diapers stamped with nitrobenzene dye have shown symptoms of poisoning.

In 1981, the Environmental Protection Agency proposed that manufacturers test nitrobenzene, saying that existing data "indicate a potential human health hazard." To date, there are no federal regulations requiring the labeling of nitrobenzene content in products.

HAVE A LITTLE SAND IN YOUR SUGAR

The chemical doctoring of foods is not a modern-day phenomenon. Food adulterants date at least as far back as ancient Rome and Athens. And 100 years ago in England and the United States, the problem was even worse than it is today.

England had regulations prohibiting food adulteration as early as the 1200s. With the growth of towns in the Middle Ages, food production moved from the home to the factory, and the pressures of large-scale manufacturing and marketing prompted merchants to resort to objectionable shortcuts. In Victorian England, cash-hungry bakers got more dough for their dough by adding alum and sulfur of copper. Dairymen sold cream thickened with flour, watered down milk, and often added chalk or plaster of Paris to perk up the color of milk from diseased cows. A conglomeration of calcium, gypsum, gelatin fat, and mashed potatoes was passed off as butter, but oleomargarine was even worse. Known as "bogus butter," it was distilled from beef fat, bleach, and other unsavory substances. To stretch sugar, grocers on both sides of the Atlantic routinely added sand. Pepper was sometimes mixed with mustard husks and floor sweepings, and coffee beans were often fortified with fake beans made of sawdust.

But while the adulterants were merely sickening, the chemical additions were downright lethal. In 1892 in the United States, federal investigators found large quantities of toxic tin chloride in molasses, aniline dyes in candy, and copper salts in canned peas. In England, candies took on bright colors from massive infusions of toxic salts of copper and lead. Gloucester cheese acquired its appealing orange hue from its red lead content. And beer contained additives like vitriol and *cocolus indicus*, known to induce paralysis, convulsions, gastroenteritis, and fatal over-stimulation of the respiratory system.

One of the most blatant cases of food adulteration occurred as recently as 1969, when a man in England was charged with selling phony grated Parmesan cheese. What he was really selling was grated umbrella handles.

THE AMERICAN CROWBAR CASE

You think *you* have headaches? Phineas P. Gage lived more than twelve years with a 3½-inch-wide hole in his skull.

A foreman on the construction of the Rutland and Burlington Railroad at Cavendish, Vermont, twenty-five-year-old Gage was tamping down an explosive charge on September 13, 1848, when he accidentally sparked the powder. The unexpected blast drove a 13¼-pound tamping iron completely through his brain and out the top of his head.

Gage was loaded onto an oxcart by his horrified coworkers and taken to a hotel about a mile away, where, with a little assistance, he climbed the stairs to a second-floor hall. There, two doctors examined Gage and cleaned his wound. He never lost consciousness.

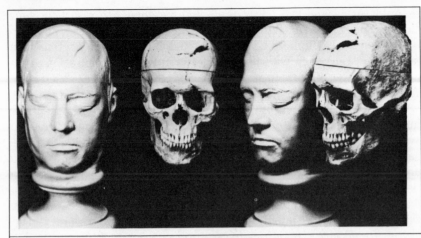

Skull and cast of Phineas P. Gage

That evening Gage endured severe hemorrhaging and vomiting but remained lucid. In the following weeks, he became intermittently delirious and lost the use of his left eye. Within two months, however, he was well enough to return home and soon resumed an active life of work and travel. He died in 1861 after a series of convulsions.

Known in the annals of medicine as the American Crowbar Case, Gage's story has baffled doctors for generations. Today, the steel rod, a life cast of Gage's head, and his actual skull are on display at Harvard Medical School's Warren Anatomical Museum.

LIVE SHORT FOR A LONG LIFE

It is often noted that the average American woman lives about eight years longer than the average American man. Scientists have tried to explain those extra years as resulting from female hormones, lack of stress, and other factors, but one element hasn't been examined: height. What if women, who average five feet, four inches in America, live longer because they are five inches shorter than the average male?

Not a popular idea, since we admire stature over shortness. Should we stop looking down on short people? Thomas Samaras thinks so. His theory is that tallness itself promotes a shorter lifespan.

After studying groups of athletes, U.S. presidents, successful businessmen, and even giants, Samaras concluded that the average age of death declined with increasing height for all of these groups. Shorter men outlived taller ones by 6 to 20 percent. Five presidents under five feet eight averaged 80.4 years at death; five over six feet one averaged only 66.8 years. Giants taller than seven feet seven averaged only 39.8 years at death.

Is there an optimum size for human beings? Perhaps we should study this question before the average gain in height for our race as a whole—one inch every thirty years—turns us into twenty-first-century dinosaurs.

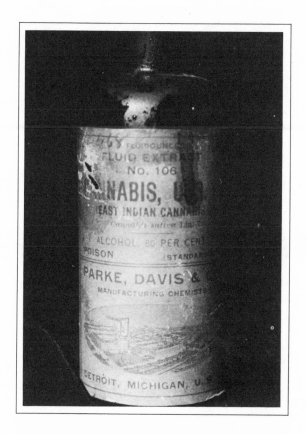

WHEN "MARIJUANA" WAS LEGAL

In 1851, marijuana extract was recommended in a U.S. drug manual for more than a dozen ailments.

In the early 1900s, the U.S. drug company Parke-Davis was a leading importer of "pot" and sold it in extract and bulk form. Bulk marijuana was purchased by Russian and Polish immigrants with respiratory ailments, who placed it on their radiators and inhaled its vapors. Imported marijuana varied in strength, so Parke-Davis began growing *Cannabis americana* in an attempt to standardize potency.

Marijuana fell into disfavor as a pharmaceutical product by the 1930s. New synthetic drugs were faster acting and offered a controlled dosage. Sensational news stories and the work of Harry J. Anslinger, the zealous commissioner of the new Bureau of Narcotics, turned public opinion against the "killer weed." However, twenty-eight medical products still contained marijuana, though it often was not on the label. The Marijuana Tax Act of 1937 made it difficult to prescribe cannabis.

The act was opposed by the birdseed industry, which annually used 4 million pounds of German hemp seed for pigeon food, and by the American Medical Association, which said "a restudy of the drug by modern means may show other advantages to be derived from its medical use." Today, researchers say marijuana could be an effective treatment for glaucoma, anorexia nervosa, heart attacks, and migraine headaches.

DR. FREUD'S MAGIC NOSE POWDER

In 1884, Sigmund Freud published research on a miraculous new drug—cocaine. The report, "Über Coca," was, in the doctor's words, "a song of praise for this magical substance." It could cure almost anything, he claimed, and he recommended it for digestive ailments, asthma, fatigue, morphine addiction, alcoholism, headache, melancholy, and pain relief. Freud himself swallowed and injected the drug. It eased his shyness, he told his fiancée Martha, and he sent her some "to make you strong and give your cheeks red color." Soon his friends and colleagues also were encouraged to try some.

Within months, "Über Coca" was translated into English, and American pharmaceutical companies took immediate notice. One claimed that cocaine "would supply the place of food, make the coward brave, the silent eloquent . . ." During the 1890s, doctors and dentists—who had access to the drug in its pure state—began using (and abusing) it themselves, as well as prescribing it widely.

Salesmen went door to door with the drug, and bartenders would, on request, add a dash of cocaine to one's shot of whiskey. Sniffing parlors catered to both wealthy and bohemian clients. Anyone could walk into a drugstore and find cocaine-based hay fever remedies, tonics, digestive aids, pills, powders, cigarettes, and patent medicines. One remedy, invented in 1886, was Coca-Cola. "The Pause That Refreshes" was sold in drugstores as a headache tonic. By 1909, there were sixty-nine imitations of Coca-Cola—all containing cocaine.

Millions of users eventually discovered that cocaine was not only stimulating but also habit-forming. Freud had called it a harmless stimulant, but within a few years of his research, doctors were seeing cases of cocaine abuse, including full-blown cocaine psychosis complete with hallucinations of insects and snakes crawling under the sufferer's skin. Cocaine abuse caused increasing alarm until 1914, when the drug was outlawed in the United States by the Harrison Narcotic Act.

THE WORLD'S MOST EXPENSIVE SPICE

Next time you're fixing dinner, go easy on the saffron. At $150 an ounce, retail, it is easily the world's most expensive spice.

Small wonder. Between 70,000 and 80,000 blossoms of the saffron crocus are required to make a single pound of the aromatic orange-red powder. Each blossom has three bugle-shaped stigmas, which must be carefully removed by hand, dried over charcoal fires, and then crushed into powder.

An ancient spice, saffron is native to Greece, Asia Minor, and Iran. Over the centuries, as traders introduced it in Europe, the Orient, and elsewhere, it came to be valued not merely as a condiment, but as a perfume, aphrodisiac, and cure-all. John Gerard, the sixteenth-century English herbalist, claimed saffron was good for the heart and lungs; the medieval Arabian physician Avicenna touted it as a great early-morning eye-opener. Pliny the Elder of ancient Rome claimed it cured ulcers. (Many of the same kinds of benefits are claimed for wild ginseng root from China—the world's most expensive herb, used in teas and tonics and available for up to $23,000 an ounce in Hong Kong.)

These days saffron is used mainly as a flavoring. So costly is it that many restaurants and grocery stores keep their supply under lock and key.

OVER-THE-COUNTER HALLUCINOGENS

In his book, *Hazards of Medication,* Eric Martin reveals a startling fact: many of the "safe" drugs which are sold in drugstores without prescription actually contain hallucinogenic ingredients in the same family as LSD, mescaline, and hashish. Among the sedatives, sleep aids, and other remedies which may cause hallucinations for the user are:

Alophen
Compoz
Contac
Donnagel
Nytol
Sleep-eze
Sominex.

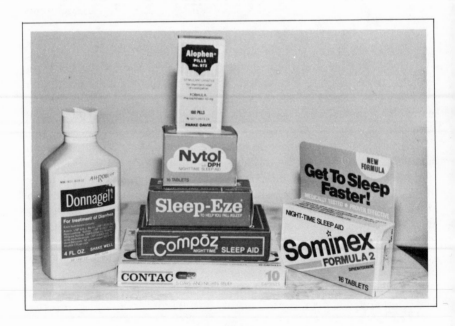

Excessive doses of these and 123 other easily available drugs may lead to confusion, delirium, and disorientation, as well as both auditory and visual hallucinations.

THE CHEWING CRAZE

Horace Fletcher taught the world to chew its way to health. In the early 1900s, almost everybody was "Fletcherizing"—including John D. Rockefeller, Thomas Edison, and many West Point cadets.

The story of Fletcherism began in 1895 when Fletcher's application for insurance was rejected because he was a poor health risk. He weighed 217 pounds—too heavy for his five-foot, six-inch frame—drank excessively, and felt rotten most of the time. He described himself as "an old man at forty on the way to a rapid decline."

To improve himself, he followed his own regimen of eating, based partly on a precept of Prime Minister William Gladstone of England, that one should chew each bite of food thirty-two times, once for each tooth. Fletcher, less exact, chewed until the food was ready to "swallow itself"—from thirty to seventy times. He also never ate when upset or when not hungry. After five months, he'd lost more than sixty pounds and was fit and healthy.

Fletcher's popular books and lectures about his method soon persuaded thousands of people to live by his example. Their slogan was: "Nature will castigate those who don't masticate."

THE GREAT EGGSPERIMENT

During World War II, three researchers in Cambridge, England, did their part for the war effort and the pursuit of scientific inquiry by tasting the cooked eggs of eighty-one different species of birds. Dr. J. Brooks, Mr. H. P. Hale, and Dr. J. R. Hawthorne ate each egg scrambled, cooked over steam. They savored seven or eight eggs at a sitting and ranked them from 10 (excellent flavor) down to 2 (inedible). The eggs of each species were sampled at least twice and the research-

251

ers were not told which particular type of bird egg they were eating.

The common chicken egg received the highest ranking (8.8), but it had stiff competition. The eggs of the coot, moorhen, and lesser black-backed gull each scored 8.3, while the kittiwake egg finished with an 8.2.

Brooks, Hale, and Hawthorne were particularly repelled by the bitter and disgusting tastes of the eggs of the eastern house wren (3.2), the blue tit (3.3), and the reed warbler (3.4). Blue tit eggs were described as "fishy tasting," despite the fact that blue tits don't eat fish. The worst-tasting egg was that of the ordinary wren, which possessed no redeeming qualities and scored a rock-bottom 2.

Most curious were the eggs of the oyster-catcher, which had a different taste each time they were cooked. The first sample reminded the researchers of the smell and taste of onions (4.3), while the second batch had a nutty flavor (7.7). A third round of oyster-catcher eggs proved inedible, having the odor and flavor of hemp (3.7).

The experimenters concluded that small birds ensure the continuation of their species by producing eggs that are distasteful to birds of prey and other predators.

FRESHEST IDEA IN YEARS

Something was rotten in the state of France in the eighteenth century—namely, the food. Because there was no satisfactory means of keeping food fresh, malnutrition and food poisoning were killing thousands of Napoleon's soldiers.

In 1795, the French government challenged the nation's inventors: Devise a way to keep food fresh and win a prize of 12,000 francs. Nicholas Appert, a Parisian brewer and confectioner, accepted the challenge. No one knew about bacteria and sterilization in those days, but Appert had a hunch that storing food in hermetically sealed bottles and boiling them in water might be the answer. Working in a crude laboratory—where he also invented the bouillon cube—Appert designed his own wide-mouthed glass vessels, which he filled with all manner of prepared delicacies, from syrup and sugared fruits to pot-au-feu and fillet of beef. He sealed the bottles tightly with cork stoppers and wax, and boiled them for varying lengths of time. By 1804, he was able to keep food preserved for more than three months. *Voilà:* canning was born.

In 1809, Appert won the 12,000 francs. The following year he published *The Book for All Households, or the Art of Preserving Animal and Vegetable Substances for Many Years.* With the prize money he opened the House of Appert, the world's first commercial cannery. It lasted for more than a century.

LEGAL HEROIN

Heroin was introduced to the world in 1898 by Dr. Heinrich Dreser, head of the drug research department of the Bayer Company of Germany. Dreser, who also claimed credit for discovering aspirin the following year, declared that heroin was a *non* addictive substitute for morphine, from which it was derived.

Before the year was out, Bayer was happily marketing heroin as an ingredient in over-the-counter cough medicines. Soon it was also being touted as a painkiller, as well as a cure for morphine addiction. Doctors all over Europe and the Americas began prescribing heroin for headaches, coughs, and menstrual cramps. Unfortunately, literally millions of addicts were created in the twelve years it took doctors to

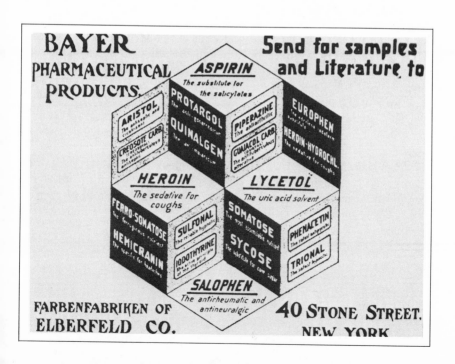

realize that heroin was just as addictive and dangerous as morphine.

By 1924 the U.S. Congress had banned the manufacture of heroin, and in 1956 all existing legal supplies were destroyed. However, by that time, organized crime had long since discovered the profitability of heroin, and its use has remained widespread. In fact, the only time that heroin is in short supply in the United States is when the Longshoremen's Union is on strike and ships stand unloaded.

Recently there has been talk of making heroin legal again. The argument for legalization is twofold:

1) It would take away from organized crime one of its biggest businesses.

2) Addicts, able to purchase heroin easily, would no longer need to steal to keep up with the superinflated prices being charged by pushers.

And this time it wouldn't be prescribed as an ingredient in cough medicines.

ONE SQUARE INCH OF SKIN

Human skin is *not* only skin deep. In fact, it is among the body's most complex organs. Of its three main layers, only the paper-thin epidermis is normally visible. Beneath the epidermis is the dermis, and below that is the subdermis. In a square inch of skin, you will find: 20 blood vessels; 65 hairs and muscles; 78 nerves; 78 sensors for heat, 13 for cold, 160–165 for pressure; 100 sebaceous glands; 650 sweat glands; 1,300 nerve endings; and 19,500,000 cells.

The sweat glands do double duty, helping to eliminate wastes and cool the body. On a hot day, the skin can release up to 2,500 calories of heat.

The body's largest organ, the skin measures about twenty-one square feet in an average adult. It accounts for 15 percent of total body weight and provides a protective shield against bacteria and viruses. It also absorbs shocks that might otherwise damage the bones and internal organs.

MITES ON YOUR FACE

What has a wormlike body, four pairs of stubby legs, and is crawling in colonies on your face? Tiny mites called *Demodex folliculorum* and *Demodex brevis.*

The creatures can be found on just about everybody, says Dr. Matthew Douglas of the University of Kansas, and they have inhabited mankind throughout the ages. Don't try to scrub them off—it's a futile gesture. Besides, they seem to do no harm and may even be doing some good.

The *folliculorum* inhabits the hair follicles, especially around the nose and eyes. Its fellow parasite, the *brevis,* prefers to live in the sebaceous, or oil, glands. The mites may be earning their keep by cleansing the follicles and unclogging the glands.

If you have a magnifying glass of 30-power or better, you might be able to get a look at your guests. Take a clean index card and closely scrape your eyebrows. Place the edge of the card into a shallow dish containing a few drops of clean water. You'll have to look closely, because the tiny *Demodex* is almost transparent.

12

DAILY LIVING AND ENTERTAINMENT

MAIL-ORDER HOUSES

Since 1893, Sears, Roebuck and Co. has sold virtually everything through the mail—including houses.

Sears introduced its first catalogue for mail-order houses in 1908. It experimented with financing plans and for several years offered a "no money down," fifteen-year loan that included money advanced for labor costs. The build-it-yourself house kits were shipped by rail in large crates and included shingles, windows, precut lumber, and all other necessary building materials, along with blueprints and assembly instructions.

These were not ticky-tacky plywood boxes, but spacious, solidly built homes. The 1918 edition of Sears's *Modern Homes* catalogue listed more than 100 models, including a six-room cottage which sold for $765 and the exclusive "Magnolia"—a two-story mansion with a basement, solarium, nine-foot ceilings, inlaid oak floors, and servants' quarters.

More than 100,000 homes were sold by mail in the United States before 1937, and many are still around. The Depression made it impossible for Sears to profit by selling mail-order houses. However, kit houses once again are being produced and sold successfully by many U.S. companies.

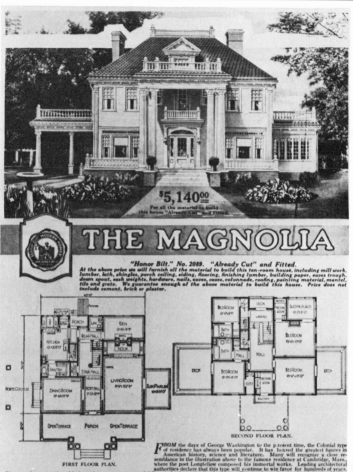

$5,140⁰⁰

For all the material to build
this house "Already Cut" and Fitted.

THE MAGNOLIA

"Honor Bilt." No. 2089. "Already Cut" and Fitted.

At the above price we will furnish all the material to build this ten-room house, including mill work, lumber, lath, shingles, porch ceiling, siding, flooring, finishing lumber, building paper, eaves trough, down spout, sash weights, hardware, nails, eaves, cases, colonnade, roofing, painting material, mantel, tile and grate. We guarantee enough of the above material to build this house. Price does not include cement, brick or plaster.

FIRST FLOOR PLAN.

SECOND FLOOR PLAN.

FROM the days of George Washington to the present time, the Colonial type of residence has always been popular. It has housed the greatest figures in American history, science and literature. Many will recognize a close resemblance in the illustration above to the famous residence at Cambridge, Mass., where the poet Longfellow composed his immortal works. Leading architectural authorities declare that this type will continue to win favor for hundreds of years. There can be no question of its imposing appearance, graceful lines and other attractive features. This is a house for the discriminating builder who is willing to invest a fair amount for the largest returns in comfort, convenience and extra high quality.

First Floor A Colonial front door opens from the porch into the reception hall, which has French doors leading to the living room and the dining room. French doors also lead from the living room to the solarium or sun parlor. A massive but graceful stairway leads from the hall to the second floor. There is a rear hall back of the stairway, with doors leading to the kitchen, the den and the rear porch. The kitchen has a nicely arranged breakfast alcove lighted by three fancy windows. A china case over each seat in the alcove. See illustrations on the opposite page. Rooms are 9 feet 6 inches from floor to ceiling.

We furnish oak flooring, oak doors and birch trim for the reception hall, living room, dining room and sun parlor. Yellow pine flooring, doors and trim for the rest of the first floor. With the exception of the French doors for the living room, dining room and sun parlor, all other inside doors are the latest two-panel design. For the second floor we furnish yellow pine flooring and trim with five-cross panel solid white pine doors.

Second Floor There are four bedrooms with closets, two bath rooms and a sleeping porch on this floor. One of the front bedrooms and one of the rear bedrooms have dressing rooms, with extra compartments for dresses and hats. Other conveniences are shelves in the closets, a special broom closet and a stairway to the attic. Note that the servants' quarters are completely separate and have a stairway from the kitchen. Rooms are 9 feet from floor to ceiling.

Basement An excavated basement under the entire house, 7 feet from floor to joists, lighted with basement sash.

A pair of French doors lead from the stair landing to the deck and a French door from dressing room to front of balcony.

Painted two coats outside, your choice of color. Varnish and wood filler for interior finish.

Built on a concrete and brick foundation, frame construction, No. 1 yellow pine framing and dimension lumber.

Our Guarantee Protects You—Order Your House From This Book.
Price Includes Plans and Specifications.

EXCLUSIVE: THE WORST HOUSEHOLD TASKS

Washing dishes is the least favorite household task of American women, according to an exclusive poll of 1,352 women commissioned by "Significa" and conducted by the Gallup Organization of Princeton, New Jersey. The second-most hated task is cleaning the bathroom, followed closely by ironing and scrubbing floors.

Women in the Western states have a particular distaste for vacuuming, while dusting is least popular in the Midwest. Women who never graduated from high school are the most likely to object to cooking, although they don't seem to mind doing laundry and ironing.

Here are the final results of our exclusive Gallup poll, in order, with the percentage of women who called that household chore "the worst":

1.	Washing dishes	17%
2.	Cleaning bathroom	9%
3.	Ironing	8%
4.	Scrubbing floors	7%
5.	Cleaning (nonspecific)	7%
6.	Vacuuming	6%
7.	Washing windows	5%
8.	Cooking	5%
9.	Dusting	5%
10.	Laundry	5%
11.	Cleaning oven	5%
	Miscellaneous	11%
	Don't know	10%

ALASKAN ESKIMOS DO NOT LIVE IN IGLOOS

If you believe Alaskan Eskimos live in igloos, you've been snowed. The only igloos in that state—or anywhere in western Canada—are in museums and picture books. Most Eskimos in those areas have never seen an igloo.

To be sure, natives of Greenland, Canada's Baffin Island, and some other areas have for centuries built and lived in the dome-shaped snow houses. Working alone, an experienced builder can hack out the blocks of packed snow for a modest-sized igloo and assemble them in an hour or two. It's a useful skill, especially if you're caught unprotected with a storm brewing.

Where do Alaskan Eskimos live, then? Many inhabit the same conventional wood homes you see in any American town. In coastal villages, more primitive-looking wooden shacks are common. Since the coastal region lacks trees, building materials often must be flown or shipped in.

Archeological records show that up to 5,000 years ago, Eskimos in Alaska lived in huts fashioned from blocks of sod or in tents made from the skins of caribou, walrus, and polar bear.

WHAT'S A MOTHER TO DO?

Alice Hamilton of West Dallas, Texas, held an unenviable distinction in the annals of motherhood: Both of her sons were listed as "Public Enemy No. 1."

Mrs. Hamilton's older boy, Floyd, fell in with the notorious Bonnie and Clyde gang. But it was a prolonged armed robbery rampage in 1938

Alice Hamilton with her son Raymond in a Texas courtroom

that earned him his public-enemy status. He drew two sentences totaling fifty-five years, served time in Leavenworth and Alcatraz, and was released in 1958.

Her son Raymond, also a Bonnie and Clyde gang member, shot and killed an Oklahoma sheriff and his deputy in 1932, one of several crimes for which he was sentenced to a total of 263 years in jail. He broke out less than two years later but soon was arrested after a shoot-out with Texas Rangers. While awaiting trial, he escaped from Huntsville Prison in Texas. During the break, a prison guard was killed, and Raymond was branded Public Enemy No. 1. He was quickly recaptured and executed in the electric chair in 1935.

"I was taught to love and honor God and that hard work is good for the soul," Mrs. Hamilton once said. "And that's what I taught my sons." Evidently Raymond never got the message, but Floyd became a born-again Christian after leaving prison. He now spends time preaching to prisoners.

SUBVERSIVE KINDERGARTEN

For the years 1851–60, the Prussian government banned a dangerous institution—the kindergarten. The kindergarten movement, founded by Friedrich Froebel in 1837, was in its infancy.

Froebel, whose unhappy childhood gave him a special affinity for children, was fifty-five when he set up his Child Nurturing and Activity Institute in the German village of Blankenburg. Luckily, he came up with a better name—the German word *kindergarten*—"children's garden"—during a walk in the woods. A kindergarten, he believed, should be a place where children are "cultivated in accordance with the laws of their own being, of God, and of Nature."

It all sounds very innocent—and was. Yet in 1851, the Prussian minister of education banned kindergartens as socialistic institutions that taught atheism. It is probable that the minister had confused Froebel with his radical nephew Karl; but though this possibility was pointed out to him, he did not rescind the decree. Elsewhere, however, kindergartens flourished, promoted by liberals incensed at the Prussian decree. And they flourish today, even in Germany.

CHILD-BEATING—AT SCHOOL

Each year, 1.5 million schoolchildren in the United States are physically punished under the authorization of principals and other school administrators. This figure does not include informal slappings or beatings meted out by teachers, coaches, bus drivers, and other school employees.

The schools most inclined to punish are those in Florida, followed by those in Arkansas and Mississippi. In Florida, one out of eight public school students receives corporal punishment in a typical year. The national average is one out of twenty-eight. Black schoolchildren are victimized most often; one out of three is punished nationwide in a typical year.

Awards of commendation go to six states—Hawaii, New Jersey, Massachusetts, Maine, New Hampshire, and Rhode Island—which refuse to allow corporal punishment.

MEN WHO WERE RAISED AS GIRLS

During Victorian times, mothers often dressed little boys as girls for their first few years because dresses made diaper-changing easier. But some mothers, before and since, carried this practice to extremes. For example:

North Pole explorer Robert Peary's mother sent her little "Bertie" out to play in frilly clothes and a sunbonnet.

General Douglas MacArthur often said, "My first memory is that of a bugle call." His next memories perhaps were those of being dressed in skirts and wearing his hair in long curls until he was eight. Author Ernest Hemingway was another "macho" man whose mother's whim was to dress her son in feminine attire.

Artist Peter Paul Rubens, at the age of twelve, served as one of three pages at the court of Countess Matilda de Lalaing. For amusement, Matilda and her female friends dressed the three boys in lacy underwear and sumptuous gowns, plucked their eyebrows, and made them wear women's wigs and makeup.

German poet Rainer Maria Rilke was raised as a girl for his first six years. His mother had wanted a daughter and was so disappointed that she even called him "Sophie." Another disappointed mom was Speranza Wilde, mother of wit and playwright Oscar Wilde. She clothed

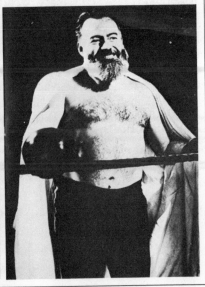

Ernest Hemingway in feminine dress   . . . and macho attire

Oscar in blue velvet dresses and so many trinkets that one contemporary writer likened him to "a little Hindu idol."

Novelist Thomas Wolfe was the last of seven surviving children. Said his mother, "He being the baby, I kept him a baby." She breast-fed him until he was 3½, slept with him until he was 6. She curled his long hair every day and ignored his pleas to cut it. Once, when some older boys called him a girl, Tom opened his trousers to prove otherwise. At nine, Tom caught head lice, and his mother finally let his curls be cut.

Of all the famous men brought up as girls, wit and critic Alexander Woollcott probably enjoyed it the most. His older sister and her teenage friends took pictures of little Aleck in dresses and makeup. In college, Aleck founded a drama club and played the female leads in its plays. He even went to parties in women's clothes, handing out calling cards that read "Alexandra Woollcott."

THE SQUAW MAN

Chroniclers of the early West have recorded that American Indians took a dim view of cowardice in battle. They often punished the fainthearted with death. But one male offender was forced to dress and live as a woman for the final sixty years of his life.

In 1878, the U.S. Indian Bureau dispatched Nathan Meeker to the White River Agency in western Colorado to "civilize" the Utes. A social reformer and utopian, Meeker thought he could teach the nomadic Utes to live in houses and be farmers. The Utes wanted no part of him. But Meeker had a job to do, and when the Utes continued to balk, he summoned the cavalry. In retaliation, the Utes slaughtered Meeker and six of his men.

One Ute brave named Yugasie refused to join the massacre. When the dust had settled, he was ostracized from male society and forced to dress, live, and work as a squaw for the rest of his days. Although he lived to be nearly 100, Yugasie never protested his enforced transvestism and docilely went about his daily chores, which included sewing the blouses and ankle-length skirts he wore. Actually, Yugasie's so-called punishment was not as severe as it sounds. Many Indian tribes tolerated transvestism; some Indian men even chose the homosexual or quasi-female existence. Yugasie, however, was offered no choice.

NO-SEX CEREALS

Cold breakfast cereals were originally produced to dampen human sex drives. Three men in particular—Sylvester Graham, James Caleb Jackson, and John Harvey Kellogg—helped steer the American public away from ham and eggs and toward cold-processed grains and milk.

Sylvester Graham was a self-styled doctor in the early 1800s. He recommended no sex for men before age thirty, and not more than one sexual indulgence per month thereafter. To calm sexual arousal—which seems inevitable given that Spartan schedule—he suggested a bland diet featuring "Graham bread," made with home-ground whole wheat. His theories were pooh-poohed by many, including commercial bakers and essayist Ralph Waldo Emerson, who dubbed him "the prophet of bran bread and pumpkins."

Graham opened boardinghouses where healthful diets were provided for residents. His establishments helped promote the popularity of water-cure resorts, like Our Home on the Hillside in New York, owned by James Caleb Jackson. As a sideline, Jackson prepared Graham-derived health foods, including cereals.

Inspired by visits to Jackson's establishment, the Seventh Day Adventists built a similar resort in Battle Creek, Michigan. In 1876, John Harvey Kellogg became the superintendent there. Believing that "irritating" foods stimulated erotic feelings, he also manufactured cold cereal. If children ate it, said Kellogg, they wouldn't fall prey to the sin of "self-pollution," a euphemism for masturbation. In 1906, his younger brother, Will Keith Kellogg, began the breakfast cereal empire that bears his name.

A EUNUCH SITUATION

Eunuchs (castrated males) still exist in the world, although they no longer serve as harem attendants. It is estimated that today there are about 3,500 hijras, or eunuchs, in Bombay, India. As recently as ten years ago in Afghanistan, castrated boys sometimes were traded for horses and cattle to serve as sexual slaves. And in the 1950s in Scandinavia, 250 males were castrated—mostly for criminal acts, but some merely for being "troublesome." The Nazis sexually butchered scores of "undesirable" men, including homosexuals and the retarded.

Indian and Pakistani hijras are initiated at an early age, perhaps as young as six or as old as sixteen. Likely candidates are convinced or coerced into believing that they will earn good money and will always have the security of a close-knit community life. The initiates become eunuchs during an eleven-day ritual. On each of the first ten days, a priest asks the initiate, "Do you want to become a eunuch?" to which the boy answers "yes." At dawn on the last day, the boy is held by four eunuchs, drenched with cold water and mildly anesthetized, then suffers the excision of his genitals. (This usually means that the penis is cut off, but sometimes the scrotum, or occasionally both, are removed.) Some die.

Hijras wear women's clothes and display feminine mannerisms. They can still enjoy sexual feelings and desires, but they can no longer procreate. They work as prostitutes to male customers, mostly as passive partners. They are also singers and entertainers who celebrate births and marriages for money.

When hijras die, they are escorted upright to the graveyard in the middle of the night, to keep the death as private as the life had been living in the hijra community.

SEX FOR NAILS

The poet Christopher Marlowe wrote of "the face that launched a thousand ships." Ironically, the faces—and other charms—of lovely Tahitian maidens very nearly *sank* a ship.

In 1767 explorer Samuel Wallis discovered the Tahitian Islands. The crewmen of his ship, the *Dolphin,* were soon enjoying visits to the tropical paradise. It wasn't long before the sailors learned a thrilling fact: the enticing island girls offered them hours of lovemaking in trade for a commodity rare to the Tahitians—the iron nails that held the *Dolphin* together. The natives used iron to make fishhooks and to bore holes in the planks of canoes. Wrote a *Dolphin* crew member, "Their love of iron (Nails) is so great that the women (or rather Girls, for they were very young and small) prostitute themselves to any of our People for a Nail, hardly looking upon Knives, Beads, or any toy."

At first, Captain Wallis was either unaware of the situation, or chose to ignore it. Eventually, however, he forbade the traffic in nails, but the crew ignored his command. The *Dolphin* was literally falling apart at the seams. The men's hammocks, once held up by nails, lay on the ground. What's more, the Tahitian women began to demand longer nails (the most beautiful girls could only be had for the longest nails).

Finally, a crisis occurred. Wallis refused to grant shore leave until the guilty parties confessed. The men held a trial among themselves and exchanged accusations of running up the prices by trading overly large nails. When the accused men responded that they had received double value for the bigger spikes, this sexual bragging led to a fistfight. In the end a scapegoat, Mr. Pinckney, was blamed. (His efforts had apparently caused the ship's mainsail to collapse.) Pinckney was flogged, and shore leave was ended.

The Tahitians later claimed that they had been led to believe that it was customary among white people to fornicate freely and openly. They thought it was the white man's way of saying "Hello."

MARRIED PRIESTS

Pope John Paul II has emphatically stated that Roman Catholic priests must remain single and chaste. But the Church has not always been so strict, and the rules have often been broken.

Christ's disciple St. Peter, who is considered the first pope, was a married man. Marriage was not outlawed for the Catholic clergy until the fourth century. A tug-of-war between the ideal of celibacy and the realities of carnality has existed ever since. There have been several popes who were married before being ordained, such as Clement IV (1265–68), who had two daughters.

During the Dark Ages, many priests were married—including Marino, who could drive caterpillars out of the fields with holy water, and St. Swithin, rainmaker and healer. Some created dynasties, passing on their wealthy benefices to their sons. The crackdown came in the eleventh and twelfth centuries. Married clergy were driven from their homes, their wives and children scorned by the Church. Even so, the prohibition didn't entirely work—witness the medieval German word for bastard, *pfaffienkind*, meaning "priest's son."

After the Revolution, the French Constitution of 1791 allowed clerical marriage, and thousands of priests took advantage of it. The Concordat between Napoleon and Pope Pius VII later gave them the choice of remaining in the Church as married laymen or resuming clerical celibacy. Two thousand chose marriage. Talleyrand, minister of foreign affairs, was refused such dispensation because he had formerly been a bishop.

Nowadays, if a married minister of another faith converts to Catholicism and becomes a priest, he may remain married "by way of exception," which means that the new priest's marital status has been specifically and personally approved by the pope. In the United States, a special commission exists to review the cases of Anglican ministers in this situation, but the decision to grant them permission to remain married rests solely with the pope. About 4,000 priests (1 percent of those in the Roman Catholic Church) leave each year, most of them planning to marry.

NAPOLEON'S ADOPTED CHILDREN

In 1805, Napoleon Bonaparte adopted thousands of children. It was after the battle of Austerlitz on December 2, 1805, perhaps his greatest victory, won by brilliant tactics that completely fooled the Austrian and Russian forces. Of the allies' 90,000 men, 26,000 were listed as casualties. Of France's 68,000 men, 9,000 were listed as casualties.

In a speech the next day, Napoleon congratulated his men: "Soldiers, when all that is necessary to assure the happiness and prosperity of our country shall be accomplished, I will lead you back to France. . . . My people will see you back with joy, and it will suffice you to say, 'I was at the battle of Austerlitz,' for people to answer, 'There stands a brave man.' " He announced that there would be a holiday given for them upon their return to Paris. He also adopted the children of all French soldiers killed at Austerlitz, ordering the state to pay for their support and education, to find husbands for the girls and jobs for the boys. In addition, he permitted his new children to add the name Napoleon to theirs.

GHOST MARRIAGES

The Masai of East Africa—one of the last purely pastoral people in existence—are probably best known for their unusual diet, which is dependent upon cattle milk, beef, and cattle blood.

When a young Masai warrior dies without having married and having had children, it sometimes happens that the members of his family, unwilling to let his name be forgotten, confer with the rest of the clan to find a bride for the dead man. Once chosen, this woman looks after his cattle and is allowed to have children by any man she wishes. The first son of this "ghost marriage" inherits the dead warrior's property, as well as his name.

SMOCK MARRIAGES

In the eighteenth century, widows sometimes remarried clad only in a smock or wearing nothing at all. This custom was based on the notion that, according to common law, a man who married a woman with few or no clothes would not be responsible for her debts or those of her first husband. Without an estate, the thinking went, the widow-bride could not pass on any liability to her new husband. Jurist Francis Wharton called this concept "a vulgar error."

These "smock marriages," which originated in England, were not uncommon in the New England colonies during the early 1700s. The custom varied according to the region. In some places, the marriage took place after the groom and his scantily clad bride had crossed a highway one or more times. In other areas, the bride, often naked, stood in a closet and put out one arm during the wedding ceremony. Sometimes the bridegroom lent wedding clothes to his bride-to-be, keeping her modest while he protected his money.

WASHINGTON'S MOMMIE DEAREST

The father of our country really had his hands full with his mother. Mary Ball Washington was domineering, petulant, and an insufferable nag—as much a royal pain to her son as was the English monarchy.

George Washington was the eldest of Mary's six children but, many historians believe, far from her favorite. While he gave her plenty of money and a fine house, Mother Washington kept up a steady salvo of complaints that George was forsaking her for his career. Sometimes she carped publicly. Once, when George was away on military matters, she initiated a petition in the Virginia legislature for a pension to make up for the stinginess of her son, the general. Humiliated, Washington quickly quashed the request.

After the Revolution, Mother Washington grew even more clutching and cantankerous. George suggested that she move in with one of her children—but he made it very clear she was not welcome at Mount Vernon. She lived to see him inaugurated as president in 1789 but died four months later.

Washington saying last good-bye to his mother:
He probably felt relieved

THE WOMAN IN THE BASEMENT

Patrick Henry, famous for having said, "Give me liberty, or give me death," confined his wife, Sarah, in a basement bedroom during the last years of her life.

As a bride in 1754, Sarah Henry was pretty, sweet-tempered, and quite sane. Her father gave the newlyweds a 300-acre Virginia tobacco farm, six slaves, and a loan. Patrick Henry studied for the bar and by the early 1760s had a successful law practice, where he cultivated the oratorical skill that helped him to become one of the great civil leaders of the American Revolution.

She had married for love, but nearly twenty years and six children later, Sarah developed a keen hatred for her family. Although she was treated tenderly, her condition worsened. When her behavior became uncontrollable, she was placed in a basement bedroom—which did have two windows and an open fireplace—where she was cared for by the family housemaids. This may have been a kind alternative to placing her in the nearby mental hospital—in those days, the insane were considered criminals or sinners. Or perhaps Henry, later a leading proponent of the Bill of Rights, was concerned for the family's reputation.

Sarah's death in 1775 greatly affected Henry. He gave up all reminders of her and seldom spoke her name.

THE RIVALS

Abraham Lincoln and Stephen Douglas were famous political rivals. Although it is little known, they were romantic rivals as well. At one time, they each sought the hand of the same woman in marriage.

Both Lincoln and Douglas noticed a young lady named Mary Todd when she moved to Springfield, Illinois, in 1839. Mary was an accomplished flirt, but she vowed to marry only for love.

Her family hoped she would choose Douglas, a lawyer who, like Mary, had ambition and social standing. Some said he might even be president one day. Called "the Little Giant" because he stood just over five feet tall, Douglas was handsome, with a powerful voice.

But another lawyer had caught Mary's eye. This one, Abe Lincoln, was a gangly six feet four, with ill-fitting clothes and rustic manners. Four years older than Douglas, he'd been a state legislator since 1834. But to Mary's family, he lacked class, money, and looks.

By late 1840, Mary and Lincoln were engaged. Once when Lincoln arrived late at a party, he found Mary flirting animatedly with Douglas. Within a few days, Lincoln broke their engagement. After a painful separation, however, they were married in November 1842.

Sixteen years later, Lincoln and Douglas were again rivals. This time the issue was slavery. Their famous debates continued until the Civil War. Commented Mary during an 1858 debate: "Mr. Douglas is a very little, *little* giant by the side of my tall Kentuckian, and intellectually my husband towers above Douglas just as he does physically." Lincoln lost the Illinois Senate seat to Douglas in 1858 but won in 1860 when the two vied for president.

At Lincoln's inaugural ball, his first lady, dressed in blue, took the arm of Stephen Douglas, and the two danced—as they first did twenty-two years earlier.

SAY IT WITH FLOWERS

Do flowers enrich one's love life—especially one's sex life? There have been a number of important people who did feel that flowers add a certain stimulation to romance.

Cleopatra, who found powerful men irresistible, was one such believer in flower power. After Julius Caesar's assassination, she set out to seduce his successor, Mark Antony. She formally introduced herself to the Roman leader by appearing on a golden barge with flower gardens on deck. Then the Egyptian queen filled a banquet hall several feet deep with rose blossoms and intoxicated Antony with the scent. Eventually the couple had three children.

In 1844, the French playwright Alexandre Dumas developed a passion for Lola Montez, dancer and femme fatale. Strewing the floor of his chambers with rose petals, he led her to the couch, which he called his "theater designed for the act of love." Afterward, Lola would comment only that Dumas was "the most brilliant conversationalist I have ever met."

To Rudolph Valentino, the screen's "Great Lover" of the 1920s, Hollywood extravagance was natural. Actress Pola Negri was at first terrified—but hypnotized—by his amorous attentions. Finally, Valentino paid her a call with an armful of roses. After the two enjoyed dinner, he plucked the petals from the bouquet and scattered them on her bed. Said Pola, ". . . on this floral bower, we rejoiced until dawn broke."

UNMIXED COMPANY

The extreme of prudishness occurred in 1863 when Lady Gough's *Book of Etiquette* advised hostesses to redo their bookshelves by separating books by single male authors from those by single females—presumably to prevent the authors from taking literary license.

Frances Maria Gough, daughter of a British general, married Sir Hugh Gough, who eventually became a celebrated field marshal. Married for fifty-six years, Lady Gough gave birth to five children and one book on etiquette, published in the last year of her life.

We have never been able to find a copy of Lady Gough's rare *Book of Etiquette.* But we learned that a half century ago, someone read it and on page 80 found the following admonition:

"The perfect hostess will see to it that the works of male and female authors be properly separated on her bookshelves. Their proximity, unless they happen to be married, should not be tolerated."

NO CLERGY ALLOWED

Since its opening in 1848, no clergyman of any faith has been allowed past the entry gates of Philadelphia's Girard College.

In his will, financier Stephen Girard left $6 million of his $7 million fortune to set up a free elementary and secondary school for white orphan boys. The will stated, in part, "I enjoin and require that *no ecclesiastic, missionary, or minister of any sect whatsoever, shall ever hold or exercise any station or duty whatever in the said college; nor shall any such person ever be admitted for any purpose, or as a visitor, within the premises . . .*"

In a suit to break Girard's will, lawyer Daniel Webster called this stipulation an "odium to the whole clergy" and accused Girard of being a freethinking atheist. This was untrue. Girard only wanted to protect the boys from the early nineteenth-century religious squabbling, or as he put it, "to keep the tender minds of the orphans free from the excitements which clashing doctrines and sectarian controversy are so apt to produce." A nominal Catholic and a Mason, he was sympathetic to the anticlerical attitude of the Quakers.

At Girard, boys go to religious services run by laymen on weekdays and Sundays. Presidents of the school have included an editor of a religious magazine, a professor in a Methodist seminary who was also a president of the American Bible Society, and a Presbyterian elder.

The original ruling in the will still stands—no clergyman has ever walked the grounds of the school or darkened its doors.

THE WOMAN WHO DIDN'T COME TO DINNER

Tonight, like every evening since the year 1576, there is an extra place setting for dinner at Howth Castle in Howth, Ireland, near Dublin, for a guest who never appears—a lady who died 380 years ago.

The missing guest is Grace O'Malley, swashbuckling daughter of an Irish chieftain, who led a fleet of pirates in plundering merchant ships from her base on Clare Island off County Mayo. Her seamanship, courage, and popularity among her crew were widely renowned. She once joined in fighting off marauders the day after giving birth to a child.

Grace's reputation on the high seas brought her to the attention of another powerful woman of the period, Queen Elizabeth, who invited her to England for a visit. In a celebrated meeting between these two strong women in 1593, Grace refused to kowtow before royalty and spoke with Elizabeth as an equal, as one queen to another.

Seventeen years earlier, after traveling from England to Ireland, Grace sought a few days' lodging at Howth Castle but was coldly turned away. Furious at such an insult, Grace kidnapped the son of the Lord of Howth and held him in hiding, promising to release him only if her ransom demand was met. The Lord, said Grace, could have his son back if he promised perpetual hospitality for Grace O'Malley—a dinner setting at his table always ready should Grace happen to drop by. The Lord conceded the ransom, his son was returned, and he thereafter kept a place for Grace O'Malley at his table for the rest of his life, although she never returned. The Lord's descendants, and all descendants thereafter, continued to maintain the extra dinner setting.

HOLLYWOOD ON THE POTOMAC

Before becoming chief executive in the White House, Ronald Reagan starred and was featured as an actor in fifty-three Hollywood motion pictures, including *King's Row* with Ann Sheridan. And his wife, First Lady Nancy Reagan, was an MGM contract actress who played in such films as *East Side, West Side* with Barbara Stanwyck. Both Ronald and Nancy Reagan appeared in the 1957 film *Hellcats of the Navy*.

Are the Reagans the first cinema actors to inhabit the White House? They are not. There was one ahead of them.

Patricia Ryan—better known as First Lady Pat Nixon, wife of President Richard M. Nixon—appeared before Hollywood cameras at least half a dozen times as an actress. In 1935, when she was a student at the University of Southern California, Pat Ryan was paid $25 for a walk-on role in *Becky Sharp*, the first full-length Technicolor picture, starring Miriam Hopkins. Pat had one speaking line, but both she and the line were cut from the film before it was released. In 1936, Pat Ryan

Glamour girl
Pat Nixon

appeared as an extra in *The Great Ziegfeld,* starring Luise Rainer and William Powell. Her farewell appearance as a movie extra was in *Small Town Girl,* starring Janet Gaynor and Robert Taylor. A year after graduating from movies and USC, Pat Ryan took up acting again in the Whittier Little Theater. She played a small role in a stage play called *The Dark Tower.* Appearing with her, as leading man, was a newcomer named Richard M. Nixon.

WHEN THE VATICAN "WENT HOLLYWOOD"

Movie actor-director Vittorio de Sica eluded the net of the Nazis in World War II with a good excuse—he was directing a film for His Holiness, Pope Pius XII.

Like many Italian artists, De Sica hated the Fascists. He looked upon Mussolini as ridiculous, despised the Nazis, and hid Jews in his own apartment. Luckily, when Nazi propaganda minister Joseph Goebbels asked De Sica to head the Czech Fascist cinema, he was able to say that he had already been hired to make a movie by a higher authority—the Vatican.

The theme for the film, *La Porta del Cielo* (The Gates of Heaven), was suggested by Pope Pius XII. It concerned several people searching for miraculous cures. In charge of production was Father Giovanni Montini, later Pope Paul VI.

De Sica managed to string out the making of the picture under the wing of the Vatican for two years. When Rome fell to the Allies, he finished the Church-financed film in one day and went on to produce his postwar neorealist films, among them the Academy Award-winning *Bicycle Thief* and *Shoeshine.* The Vatican-backed *La Porta del Cielo* was never released. Those who have seen it give it mixed reviews.

STARRING PANCHO VILLA

In probably the most unusual motion picture ever made, Mexican guerrilla leader Pancho Villa conducted much of a real revolution according to a prepared movie script.

In March 1914, Harry Aitken, president of Mutual Film Corporation of New York, decided to make a feature film called *The Life of General Villa*. Aitken met with Pancho Villa—a "serious, dignified man," not an "uncouth bandit"—in Juarez, Mexico, and agreed to pay him $25,000 in gold (Villa had once killed a man who tried to pay him in paper money) if he would stage and act in a real revolution. One stipulation in the contract was that if a battle went poorly, Villa would fight it again to give the studio better footage. The contract was not difficult for Villa to carry

Cinema hero Pancho Villa

out because he, along with Venustiano Carranza and Emiliano Zapata, was already leading an uprising against the Mexican dictator General Victoriano Huerta in Mexico City.

The film, backed by the Wall Street banking firm of Kuhn, Loeb, was to be directed by D. W. Griffith. At the last moment, Griffith decided to direct another picture, *The Birth of a Nation,* for Mutual, and Christy Cabanne was made the new director, although the battle sequences were directed by Raoul Walsh, later to gain Hollywood renown as the director of such films as *What Price Glory?* and *High Sierra.*

Villa held up the battle for Ojinaga until Raoul Walsh could get his five cameramen into place. This allowed Huerta's federal troops time to reinforce, but Villa overran them anyway. One problem during filming was that Villa was executing his prisoners too early, while it was still dark. "I used to get him to put off his executions," Raoul Walsh told movie historian Kevin Brownlow. "He used to have them at four or five in the morning, when there was no light. I got him to put them off until seven or eight. I'd line the cameramen up, and they'd put these fellows against the wall and then they'd shoot them." Walsh also convinced Villa to delay all fighting until 9:00 A.M., when the sun was out, and cease fighting at 4:00 P.M., when darkness set in. Sometimes, during a battle, the director would get Villa to stop the killing until cameras could be moved to a new angle. Walsh tried to take pictures of Villa in actual combat, but it was too difficult. Then Villa agreed to act out his role as leader for the filming. "We'd set up at the head of the street," said Walsh, "and he'd hit that horse with a whip and his spurs and go by at 90 miles an hour. I don't know how many times we said, *'Despacio, despacio—* slow—Señor, please!'"

After a victory at Durango, Villa and Carranza, joined by Zapata, overthrew Huerta and entered Mexico City. Then Carranza turned on the other two and took over the government until he himself was deposed in 1920. After that Pancho Villa went into retirement. As for the movie, when Walsh brought it back to the Mutual studio, it was found that the battle scenes were dull and unbelievable. Most of them were reshot on the studio lot.

All prints of the film have been lost.

FIRST MOVIE NUDE

The first leading actress to appear stark naked in a feature film was Annette Kellerman, in Fox Film Corporation's *A Daughter of the Gods* in
1916. A professional swimmer, Kellerman had already created a sensation when, in 1911, she had daringly worn the first one-piece swimsuit.

A Daughter of the Gods was planned as an elaborate spectacle. Kellerman was called on to jump from a 100-foot-high tower, throw herself
into a pool full of crocodiles, crash against rocks, and tumble down a
waterfall. She romped through many of her scenes in the buff.

The film was shot on location in Jamaica. No expense was spared.
Director Herbert Brenon restored an old Spanish fort, constructed a
Moorish city and a city of gnomes, erected the tower for Kellerman's
spectacular dive, and imported twenty camels for one five-minute scene.
Despite all these trappings, and the star's sensational nudity, the story
was so dull that even the presence of its undraped actress failed to raise
eyebrows.

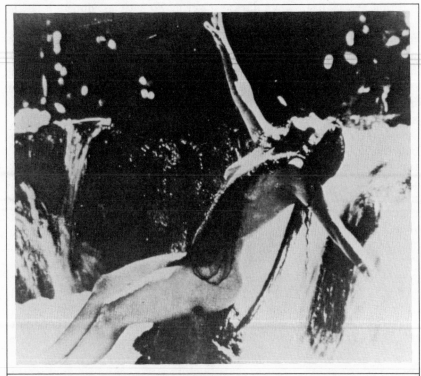

Annette Kellerman in *A Daughter of the Gods*, 1916

The real excitement happened off camera. Unimpressed with director Brenon's efforts, William Fox had the film re-edited and removed Brenon's name from the film credits. Fox also barred the director from the premiere. Brenon showed up anyway, disguised behind a luxurious set of false whiskers. He reportedly enjoyed the show.

THE CENSORED DOCUMENTARY

The U.S. government once confiscated a film it had commissioned. Oscar-winner John Ford was codirector.

During World War II, Ford headed the U.S. Navy documentary film unit. In 1942, he was asked to make a feature-length film on the Pearl Harbor attack. Ford put cinematographer Gregg Toland in charge.

The film, called *December 7th,* showed America's lack of prepared-

December 7th, 1941

ness for such an attack—in uncompromising detail. The military didn't like it. The White House issued a directive allowing censorship of Ford's footage, and the navy confiscated the film.

Later, Ford took the negative of *December 7th* off the shelf and scaled it down to a twenty-minute short without the controversial material. It was shown to defense workers as a propaganda film and won a 1943 Oscar.

THE MOST POPULAR SONG

The most often played and sung song in the world? This may come as a surprise. It is "Happy Birthday to You."

The ditty did not come into being by spontaneous combustion. It actually was composed in 1893 by two Kentucky sisters living in Louisville—Mildred and Patty Hill, the first a music instructor, the second a kindergarten teacher. Patty went on to join the teaching staff of Columbia University.

As a diversion, the Hill sisters wrote little songs for youngsters. One of these they called "Good Morning to You." The published song did not catch on. Later, one of the sisters thought of changing two words of the song, substituting "Happy Birthday" for "Good Morning." Published again in 1935 as "Happy Birthday to You," it became an enduring hit around the world.

Contrary to popular belief, the song is not in the public domain. After Mildred Hill died, Patty set up a foundation to accept royalties for each entertainment usage. TV host Merv Griffin told us that every time he allows the song to be played or sung on his show, he has to pay a fee to the Summy-Birchard Music Company in New Jersey, which in turn pays a share to the sisters' foundation.

THE SILENT AUTHORS OF "SILENT NIGHT"

Only by happy coincidence did the names of the true authors of the song "Silent Night" come to light—thirty-six years after they wrote it.

It all began in 1818 in a church in the little Austrian town of Oberndorf. Shortly before Christmas Eve—so the story goes—a mouse ate a hole in the leather bellows of the church organ, effectively silencing it. Other accounts of damage to the organ placed the blame on the Salzach River, which periodically flooded the church. Because it was continually damp, the organ eventually rusted.

In either case, the itinerant organ-mender was not due in town for months, and music was needed for the Christmas Eve mass. In 3½ hours, Franz Grüber, the organist, composed music for a poem written by Josef Mohr, a priest. It began *"Stille Nacht, Helige Nacht"* ("Silent Night, Holy Night"). On Christmas Eve, the two men sang their composition accompanied by a guitar and children's chorus. They were a great success.

The following May, when the organ-mender turned up, Grüber gave him a copy of the song, which the man then circulated in his travels. By 1831—thirteen years later—the Strasser family quartet was billing "Silent Night," one of their numbers, as a Tyrolean folk song by "Authors Unknown."

Time went by, and soon the now-popular song was being attributed to several famous composers. In 1854, the leader of the king's orchestra in Berlin wrote to the choir director of the Benedictine school in Salzburg, asking for a copy of "Silent Night" by Michael Haydn, brother of the more famous composer Franz Joseph Haydn. The choir director asked a student—who just happened to be Felix Grüber, Franz Grüber's son—to find a copy. And you can guess the rest.

FROM HARVARD FIGHT SONG TO NAZI MARCH

The Nazi marching song with the refrain "Sieg Heil, Sieg Heil" was adapted by Ernst Hanfstaengl from a Harvard football fighting song. A German with an American mother, Hanfstaengl was a 1909 Harvard grad.

Impressed with the climactic "orgasm of words" in a speech by Adolf Hitler in a Bavarian beer hall in 1922, Hanfstaengl befriended the dictator-to-be, then relatively unknown. Tall, with a prominent jaw, Hanfstaengl (nicknamed Putzi, for "little one") played the piano with enthusiasm. While he banged away on an upright, Hitler would whistle along and march up and down, waving his arms like a band conductor.

Putzi once played some Harvard fight songs for his friend, explaining how they were shouted in unison to whip up the passions of the Harvard side. Hitler said, "That is what we need for the movement, marvelous." So Putzi turned one of the songs into the Nazi march that was played by the brownshirts on the day Hitler gained power in Germany. "Rah, rah, rah" was changed to "Sieg Heil." Hanfstaengl also wrote other Nazi marches.

Disillusioned by the Hitler regime, Hanfstaengl later came to Washington, D.C., where he was informally interned and spent most of World War II as an adviser on German affairs.

GOOD NEWS FOR MUSIC LOVERS

In this period of federal frugality, not every government program has had to trim expenses to the bone. For fiscal year 1982, U.S. military bands were allocated $89.7 million—more than four times the $19.3 million set aside for the Arms Control and Disarmament Agency.

Lest you feel the administration's priorities are askew, remember that military bands "contribute to the morale and efficiency of the armed forces," according to a Defense Department spokesman. The ACDA, on the other hand, merely advises the president and the secretary of state on arms control and disarmament activities and participates in negotiations with other countries seeking international agreements to control, reduce, or eliminate conventional and nuclear arms.

You may feel the ACDA deserves at least as big a piece of the federal budget as the military bands, but obviously the budget-makers are marching to a different drummer.

UNNERVING NOTES

One of the lesser-known inventions of Benjamin Franklin is the glass harmonica. Playing it gave him great pleasure, but some others who tried it—and their audiences—suffered serious side effects.

In 1761, Franklin built a mechanized instrument using twenty-four glass bowls of various sizes. While the bowls revolved, the player touched the rims with moistened fingertips, producing a rich range of notes.

The glass harmonica quickly gained wide popularity and drew the attention of serious musicians like Mozart, who composed a piece especially for the instrument. It also gained the attention of Franz Mesmer, who used the instrument as an aid in his new healing technique, "mesmerism," which made use of hypnosis. However, the glass harmonica fell into disrepute during the 1780s, when rumors spread of its harmful effects. Its music was said to make women faint, send dogs into convulsions, cause sleeping girls to wake up screaming, and even bring on the deaths of very young children. Some authorities banned the use of the instrument in their towns.

The merit of these charges was never established, but three glass-harmonica virtuosos suffered nervous disorders from the high tone of the instrument and from the vibrating of the glasses against their fingertips. They were obliged to give up playing the harmonica. Some players tried to overcome the vibration problems by using violin bows instead of their fingertips, but the effect just wasn't the same.

THE HAWAIIAN MUSIKMEISTER

Hawaiian band music—the type we often think of as native to the islands—was really made popular by a German.

In 1872, members of a German military band spent time rehearsing each day while their ship was docked in Honolulu harbor for repairs. Their music enchanted passersby, including Hawaiian King Kamehameha V, who sent an unusual request to Emperor Wilhelm of Prussia: would he designate one of his officers to organize and direct a Royal Hawaiian Band?

Obligingly, Wilhelm dispatched Captain Henry Berger to Honolulu. Dapper and elegantly bewhiskered, Berger was the very model of the modern Prussian bandmaster. Over the next forty-three years, he was credited with writing the music for some seventy-five of the best-loved songs of Hawaii, including "Hawaii Ponoi," and for his arrangements of such favorites as "Aloha Oe," written by Queen Liliuokalani.

To be sure, Berger, who died in 1929, often protested that he was no more than a talented scribe, listening to native tunes and committing them to notation. There may, however, be more to the story than that, much of his music, so richly evocative of the islands' very essence, bears an uncanny resemblance to German folk tunes.

ONE-SUBJECT PAINTER

For twenty years, in the days before cameras, Ralph E.W. Earl painted one subject—Andrew Jackson—over and over again.

Earl's countless portraits—which were passed out to visiting voters and sold to politicians—include Jackson as hero of the battle of New Orleans; Jackson as president talking with guests; Jackson strolling the streets of Washington; Jackson on a horse; Jackson working at his desk; Jackson as an old man in a shawl, and more. It seemed that Earl was always there, wielding his brush in a continuous effort to preserve the president's image for all time. "Old Hickory" paid Earl $50 a painting, and politicians knew it was wise to buy one of these portraits by the man known as "the King's painter." If not an investment in great art, it might be an investment in a political future.

Earl's career as a Jackson intimate began in 1818, when the itinerant painter married Jane Caffrey—who was the niece of Jackson's wife Rachel. A few months after the wedding, the eighteen-year-old bride died, and the Jacksons took Earl into their home. He spent the rest of his life with them. After Rachel's death in 1828, Jackson depended on Earl for companionship.

The portraits, while not always physically accurate, do convey Jackson's strong personality. In fact, Jackson's best likeness is a one-inch daguerreotype, harbinger of a photographic future that put men like Earl out of business.

THE LARGEST PAINTING IN HISTORY

In 1846, New York-born artist John Banvard unveiled the world's largest painting. Twelve feet high and three miles long, it was titled *Panorama of the Mississippi* and depicted 1,200 miles of the Mississippi River valley from the mouth of the Missouri to New Orleans.

Banvard began his project by spending thirteen months rowing up and down the Mississippi, sketching the landscape. Then he built a studio in Louisville, Kentucky, and, using canvas specially woven in Lowell, Massachusetts, devoted the next five years to painting his masterpiece.

The painting had to be stored in huge cylinders. Audiences in Boston, New York, London, Paris, and elsewhere clamored to watch John Banvard spend two hours unspooling his unusually realistic view of America. Riverboats, forts, and Indian settlements were all shown in minute detail, as was a shipwreck that had occurred as he neared completion.

As the years went by, Banvard updated the panorama; in 1862, he added a section showing Civil War scenes.

Unfortunately, Banvard's work of art no longer exists. As it began to deteriorate from overuse, sections were cut out to be used as scenery in the opera house of Watertown, South Dakota, where Banvard and his family had settled. It is presumed that other portions were bought by vaudeville theaters for use as backdrops and curtains. We know that Banvard died in Watertown in 1891 at age seventy-six, but the fate of the bulk of the largest painting in history remains a mystery.

13

SPORTS AND GREAT FEATS

DEAD BUT NOT FOR GOOD

On May 8, 1936, the great jockey, Ralph Neves, was pronounced dead after an accident at Bay Meadows Racetrack in San Mateo, California. Yet he reappeared later in the afternoon and was back in the saddle the following day.

The incident began during the fourth race. Neves and his horse, Flanakins, were in fifth place as the field entered the far turn. Suddenly, one of the lead horses stumbled and fell against another horse, starting a reaction that brought the first four horses and their jockeys to the ground. Neves tried to swerve but Flanakins balked and Neves was sent flying. As he lay on the track, stunned, his horse landed on top of him.

Two jockeys and a spectator managed to extricate Neves, but three doctors on the scene, finding no heartbeat and no pulse, declared him dead. When the track announcer gave the news over the loudspeaker, the 20,000 horrified spectators joined in silent prayer.

Neves was wrapped in a white sheet and taken away in an ambulance which deposited his body in the cold-storage room of a nearby hospital until it could be taken to a mortuary.

Half an hour later, Neves's body stirred and he awoke to find himself in a pitch-black room. He screamed, but no one heard him. Finally he found the door and rushed out to the street. Wearing only his boots and a white sheet, Neves hailed a cab and told the frightened driver to take him to the track.

When he arrived, there were still several thousand fans milling about. He began running and was caught by two jockeys who returned him to the first-aid station. There, the same doctors who had earlier found him without any signs of life discovered that he was suffering from nothing more serious than mild shock and a few bruises.

The next day, Neves rode his mounts and he later won the leading rider title at Bay Meadows that season for having ridden the most winners.

Ralph Neves
(Left) resurrected

WYATT EARP, REFEREE

Wyatt Earp, the legendary Wild West gunslinger, once refereed an important heavyweight prizefight—and gave the victory to the fighter who'd been knocked out.

The bout pitted heavyweight Tom "Sailor" Sharkey against world middleweight champion Bob Fitzsimmons in San Francisco on December 2, 1896. Chosen to referee on the day of the fight, Earp showed up at the arena packing a .45 six-shooter, which he grudgingly surrendered to the police before entering the ring.

Fitzsimmons wasn't happy with the choice of referee, for he had heard that gamblers had bribed Earp to hand the decision—and the $10,000 purse—over to Sharkey. His fears weren't groundless. Historians today say that Earp's reputation as a just and fearless Western lawman is hokum, and that he spent most of his life as an itinerant horse thief, con man, vagrant, and gambler.

Fitzsimmons overpowered Sharkey in the early rounds, and floored him in the eighth. But Earp nullified the knockout on the grounds that Fitzsimmons had struck Sharkey below the belt. Earp awarded the bout to Sharkey on a foul. Fitzsimmons knew he was being had, and so did many of the 15,000 spectators, but the decision stuck, even after Fitzsimmons publicly claimed he was "simply robbed out of $10,000."

Four months after the Earp fiasco, Fitzsimmons won the world's heavyweight championship by knocking out James J. Corbett. Fitzsimmons had his revenge on Sharkey by meeting him again in 1900, without Earp in the ring, and KOing Sharkey in two rounds. In 1903, Fitzsimmons won the world's light-heavyweight crown, his third title.

As for Earp, he left San Francisco for Alaska to open a saloon. He died in Los Angeles in 1929.

FIRST FEMALE BOXING MATCH

In the United States today, there are about fifty women who are licensed professional boxers. Women's boxing, however, is not a new fad. The first public match between two women took place more than 100 years ago.

On March 16, 1876, twenty-four-year-old Nelly Saunders met twenty-five-year-old Rose Harland in the ring in New York City. Eager fans gathered at Hill's Theater to cheer them on as they fought for the prize:

$200 and a silver-plated butter dish. The two women, both variety dancers, had trained vigorously for the match. (Saunders was trained by her husband, a professional boxer.)

Miss Harland wore white tights and blue trunks, while Mrs. Saunders sported a white bodice and purple knee breeches. They began hesitantly. Reported the *New York Times*: "Miss Harland did not know what to do with her hands. Mrs. Saunders had a fair idea of attack and defense but could not carry it into practice." Finally, Saunders hit Harland in the face, and the match grew livelier. Harland did not come into her own until the third round, which was scored 20-all. Saunders won the four-round match by one point, and the first female boxers in history left the ring arm in arm.

TINKER TO EVERS TO CHANCE

If you believe that Tinker to Evers to Chance was baseball's greatest double-play combination and its principals were close friends off the field, charge yourself with two errors.

Shortstop Joe Tinker, second baseman Johnny Evers, and first sacker Frank Chance played together on the Chicago Cubs from 1902 till the eve of World War I. They were a crack infield, no doubt about it, and they rallied the Cubs to National League pennants in 1906, 1907, 1908, and 1910. But they were grossly overrated and far from the best. Between 1906 and 1909, they managed a paltry fifty-four double plays among the three of them—hardly the stuff of superstars.

Tinker . . .   Evers . . .   Chance

In truth, they owed their inflated reputations to these lines written by columnist Franklin P. Adams in the *New York Evening Mail* in 1910:

These are the saddest of possible words—
"Tinker to Evers to Chance."
Trio of bear Cubs and fleeter than birds—
"Tinker to Evers to Chance."
Ruthlessly pricking our gonfalon bubble,
Making a Giant hit into a double,
Words that are heavy with nothing but trouble—
"Tinker to Evers to Chance."

The poem, titled "Baseball's Sad Lexicon," made the trio overnight celebrities. To this day, the very expression "Tinker to Evers to Chance" is synonymous with precision teamwork.

Off the field, Tinker and Evers had a strained relationship at best. When Evers hired a taxi to an exhibition game in 1905 without asking his shortstop to join him, Tinker was, well, put out. Later, the two had words about it and even scuffled briefly during the game. Although they continued to play side by side with undiminished skill, they did not say a word to each other for three years.

"TAKE ME OUT TO THE BALL GAME"

"Take me out to the ball game,
Take me out with the crowd,
Buy me some peanuts and crackerjack,
I don't care if I never get back."

Although lyricist Jack Norworth (1879–1959) wrote the perennially popular "Take Me Out to the Ball Game" in 1908, he didn't see *his* first ball game till thirty-four years later, in 1942.

Norworth was on a New York City subway train when he spotted an advertisement for the old New York Giants baseball team. He pulled a scrap of paper from his pocket and started scribbling. Thirty minutes later he'd written the song.

Norworth himself sang the song in vaudeville with his wife, the celebrated Nora Bayes. They had met and married in 1907 while performing with the Ziegfeld Follies in New York and were billed as "The Happiest Married Couple of the Stage" until their divorce in 1913.

In later years, Norworth joked that he had written "more than 3,000 songs, seven of them good." His big hits included not only "Take Me Out to the Ball Game," but also "Shine on Harvest Moon" and "Meet Me in Apple Blossom Time." As for his own tardiness in being taken out to the ball game, he once said, "So what? Harry Williams wrote 'In the Shade of the Old Apple Tree' and I am sure he never saw a blade of grass. If he ever got three blocks off 26th Street in Manhattan, it was a big occasion."

BASEBALL'S LARGEST CROWD

The biggest crowd ever to attend a baseball game—100,000 spectators—was assembled not in the United States, but in Germany.

On the night of August 12, 1936, two teams of American amateurs played a seven-inning exhibition game in Berlin's Olympic Stadium, site of that year's Olympics. The contest was intended to introduce Europeans to the United States national pastime. But despite pre-game lectures on the sport in three languages, most spectators watched in hopeless confusion, cheering with equal enthusiasm whether the ball was a base hit or an easy out.

Not everyone in the stands was taken with the strange American import. Many complained that there were too many players standing still at any given moment. Better lighting might have helped too; in the glare of the lights, the crowd often had trouble following the ball.

Not until May 7, 1959, did the United States see a baseball crowd nearly as large. On that day, 93,103 fans turned out to watch the New York Yankees beat the Los Angeles Dodgers in Los Angeles at an exhibition game which was played to raise funds for ex-Dodger Roy Campanella who had been disabled in an automobile accident in 1958.

WHEN THE BALLPLAYERS CALLED THEIR OWN
SHOTS

It may seem like a sign of the times when baseball players go on strike, but the fact is that in 1890, the heroes of the American pastime took matters even further than a strike and actually formed their own league—the Players' League. Curiously, the issues were not so different from the issues of the 1981 baseball strike.

More than 100 years ago, the club owners of the National League instituted a "reserve" clause that allowed each owner the right to reserve a given number of players for rehiring the following season without competition from other owners. As "Monte" Ward, leader of the players' union, the Brotherhood of Professional Baseball Players, wrote: "Players have been bought, sold, or exchanged, as though they were sheep, instead of American citizens." When the owners announced a maximum annual salary of $2,500 for all players, the Brotherhood had heard enough. With the financial backing of a small group of capitalists, the Players' League was begun. Before long, the new league had attracted the vast majority of professional players, including most of the stars.

Stunned by the sudden turn of events, the owners, led by Al Spalding, launched a counterattack. Branding the Brotherhood "an oath-bound, secret organization of strikers" and its leaders "hotheaded anarchists," Spalding tried to bribe the most important players, but with little success. When Spalding offered superstar Michael "King" Kelly a blank check at a secret meeting, Kelly took a walk to think it over. When he returned, he refused the check, saying, "My mother and father would never look at me again if I could prove a traitor to the boys."

The 1890 season saw vicious economic competition between the National League and the Players' League. The owners threatened to withdraw advertising from periodicals that supported the players, and some newspapers refused to report the results of Players' League games. Spalding went so far as to purchase the *New York Sporting Times* in order to silence its pro-player editorials.

When the season ended, "King" Kelly's Boston team had won the Players' League pennant by 6½ games. Mark Baldwin was the leading pitcher with 34 wins, and Pete Browning won the batting title with a .391 average.

The Players' League defeated the National League in the battle of the turnstiles and even managed to purchase the National League's Cincinnati club. But both sides had lost a lot of money, and it was the owners who were able to win the war. As soon as the last game had been played, Spalding began driving a wedge between the players and their backers. He refused to negotiate with the Brotherhood, only with their capitalist backers. Within three months, the National League owners had bought out the backers of the Players' League, and the players were forced to return to their original owners. Baseball's experiment in economic democracy had ended.

THREE-SIDED BASEBALL

On June 26, 1944, the New York Yankees, Brooklyn Dodgers, and New York Giants staged one of the most unusual experiments in baseball history. As part of the drive to raise money for World War II bonds, the teams scheduled the first three-way baseball game. Following a formula devised by Paul A. Smith, a math professor at Columbia University, the teams took turns opposing each other on the field, with each team sitting out every third inning.

Before a crowd of 50,000 at the Polo Grounds, the Dodgers dominated the evening. Facing the Yankees in the first inning, they scored a run on three singles by Goody Rosen, Augie Galan, and Dixie Walker. In the second inning, the Dodgers added two more runs, this time against the Giants, on a walk to Mickey Owen, a double by Ed Stanky, and a single by Frenchy Bordagaray.

The Dodgers finished their performance with a two-run eighth inning and then watched from the bench as Giant shortstop Buddy Kerr committed two errors to allow the Yankees their only run of the game. The final box score:

	RUNS	HITS	ERRORS
Dodgers	5	9	1
Yankees	1	4	0
Giants	0	2	2

HIGH SCHOOL WIN STREAKS

The high school with the longest unbeaten streak in football is Bedford County Training School of Shelbyville, Tennessee, which went 82 games without a loss (78 wins, 4 ties) from 1943 to 1950. Tops for baseball is 66 in a row by Capitol Hill High School of Oklahoma City, Oklahoma (1952–54). The longest win streak in any boys' sport is 323 swimming victories by Woodrow Wilson High School of Tacoma, Washington (1953–82). In girls' sports two streaks have gone over 200. From 1959 to 1972, the girls' tennis team of Tucson High in Tucson, Arizona, ran up 213 straight wins. And the girls' basketball team of Baskin High in Baskin, Louisiana, won 218 in a row (1947–53).

WHEN THE VIEWERS CALLED THE PLAYS

Football fans who tune in to their favorite teams on television may find themselves wishing they were calling the plays. For fans in Columbus, Ohio, a similar wish already has come true.

When the visiting Racine Gladiators from Wisconsin squared off against the Columbus Metros in a semipro match in July 1980, about 5,000 subscribers to the two-way, interactive QUBE cable TV system did more than simply second-guess their hometown coach. They gave him orders. By punching a response button on a hand-held control unit, each household could vote on the best play out of a choice of five. Within ten seconds, the responses were tallied by a computer and flashed on a screen at the stadium (out of the players' view). Columbus coach Hal Dyer then relayed the viewers' choice to his quarterback.

Although the Metros were edged out 10–7 by the conventionally led Gladiators, it was not for lack of managerial skill. In fact, it was Columbus who scored first—early in the first quarter—on a succession of pass and running plays selected by the home audience. The play that put them over the goal line was an outside run, backed by a 31 percent plurality. Said Coach Dyer, "I don't think I could have called the plays any better."

The QUBE contest was an early and dramatic example of one of the more exciting aspects of the cable revolution—participatory TV. This particular match gave new meaning to the term "armchair quarterback."

YANKEE JUDO DANDY

Fans of the late Bruce Lee will remember that his most famous film, *Enter the Dragon,* concerns an international free-form martial arts tournament. A similar tournament actually takes place in Taiwan. In 1978 the World Martial Arts Championship was won, for the first time, by a non-Oriental—a twenty-eight-year-old blond native of San Francisco named Peter Ralston. The Asian martial arts world was rocked. Imagine how American baseball fans would feel if a Burmese man batted .450 and hit sixty-five home runs in a season with the New York Yankees.

Ralston's father was a businessman whose work took him and his

Martial arts
champion Peter
Ralston *(Left)*
and victim

family to the Far East. In Singapore, when he was nine, a friend persuaded Peter to take classes in judo. In an interview with "Significa," Ralston said he showed no special aptitude until, at seventeen, he had a sudden insight about t'ai chi ch'uan, subtlest of the martial arts. "I had the realization," said Ralston, "that the essence of the art is supposed to be *easy*, that it's not supposed to be a struggle."

Ralston is not a large man, only five feet ten, and at the time he won the championship title, weighed 156 pounds—ten pounds more than his best fighting weight. He was also suffering from a serious knee injury. Neither handicap undermined his concentration, and in the final match—with his fourth opponent—Ralston was still standing at the end, the winner.

DRIVING BACKWARD ACROSS THE U.S.

In 1930, two St. Louis youths set out to "see America backward." With this motto inscribed on their Ford roadster, interior decorator James B. Hargis and mechanic Charles Creighton successfully drove in reverse from New York City to Los Angeles and back again. They made the trip in forty-two days, with the car's gears locked into reverse and the headlights attached to the rear of the car. The pair drove nearly nonstop, usually traveling at speeds of 8 to 11 mph.

Hargis and Creighton had only one major setback during the trip. As they were leaving New York, a taxicab ran into their roadster, bashing its fender and damaging the running board. Without stopping for repairs, the forward-thinking youths proceeded backward.

James B. Hargis *(Left)* and Charles Creighton
pose with their Ford "reversemobile"

THE LONGEST SWIM

Only one person has ever swum the Mississippi River—lengthwise. He was Fred Newton, a twenty-seven-year-old Oklahoman who covered the 1,826-mile course in nearly six months in 1930—still the longest recorded swim.

Newton entered the Mississippi on July 6 near Minneapolis and figured on completing his marathon while the weather was still warm. But frequent stops were necessary, and he didn't make it to New Orleans until December 29. Covered with a protective layer of axle grease—but still shivering with cold—he emerged after a total of 742 hours in the water. Two boys in a rowboat had accompanied him part of the way.

Why did he take the plunge? No reason in particular, Newton explained. It was just "an idea." The man who holds the record for history's longest swim had no organized backing when he left Minneapolis, nor any promise of rewards. But he was greeted in New Orleans by three motorcycle policemen and several hundred admirers.

THE GREAT SURVIVOR

For 133 days, a lone Chinese seaman named Poon Lim managed to endure aboard a small life raft in the South Atlantic. His tale is one of the greatest survival stories of World War II.

Poon Lim's ordeal began on November 23, 1942, when the S.S. *Ben Lomond,* a British merchant ship, was torpedoed by a German submarine 565 miles off the west coast of Africa. Thrown overboard, Poon Lim watched his ship and all its passengers go down. After swimming for two hours, he grabbed on to an eight-square-foot wooden raft bobbing in the wreckage. In it were a few tins of biscuits, a container of water, a flashlight, and a rope. His scant rations lasted only sixty days, then he was forced to improvise.

Fashioning a crude fishing pole by attaching the hemp in the rope to a hook made from a wire spring in the flashlight, Poon Lim was able to catch small fish. Occasionally, he used bits of fish to lure sea gulls aboard the raft and promptly caught and killed them with his bare hands. For water, he converted his life jacket into a receptacle to catch fresh rain water. To keep himself physically fit, he swam daily in the ocean, always on the lookout for sharks.

On April 5, 1943, the twenty-five-year-old seaman was picked up by

Poon Lim after 133
days on a raft

a fishing boat off Salinopolis, Brazil. His rescuers marveled at the fact
that he had lost only 20 pounds from his five-foot-five frame and could
walk without aid.

For his feat, Poon Lim was awarded the British Empire medal.
When told that he held the world's record for survival on a raft, he commented, "I hope no one will ever have to break that record." It still
stands.

ROW, ROW, ROW YOUR BOAT—ACROSS THE
ATLANTIC OCEAN

Perhaps the most memorable feat in the history of individual seafaring occurred in 1896 when two young oyster fishermen from New Jersey actually rowed their way across the Atlantic Ocean from New York to England.

On June 6, 1896, thirty-one-year-old George Harbo, a Norwegian who worked in the United States, and twenty-seven-year-old Frank Samuelson, an American, got into their clinker-built eighteen-foot open rowboat in New York City harbor and set out to row themselves across the Atlantic. Their small boat, the thirty-five-inch-deep *Richard K. Fox*, was equipped with buoyancy tanks, carried ten extra pairs of oars, sixty gallons of fresh water, and cartons of canned goods.

Harbo and Samuelson each plied oars and rowed steadily for eighteen hours a day, doing most of the rowing during the cool nights. They spent one hour a day eating and five hours a day sleeping. They were favored by calm seas most of the way. Once, when the ocean was rough, their boat was swamped and they capsized. They were able to right the craft, bail it out, and save some supplies. After six weeks at sea, they stopped to board a nearby freighter to buy fresh supplies.

The pair rowed into St. Mary's in the Scilly Islands, just south of England, on August 1, 1896, having covered 3,075 miles in fifty-six days. Not until seventy years later, in 1966, did another pair succeed in rowing across the Atlantic. Two British subjects, John Ridgway and Chay Blyth, in a twenty-foot dory, made it by oar from Massachusetts to Ireland in ninety-one days—thirty-six days longer than the Harbo and Samuelson voyage.

LA SIGNORINA

Eight people have walked across Niagara Falls on a tightrope, and one of them was a woman. Little is known about the background of Signorina Maria Spelterina, who made her debut on July 8, 1876. It was a field day for the press, however, who described Maria as twenty-three years old, "superbly built," and 150 pounds of female pulchritude.

Her tightrope was a 2¼-inch, 1,100-foot-long rope that spanned the deadly gorge at a height of 65 feet. Crossing steadily, she danced back over the falls to waltz music played by a band on the riverbank.

SIGNORINA MARIA SPELTERINA IN HER HIGH ROPE PERFORMANCE.

For her second walk, on July 12, she strapped peach baskets to her feet and made the journey in eleven minutes. She returned in ten—walking backward.

Trip number three, on July 19, was executed blindfolded. For number four, on July 22, she had her ankles and wrists manacled. She was scheduled for another crossing on July 26 but didn't go.

BURRO SCHMIDT'S OBSESSION

William Henry "Burro" Schmidt was frail and tubercular, but he devoted thirty-two years of his life to a single bizarre obsession: digging a tunnel through a half-mile of solid granite in California's El Paso Mountains.

Born in Rhode Island in 1871, Schmidt went west at age twenty-four to improve his health and to prospect for gold. He made a strike in Copper Mountain, near Randsburg, California, but decided it would be pointless to work his claim unless he had first tunneled through to the mountain's far side, where he could pick up a road to the smelter.

He began serious digging in 1906, his sole companions a pair of burros named Jack and Jenny—hence his nickname. Working with crude

"BURRO" SCHMIDT
Human Mole
OF
RIPLEY'S
BELIEVE IT OR NOT

William Henry "Burro" Schmidt

hand tools, and dynamite when he could afford it, Schmidt labored day and night in total isolation. Often he worked in darkness, the air so thin that candles would not burn steadily. Meanwhile, overland road and rail links between the mountain's north and south sides were built, rendering the tunnel unnecessary. But "Burro" refused to quit.

After tunneling 1,872 feet and removing 2,600 cubic yards of rock, Schmidt broke through in 1938. He was sixty-seven. Reporters, geologists, and curiosity seekers came to see, and Robert "Believe It or Not" Ripley dubbed him "The Human Mole." Encouraged by a business partner, Schmidt turned the tunnel into a tourist attraction, which he ran until his death in 1954. You can go through it today—in much less time than it took Schmidt.

14

THE MONEY MARKET

THE TOPLESS QUARTER

The U.S. Mint once issued a 25-cent coin that many people judged to be obscene.

In 1916, the sculptor Hermon A. MacNeil was commissioned by the director of the mint to modernize the quarter. MacNeil's design showed Liberty facing east, a shield in her left hand and an olive branch in her right. Everyone at the mint was pleased with the new look, and the Liberty quarter was duly issued for public use.

But the American public was not so receptive to the new coin. Many citizens felt that MacNeil had taken uncalled-for liberties with Miss Liberty: her right breast was completely exposed, as was an indecently large expanse of her right thigh.

Thousands of letters poured into Washington, D.C., to protest the monetary lewdness. The outcry forced Congress in 1917 to authorize MacNeil to revise his design, though the lawmakers did not at any time directly address the issue of Miss Liberty's undress. Rather, Congress asked for several minor design changes, which included altering the relief of the coins to make it easier to stack them in banks. MacNeil

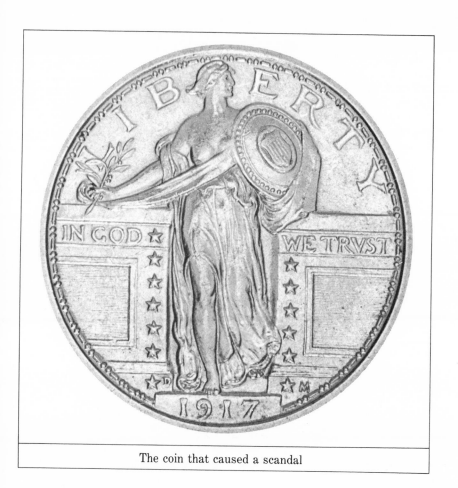

The coin that caused a scandal

obliged, and at the same time he covered Miss Liberty's breast and neck with chain mail and chastely draped her thigh. The no-longer-topless quarter remained in circulation, unprotested, until 1930.

BANNING OF "IN GOD WE TRUST"

The words "In God We Trust" have appeared on many U.S. coins continuously since 1864—except for one interval when President Theodore Roosevelt ordered the motto eliminated.

As Roosevelt saw it, money and God simply didn't mix. He felt that common coins were no place for the Deity's name. "It is a motto which it is indeed well to have inscribed on our great national monuments, in our temples of justice, [and] in our legislative halls," the president said. "But it seems to me eminently unwise to cheapen such a motto by use on coins, just as it would be to cheapen it by use on postage stamps and advertisements."

In 1907, arguing that the law merely permitted, but did not require, the motto on currency, Roosevelt authorized sculptor Augustus Saint-Gaudens to redesign the $10 and $20 gold coins—minus the familiar inscription. When the revised coins appeared, a controversy raged. Clergymen of all denominations preached loudly against the executive erasure. Some went as far as to call the president a blasphemer.

Finally, in 1908, Rep. J. Hampton Moore of Pennsylvania proposed a congressional bill to put God back on the coins. It was passed by the U.S. House of Representatives on March 16 and by the Senate on May 18. Honoring his vow not to balk Congress, Roosevelt signed the bill into law, and the stricken motto was back on the coins by July 1. But it wasn't until 1955 that the words "In God We Trust" were made mandatory on all U.S. currency. It was 1957 before the dies could be changed and paper money bearing the motto rolled off the presses according to the new law.

THE HENRY FORD CENT

In 1917, Henry Ford ordered the minting of a coin bearing his own likeness. It resembled the Lincoln penny but bore the motto "Help the Other Fellow" in place of "In God We Trust" and was engraved with Ford's portrait instead of Lincoln's.

Ford had no intention of fobbing off the funny money as the real thing, despite its deliberate likeness to the Lincoln cent. Rather, he planned to hand it out to friends and customers as a goodwill gesture. Detroit's Weyhing Brothers jewelry firm was hired to strike the die, and a million coins were ordered. However, U.S. entry into World War I scuttled the project after just a handful of coins had been turned out—but not before Ford had proved that a resourceful industrialist not only could earn money, he could make it. A Ford cent is now worth about $5.

THE MONEY-MAKER

Ever think of printing your own currency—and backing it with gold—to beat inflation? Lloyd Darland has done just that. Fed up with the dwindling value of the dollar, Darland, of Bel Air, Maryland, has his own customized currency printed in New York. He makes only $20 certificates, and at present each is worth $875 in conventional U.S. currency, or what Darland calls "green stamps."

"My currency is a better storer of value than a federal reserve note," he says. When he sells a certificate, he uses the cash to buy the gold to back it. Darland's dollars, he is quick to note, are "redeemable in gold coin by bearer on demand"; U.S. currency is not redeemable in anything. That difference has made his money a hot property in some circles.

Darland's money-making sideline raised eyebrows at the U.S. Secret Service at first. But the agency could not find him in violation of any law. Certainly counterfeiting was not an issue, since his outsize, green-and-gold bills look nothing like U.S. currency.

A college economics teacher, Darland says the government's refusal to redeem its currency in gold or silver is nothing short of unconstitutional. And unless it changes its tune, he says, there'll be a revolution.

NO LIVE MODELS FOR OUR MONEY, PLEASE

According to federal law, you must be dead to get your picture on U.S. paper money. This has not always been the case, however.

Between 1862 and 1876, when coins were scarce, the U.S. Treasury issued fractional or "postage" currency—paper money in denominations of less than $1 that resembled postage stamps. The third issue, first printed in 1864, included 5-cent, 25-cent, and 50-cent notes bearing portraits of three U.S. Treasury officials who were still very much alive. Many persons felt strongly that the living had no business appearing on paper money—especially someone as unimportant as Spencer Clark, the superintendent of the National Currency Bureau, whose bearded face adorned the 5-cent note.

In 1866, Congress ruled that "no portrait shall be placed upon any of the bonds, securities, notes, fractional or postal currency of the United States while the original of such portrait is living." The law, which did not include stamps or coins, was initiated by Rep. M. Russell Thayer of Pennsylvania, who said that, although he had nothing against Clark, "I would like any man to tell me why his face should be on the money of the United States."

The law was passed just in time to prevent circulation of a 15-cent note bearing the portraits of two living military heroes—Ulysses S. Grant and William Tecumseh Sherman. Since then, no living American has been portrayed on U.S. paper money.

THE MARTHA WASHINGTON DOLLAR

Equality of the sexes does not apply to the U.S. Treasury. Only once has a female U.S. citizen ever been pictured on the front of a U.S. paper note—and that was almost 100 years ago.

A portrait of Martha Washington appeared on the face of the $1 silver certificates of 1886 and 1891. Martha also appeared on the reverse of the 1896 silver certificate, and the Indian heroine Pocahontas was pictured on the back of the 1875 $20 bill. No other women—except for female representations of such abstract concepts as "Liberty" and "Justice"—have ever graced U.S. currency.

It wasn't until 1979, when the Susan B. Anthony dollar was minted, honoring the founder of the women's suffrage movement in the United States, that an American woman graced a U.S. coin.

LAUNDERING MONEY—LEGALLY

The U.S. Treasury actually washed, dried, and ironed dirty money from 1912 to 1918. The motive was thrift; currency was short, and a study had shown that at least 30 percent of bills turned in by banks as unfit were merely soiled. The machine developed for washing the money could handle as many as 40,000 notes a day and was operated by two people. The dirty currency was placed between two long, moving belts, then bathed in a mixture of yellow soap, water, and a germicide. Finally, it was dried and ironed.

When the United States entered World War I, paper bills had to be made of cotton rather than linen, which was then unavailable. The cotton bills could not withstand laundering, so the machines were mothballed. After the war, the Treasury considered bringing back linen bills and the washing machines, but the U.S. Secret Service opposed the idea. Washing greatly altered the paper's texture, so that washed bills sometimes couldn't be distinguished from counterfeit ones. Since then, America's

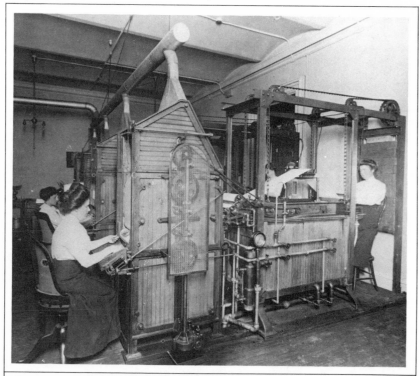

Whitewashing dirty currency

"unfit" bills have been destroyed by burning, and then, beginning in the 1970s, by shredding machines at the twelve Federal Reserve banks and their twenty-five branches. The total amount of paper money destroyed annually from 1978 to 1981 varied from a little less than $17 billion to about $27 billion.

NICKELS AND PENNIES WERE NOT LEGAL TENDER

Nickels and pennies have not always been legal tender. Title 31 of the United States Code, revised in 1965, stated that "minor coins of the United States [meaning nickels and pennies] shall be a legal tender, at their nominal value for any amount not exceeding twenty-five cents in any one payment." This meant that if you tried to pay off a debt in nickels and pennies, your creditor had every right to refuse to accept all but the first 25 cents.

Although Title 31 was implicitly repealed by the passage of the 1965 Coinage Act, it technically stayed on the books until 1982. Though rarely invoked prior to its repeal, it did figure dramatically in a 1921 court case in Durham, North Carolina. A shopkeeper named Munick went to the city water company to pay his $4.50 water bill. His payment included a roll of fifty pennies. In anger, the manager of the company, Harvey Bolton, swept the pennies onto the floor, then proceeded to slap, choke, and verbally abuse Munick.

In the case of *H. Munick* v. *City of Durham*, the North Carolina Supreme Court ruled that Bolton was out of bounds in his treatment of Munick but not in refusing the pennies. Legal tender, said the court, is legal tender. Nowadays, no matter how high his water bill, Mr. Munick would be free to pay it all in pennies.

A ZINC PENNY FOR YOUR THOUGHTS

If you looked upon the copper penny with disdain, waiting for the chance to dump that clutter of coins from your pocket, you may wish you'd saved them. Copper had become so expensive that in 1982 the government switched to a zinc-based penny. The old penny was 95 percent copper and 5 percent zinc; the new one is 97.6 percent zinc and 2.4 percent copper, and is 34 percent lighter.

The zinc penny, according to the Treasury Department, will save about $25 million annually.

Canadian "devil's face note" (see detail): An Irish nationalist was suspected of etching Satan's image amid Queen Elizabeth's curls

HIDDEN MESSAGES IN PAPER MONEY

The finely detailed designs on some currency have provided ideal camouflage for subversive messages.

On the front of several U.S. legal tender notes of 1869, 1875, 1878, and 1880, the engraving of an eagle, when turned upside down, becomes the head of a donkey. Known as "jackass notes," these bills were an embarrassment to the Republican administrations of Ulysses S. Grant and Rutherford B. Hayes. Perhaps there was a mischievous Democrat at work in the engraving department.

In 1954, the Bank of Canada unwittingly issued currency of all denominations with a picture of the devil cleverly etched among the curls of Queen Elizabeth II's hair. It was widely suspected that an Irish nationalist was responsible for defiling her majesty's image on the notes.

And in 1968, Queen Elizabeth II was again featured on an unflattering piece of currency—this time a 50-rupee note issued by the Seychelles,

then a British colony. Clearly visible in the engraving, among some palm leaves behind the Queen's head, was the word "sex." It was a case where money not only talked, it talked dirty.

WAMPUM AS HARVARD TUITION

Harvard University, founded in 1636, once accepted Indian wampum beads as tuition payment. The beads were tiny white or purple seashells that had been worked into ornamental strings or belts.

Because English money was so scarce in the colonies in the early seventeenth century, a Harvard student had the option of paying his fees in a number of commodities that would "supply the necessityes of the Colledge." This usually meant crops or livestock, and many a Harvard man arrived at school with a cow or a flock of chickens at his heels. Still others turned up with nonedibles, such as hardware, textiles, buttons, and footwear.

At times, the students would eat the school into the red, being especially punishing to the stocks of beer and bread. When this began to happen, the college steward would randomly select a student who owed tuition and send him back to the farm with an order for whatever commodities were in short supply.

If a present-day Harvard undergraduate were required to ante up in this manner, he would owe $8,195 worth of groceries for a year's tuition.

23-DIGIT INFLATION

If you find double-digit inflation painful, imagine living with the triple-digit rates plaguing Israel (130 percent inflation) and Brazil (119 percent). In Argentina, the perennial champion of modern world inflation, residents are happy now with an 82 percent inflation rate—half their 1979 level, and a mere fraction of the 347 percent peak of five years ago. But even these levels of inflation pale before the world's all-time record.

No, the famous hyperinflation of the German mark in 1923 is not the world's record. That distinction is held by Hungary, whose inflation in 1946 was a *thousand* times worse. In 1939, just before World War II, one American dollar bought 3.38 Hungarian pengös. In July 1946, the same dollar was worth 500,000,000,000,000,000,000 (500 million trillion) pengös, or the equivalent of a 23-digit inflation rate for that period, as such rates are mathematically figured. Never before—or since—has so much been worth so little.

After the war, rural Hungarians quickly abandoned money in favor of barter, but people in Budapest had to cope with the monetary system. Wages were raised daily, but prices rose by the hour. Shoppers carried their money in large bags, as high-speed presses raced to turn out currency notes in ever larger denominations. Savings evaporated and the moneyed classes were wiped out. The $100,000 worth of pengös one had banked in 1939 weren't worth the trouble it took to withdraw them in 1946. Not when a haircut cost 800 trillion pengös in Budapest, and the average annual income there would buy only $50 worth of merchandise on the black market—the only place where consumer goods could be purchased.

CHRISTMAS MONEY

Today, of course, George Washington's portrait can be found on all our $1 bills, Abraham Lincoln on our $5 bills, and so on. But back before the National Bank Act of 1863 was passed during Mr. Lincoln's administration, individual banks could issue their own currency. And several chose to decorate their bills with none other than Santa Claus.

Perhaps the jolly old gent was a natural choice for the St. Nicholas Bank of New York City, but he was also honored by the Pittsfield Bank in Pittsfield, Massachusetts, the Howard Banking Co. of Boston, the White Mountain Bank in Lancaster, New Hampshire, and the Central Bank of Troy, New York, whose $3 Santa bill of 1850 is depicted below.

All of these various Santa Claus bank notes were printed in New York City, and they now fetch $200 to $300 from collectors. You would be extremely lucky, of course, to find one today—but if you're very, very good . . . who knows?

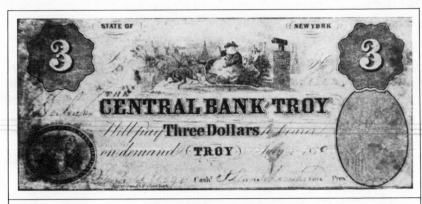

Santa Claus on a $3 bill

WHEN THE U.S. WASN'T IN DEBT

While the very notion of a trillion is unreal and incomprehensible to most Americans, it's a concept we'll have to get used to. In October 1981, the U.S. national debt topped $1 trillion. And while the United States has been in the red almost continuously since the Revolutionary War, there was one brief interlude over a century ago when the U.S. government was debt-free.

As the term implies, the national debt is the total amount of money owed by the government to its creditors, who include the Federal Reserve System, foreign investors, commercial banks, state and local governments, and individuals holding U.S. savings bonds. During the 1981 fiscal year, the interest alone on the national debt was a staggering $96.5 billion, or 14 percent of all federal spending.

While many cite extravagance and needless borrowing as the chief causes of U.S. indebtedness, these are only part of the picture. Historically the real villains have been inflation, soaring interest rates, and such heavy expenses as wars and sweeping social reforms. In 1940, for example, the national debt stood at a manageable $43 billion, but by the end of World War II, it had ballooned to $258.7 billion. Still, the debt has never grown with anything approaching the breakneck speed of the last decade. In 1970, it was about $370 billion—just 37 percent of today's figure.

That brief interlude when the United States was not in debt was 1835–36, during President Andrew Jackson's second term. After the close of the War of 1812, the country had experienced tremendous growth, and the federal coffers were overflowing with money from import tariffs and the sale of public lands. In December 1834, Jackson gleefully reported to Congress that federal assets would top debits by New Year's Day. By early 1836, the nation had a surplus of $37 million, and all but $5 million of it was divided among the states. Then came the panic of 1837, and the government was again plunged into debt, never to climb out again.

YOUR BIGGEST EXPENSE

If you are an average wage-earner in the United States, you work 2 hours and 44 minutes of every 8-hour day for the government. Of that time, your wages for 1 hour and 51 minutes go for federal taxes, and those for 53 minutes go for state and local taxes. Economists at the Tax Foundation, Inc., a nonprofit organization based in Washington, D.C., have assembled these figures based on estimates as of April 1982.

The government takes the biggest bite by far from your paycheck—in fact, nearly twice as much as housing and household operation, the runner-up (1 hour and 30 minutes). You work 1 hour and 5 minutes out of every 8 hours to pay for food and drink, 42 minutes for transportation, 30 minutes for medical care, and 22 minutes for clothing. Savings are merely part of the 47 minutes allotted to "miscellaneous."

UNUSUAL TAXES

Ever since Roman times, lawmakers have taxed their ingenuity to devise strange and unusual tax laws. Anything to dig up a dollar.

In the first century A.D., the Roman emperor Vespasian levied a tax on urine—a lucrative source of revenue, since it was a highly valued cleaning or leather-tanning agent. At one time or another, Romans also were taxed on their children and slaves, on the doors of their houses, on acts of prostitution, and, under Emperor Caligula, on "the pleasures of matrimony."

In England, conversely, bachelors paid a tax, levied in 1695. England and Ireland also enforced a "window tax" in the seventeenth and eighteenth centuries, with homeowners assessed according to the number of windows in their houses. Unshaven Russians paid a tax for their beards, enacted in 1702.

The United States, too, has had its share of unusual taxes, such as the 1886 federal levy on oleomargarine, enacted to protect the butterfat industry. On the federal level, that tax was not lifted until 1950. Indiana imposes a sales tax on ice used to cool alcoholic drinks, but not if it's used to cool bottled soda or watermelons. In New York, you do not pay tax on salted or buttered popcorn, but you do on the caramel-coated variety. Also in that state, canned tuna for humans is not taxable, while cat-food tuna is.

Try too hard to figure out the logic, and you may overtax your brain.

HOW THE WITHHOLDING TAX BEGAN

Although few things seem as permanent as the federal withholding tax, it was instituted in 1943 only as a *temporary* wartime measure. Yet somehow, once the war was ended, the withholding tax remained.

Its precedent was a "collection-at-source" income tax that had been in effect from 1913 to 1916. When President Franklin Roosevelt called for increased revenues to finance the war effort, Congress revived the tax at the suggestion of the Treasury Department and Beardsley Ruml, chairman of the Federal Reserve Bank of New York. The rationale was simple: by having employers deduct income taxes from their workers' paychecks, the government could generate funds quickly and improve its cash flow.

As a result, self-employed people only pay taxes quarterly, while wage-earners, who regularly pay withholding tax, are deprived of the opportunity to invest that portion of their earnings.

WORTH HIS WEIGHT IN GOLD

Most people try to lose weight. The late Aga Khan III, spiritual leader of 20 million Ismaili Moslems, viewed his expanding waistline with approval. Five times during his reign, his subjects honored him with his weight in jewels and precious metals.

The first time was in 1936, to commemorate his fiftieth anniversary as official leader of the Ismaili sect. In front of 30,000 believers in Bombay, the Aga sat in the pan of a large scale while attendants loaded the counter-pan with 220 pounds of gold bullion, enough to balance his bulk. The gold, donated by his followers, was worth $125,000. The ceremony was repeated in Nairobi.

Ten years later, the faithful in Bombay celebrated the Aga's dia-

Aga Khan III watches as attendant loads 234½ pounds of diamonds on a scale in Bombay, 1946

mond jubilee. They unloaded diamonds to match his weight, now up to 243½ pounds. The gems were sold for nearly $4.5 million. Again, the ceremony was repeated in Nairobi.

The last weigh-in was in Karachi in 1954. This time, the scale was rigged as a gesture of economy: a mere 15 ounces of platinum, valued at $230,000, balanced the holy man's 215 pounds.

On each occasion, the proceeds were donated to charities, supplemented by about $1 million from the Aga's own considerable fortune. When his grandson succeeded him in 1957 as Aga Khan IV, he rejected the practice as not befitting a modern monarch.

THE COMMUNIST CAPITALIST

If Karl Marx is Communism's best-known prophet, surely Friedrich Engels runs a close second. Engels collaborated with Marx on the writing of *The Communist Manifesto* in 1848, ghostwrote many newspaper articles for him, and on his own penned such anticapitalist diatribes as *The Conditions of the Working Class in England in 1844.*

But the cofounder of modern Communism was no oppressed proletarian. He was an outright capitalist. For many years, he was a high-paid executive in just the sort of factory he so savagely depicted in his writings.

Engels was born in Prussia in 1820, son of a well-to-do textile magnate. It was while traveling through Cologne in 1843 that Engels met a young radical named Karl Marx, although their most fruitful collaboration would take place in London. In the 1850s, Engels moved to Manchester, England, to work in his father's textile firm there. He lived a markedly comfortable life, with memberships in the stock exchange and exclusive clubs, and entertained lavishly—all the while supporting Marx with frequent checks and maintaining their collaboration.

Engels sold his partnership in the business in 1869 for enough cash to retire in style and spent the rest of his life urging the downfall of the very class to which he belonged.

THE WEALTHY COMMUNIST

Until his death in November 1982, Leonid Brezhnev was the leader of the most powerful Communist country in the world, but his life-style was so extravagant that Marx and Engels, the founders of Communism, would surely have condemned him as an enemy of the people.

Although Brezhnev continued to mouth the myth that the USSR is a classless society, he personally owned two yachts and maintained a fleet of fancy foreign cars, including a Rolls-Royce Silver Cloud, a Citroen-Maserati, a steel-blue Mercedes, and two gifts from Richard Nixon, a Cadillac and a Lincoln Continental.

While most citizens of the Soviet Union waited in line for rationed products, Brezhnev and other Communist Party leaders shopped at special stores, paying their bills with funds from "open accounts" at the State Bank. Brezhnev's Moscow apartment and his country house were tended by servants and furnished with the latest Western gadgets as well as his famous collection of antique clocks.

His favorite gadget helped him to fight his tobacco habit. It was a locked cigarette case with a timer that forced Brezhnev to wait for his next smoke. However, unlike the rest of the people in the USSR, who have no choice but to wait for goods, Leonid Brezhnev set his own timer.

Now let's watch the life-style of his successor, Yuri Andropov, and see if he, too, will live like a capitalist in a Communist society.

THE BLUE JEANIUSES

Blue jeans were invented by two impoverished men—one a peddler, the other a tailor.

Levi Strauss, a Bavarian Jew, emigrated to America in 1848. At first, he made a meager living in New York City as a door-to-door dry goods peddler. Later, in San Francisco, Strauss cut and stitched a piece of heavy tent canvas and created the first pair of Levi jeans. The sturdy pants caught on, and he soon had a thriving business.

The brown cloth that Strauss dyed blue was imported from Nîmes, France. It was called "serge de Nîmes"—and thus was born the word "denims." A similar cloth was brought from Genoa, Italy. "Gênes," the French name for Genoa, was Americanized to "jeans."

In 1872, Strauss received a letter from a struggling tailor named Jacob W. Davis. After years of hardship in Nevada, Davis had suddenly

Loggers wearing
early $3 denims

Levi Strauss

become successful selling his own brand of $3 denim and duck-cloth pants. He wrote to Strauss: "The secratt of them Pents is the Rivits that I put in those Pockets."

The two men joined forces, and their riveted denims swept the country. There have been few changes in the pants' design since 1873, though one notable alteration was made in 1933. Walter Haas, Sr., president of Levi Strauss, went camping wearing the original model 501 jeans, which had a copper rivet at the crotch. Relaxing by the campfire, Haas suffered "hot rivet syndrome" in a most sensitive area of his anatomy. The dangerous rivet was banished at the next Levi Strauss board of directors meeting.

W. C. FIELDS'S HIDDEN FORTUNE

As a young vaudeville performer, W. C. Fields barely eked out a living. Many years of poverty and near starvation left him with a recurring dream: he was alone in a strange city with not a penny to his name and being chased by the police. He awoke from these dreams in a cold sweat. This upsetting vision preyed on Fields's mind, and he began a series of eccentric encounters with banks all over the world.

Terrified of being broke, he would open a bank account under a fictitious name wherever he happened to be. These accounts varied from small sums—the loose change in his pockets—to as much as $50,000. Fields favored whimsical pseudonyms for his bank books, such as Figley E. Whitesides, Sneed Hearn, Ludovic Fishpond, Aristotle Hoop, Dr. Otis Guelpe, and Cholmonley Frampton-Blythe. In time, he began waking up from his nightmares saying to himself, "Forget it—you've probably got a bank account in that town."

Because Fields neglected to fully keep track of his accounts, only twenty-three of them were listed by him before his death in 1946. He had told a friend that he recalled opening at least 700. His mistress of many years, Carlotta Monti, told us that there is still about $1,300,000 outstanding—and lost forever—until Figley E. Whitesides and his friends come along.

TAKE A LETTER, MR. TWAIN

Today, 99.2 percent of all secretarial jobs in the United States are held by women. However, a century ago, offices were off limits to women, and stenographers and secretaries were always men.

The picture started changing in the 1870s when there were more office jobs than men to fill them. Some 15 percent of all clerical workers in the United States were women by 1890, 24.2 percent by 1900. During World War I, the figure rose higher as thousands of male office workers swapped their steno pads for machine guns, and women took over their jobs.

But women were not exactly welcomed into the office with open arms. Many men felt they were losing their jobs to women who would be expected to put up with much lower salaries and abominable working conditions. A 1909 survey of fifty-five London offices found that only half provided separate rest rooms for female employees.

The male secretary's plight wasn't all that much better, but that didn't stop Mark Twain, Lyndon Johnson, Carl Sandburg, and other notables-to-be from taking secretarial jobs when they were younger. Long before he became secretary of state, Dean Acheson was secretary to Supreme Court Justice Louis Brandeis. . . . As secretary to novelist Sinclair Lewis, John Hersey took dictation, typed manuscripts, chauffeured his boss around, and bought him chocolates. . . . Filmmaker Irving Thalberg worked as a secretary for a few years for Universal Pictures mogul Carl Laemmle before becoming an executive at the MGM studios in 1924. . . . In 1912, future journalist Walter Lippmann was hired as secretary to the socialist mayor of Schenectady, New York, quitting after four months in disgust over the political machinations he witnessed.

In 1930, novelist John O'Hara worked as columnist Heywood Broun's secretary. It was a better deal than most—$35 a week plus free lunch at Broun's penthouse apartment.

FROM RICHES TO RAGS

Two founding fathers of American business, whose enterprises remain household words to this day, ended their careers as low-level employees of their own firms.

Gustave Brachhausen was an inventor and engineer from Germany who started a factory in New Jersey in the 1890s, first producing music boxes. Later the company switched to the manufacture of a vacuum cleaner called the Regina Electrikbroom.

In 1915 Brachhausen sold his business for $1 million but soon lost all his money. In 1919 he returned to the factory he had founded—as a tool and diemaker, later becoming a night watchman.

Alvah Curtis Roebuck was a watch repairman from Indiana who went into the business of selling watches through the mail in the 1880s with former freight agent Richard Sears. His partner's aggressive marketing and advertising techniques made Roebuck so nervous that he decided, in 1895, to sell his one-third interest for $25,000.

After Roebuck went broke in the 1929 crash, his old firm, now a thriving mail-order and chain-store operation, put him on the publicity department payroll to make goodwill tours. Wherever Roebuck appeared, according to a business historian, "customers came in from as far as a hundred miles away to shake the hand of the man whose name had been a byword in their families."

THE MINER WHO LOST A $20 MILLION BET

A prospector once lost $20 million on a bet that he could outrace a horse.

On July 4, 1880, George Warren, in a drunken stupor, challenged George Atkins to a race in Charleston, Arizona. A crowd gathered to watch the outlandish contest: the two were to race 100 yards to a pole and back—Warren on foot, Atkins on horseback. Should he win, Warren would take Atkins's horse. Should Atkins win, his prize would be Warren's one-ninth share in the Copper Queen mine in Bisbee, Arizona.

Warren knew he couldn't outrun a horse on a straightaway, but counted on his ability to make a tighter turn around the pole. He figured wrong. He lost the race and his share in the mine. The Copper Queen eventually paid out approximately $180 million. Warren's share would have come to $20 million.

It wasn't all he lost. A year later, the courts judged Warren insane and allowed him to be stripped of three other mining claims. He wandered off to Mexico, went heavily into debt, and returned to Bisbee, where he lived out his life in near poverty, a stone's throw from the Copper Queen.

Warren's fame did not die with him, however. The miner depicted on the Arizona state seal is based on a photograph of Warren.

George Warren

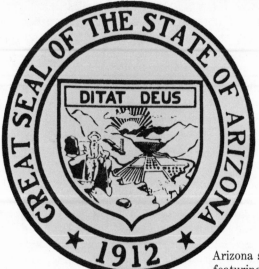

Arizona state seal
featuring the unfortunate Warren

WORLD'S BIGGEST DOWRY

A Bolivian tin magnate once gave his daughter a $22.4 million wedding dowry—the largest ever recorded.

Known as "the Bolivian Tin King," Simón Iturri Patiño at one time controlled over 50 percent of Bolivia's tin industry and had a personal fortune estimated at $1 billion, eclipsing by far the country's national budget. In 1929, on the eve of his daughter Elena's marriage to the Marqués del Mérito, a Spanish grandee, Patiño presented her with a check—in francs—which was equivalent to $22.4 million. According to unverified reports, wedding guests could view the check displayed in a glass showcase in the main salon of Patiño's Paris mansion, where the reception was held; red and green spotlights added a dramatic touch. The father of the bride also gave the newlyweds five Rolls-Royces.

Although Patiño made his fortune in Bolivia, he left the country in 1924, never to return, because the high altitudes there, he claimed, were bad for his health. For many years he lived in aloof splendor in Paris and New York City where he was known as "The Tin Hermit." At the time of his death at age eighty-one in 1947, he was reputed to be one of the world's five wealthiest men.

IT PAYS TO BE NICE TO KINGS

In the 1930s, a New York City retiree was receiving a pension of $200 a year from Great Britain as a reward for his ancestors' kindness to a future English king almost three centuries before.

The future king was Charles II. When his father, Charles I, was beheaded by Oliver Cromwell in 1649, the young heir fled to Scotland, where he mapped out plans to restore the monarchy. In 1651, he invaded England but was routed at Worcester and forced to flee for his life. His first hideout was the home of some farmers—George, John, William, Richard, and Humphrey Penderel—who helped the fugitive disguise himself and escape into the night. Many other loyal Royalists secretly fed and sheltered Charles over the next six weeks and helped spirit him out of England to safety in France. Charles II finally gained the British throne in May 1660.

Charles never forgot his benefactors. After his coronation, he gave them all generous pensions, titles, military commissions, cash, jewels, and costly trinkets. But a special reward was reserved for the five Penderel brothers—a pension to be paid in perpetuity from a special trust fund. Over the next three centuries, scores of their descendants on both sides of the Atlantic benefited. Among them was a retired laundryman, George Washington Pendrell (who had Americanized his name), living in Manhattan.

THE WORLD'S CHAMPION COMPLAINER

Anyone who has ever been upset over goods or poor services can take a lesson from a champion consumer who has received more than $100,000 as a result of his systemized method of complaining to stores and businesses.

For nineteen years, Ralph Charell, a media executive based in New York, has refused to buckle under to faceless bureaucrats and irrational computers. His long list of adversaries includes conglomerates, major public corporations, bankers, brokers, doctors, lawyers, department stores, public utilities, landlords, hotels, and restaurants. The compensation/refunds have ranged from $6.95 (for a mail-order book that was never delivered) to $25,000 (from a 1969 eviction-relocation dispute with an apartment landlord).

Many dissatisfied consumers, says Charell, do not stand up for their rights because they mistakenly believe complaining takes more time than it is worth. He spends an average of ten minutes a day composing letters, making phone calls, and other assorted duties. The author of *How to Get the Upper Hand* and *How I Turn Ordinary Complaints Into Thousands of Dollars*, Charell asserts that all it takes is perseverance and confidence.

And the rewards can be psychological as well as financial. Says Charell: "To be able to deal effectively with indifferent or incompetent professionals, arrogant clerks, sneering sommeliers—to reach the unreachable Mr. Big—is a valuable skill that can be learned and developed."

BANK WITHOUT GUARDS AND LOCKS

During a recent trip to the island of Yap in western Micronesia, we had the privilege of visiting the only bank in the world which is unguarded and unlocked. In fact, all of the bank's money is openly displayed and may be handled and studied after obtaining permission from the village chief.

The Stone Money Bank of Balabat contains thirty large, dough-nut-shaped stones which are the traditional form of currency for Yap. Although the U.S. dollar is now in common use, stone money is still used for large purchases. Because of the size of the stones, there is no chance

One of the authors of *Significa* with a piece of Yap currency

of them being stolen, and when ownership changes, the money stays in the bank.

The value of the stone money of Yap is based not on size, but on the difficulty that was encountered in bringing each stone to Yap. (Most of the stones came from the Palau Islands, 275 miles away.)

In 1872, an American adventurer named David O'Keefe organized the islanders and began a business importing stone money from Palau to Yap. At first, the money was greeted with great enthusiasm, but because of the ease with which large quantities were obtained, O'Keefe's stone money, like most of the currencies of the world, has suffered severe inflation and is now almost worthless.

THE $24 MANHATTAN HOAX

Textbooks teach that Peter Minuit bought Manhattan from the Indians in 1626 for only $24, the greatest real estate bargain ever. But it was those Indians who came out ahead, because the island wasn't theirs to sell. Minuit paid the wrong tribe.

Minuit, director-general of the Dutch colony of New Netherland, purchased Manhattan from the Canarsee Indians, who were native to Brooklyn. After pocketing the proceeds—60 gilders' worth of beads, needles, fabric, buttons, and fishhooks—the Canarsees departed. It was only later that Minuit learned he'd been swindled. Most of Manhattan belonged to the Weckquaesgeeks, who were angered at being left out of the deal and warred sporadically with the Dutch for years. In the interests of peace, the Dutch finally paid them for Manhattan too.

But for business acumen, the Canarsees had nothing on the Raritan Indians. They sold nearby Staten Island six times.

NEW YORK CITY TO WASHINGTON: "THE TIME HAS COME TO PAY UP!"

The U.S. government owes New York City more than $11 billion.

After British forces had captured Washington, D.C., in the War of 1812, other major cities, such as Philadelphia and New York, built fortifi-

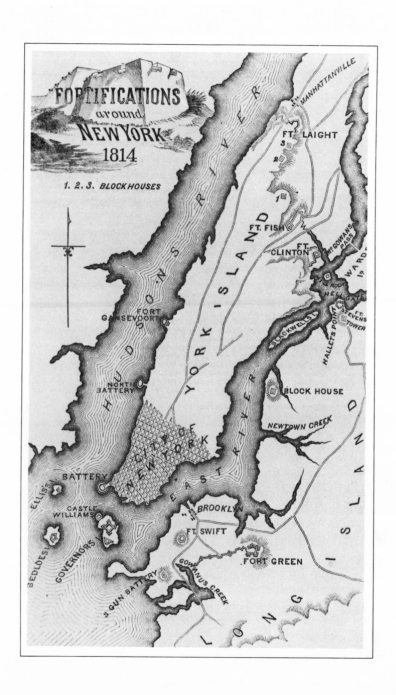

FORTIFICATIONS around NEW YORK 1814

1. 2. 3. BLOCK HOUSES

cations as a precaution. In 1814, Brig. Gen. Joseph Gardner Swift, as chief U.S. Army engineer, oversaw the construction of the fortifications in New York City's Harlem Heights section and in Brooklyn Heights, then part of the settlement of Brooklyn (now New York City). The labor was performed by several thousand civilian volunteers. Meanwhile, federal militia strength in the metropolitan area swelled to 17,000.

Since the federal government was bankrupt, the city of New York spent its own funds on the projects—a total outlay of $933,007.90. But the British invasion never materialized. On December 24, 1814, England and the United States signed the Treaty of Ghent, ending the war. In February 1815, Alexander Dallas, the secretary of the treasury, notified New York officials that President James Madison had authorized him to repay the debt in "stock and Treasury notes," rather than in currency. The city fathers didn't care for the idea—they wanted cash.

They shouldn't have quibbled. On March 11, 1818, Secretary of War William H. Crawford rejected New York City's entire claim for reimbursement on the grounds that there was no valid documentation of the loan. The War Department, he said, had no record of authorizing New York to construct the fortifications.

And that's where the matter stands today. Totaling up the original principal of nearly $1 million, plus 5 percent interest compounded annually, the United States today owes New York City more than $11 billion.

STRIKE ONE

The sturdy strikers of Poland's Solidarity union may be interested to know that the first labor strike in American history—in 1619, more than a year before the Pilgrims landed at Plymouth—was called by a group of Poles.

In 1608, the British-owned London Company set up a glassworks at the Jamestown settlement in what is now Virginia. Its initial work force consisted of eight skilled Polish glassblowers. They gained a reputation for diligence and craftsmanship, and more Poles were recruited for other work as well.

As far as their neighbors were concerned, the Poles were citizens of Jamestown. But when the election of the Virginia House of Burgesses—the first American legislative body—was set, it was announced that only those of "English stock" would get to vote. Unfair, the Poles told the governor, George Yeardley. But he stood pat, and the Poles walked off their jobs.

The strike hobbled local industry and finally forced the governor's hand. On July 21, 1619, the Poles' demands were met in full, ending the walkout.

DOWN WITH THE 24-HOUR DAY

There may be twenty-four hours in a day as far as your kitchen clock is concerned, but as far as your body clock is concerned, there are twenty-five.

In experiments conducted at both the Max Planck Institute in West Germany and the Laboratory for Human Chronophysiology in New York City, test subjects were isolated from the outside world and deprived of any indication of the time of day, such as clocks and windows.

Sleeping and waking according to their own biological rhythms, the subjects invariably fell into a twenty-five-hour cycle. Indeed, to keep step with the twenty-four-hour solar day, scientists say, we retire an hour earlier each night to rise an hour earlier each morning than is necessitated by our biological clock.

But the discrepancy between solar and biological days is not bad, for it conditions us to be flexible and allows us to adapt readily to seasonal changes. So let's let it stay—that good old twenty-four-hour day.

UNEMPLOYMENT KILLS

A rise in unemployment brings about a rise in mental illness, crime, alcoholism, infant death, and serious disease. This was proved statistically by M. Harvey Brenner, a professor at Johns Hopkins University, who studied U.S. economic history for sixteen years.

Effects are cumulative. For example, in the first three years after a peak, imprisonment and suicide go up; in the next three years, there is a rise in deaths from chronic diseases.

Brenner prepared an estimate for Congress on the effects of a 1 percent rise in unemployment: a 4 percent rise in state prison incarcerations,

5.7 percent in murders, 4.3 percent in male and 2.3 percent in female admissions to mental hospitals, 4.1 percent in suicides. Within six years, the death rate from serious diseases would go up 1.9 percent.

Oddly, the Great Depression, our worst economic disaster, did not cause as great a rise in mental hospital admissions as would be expected. Brenner attributes this to a "same boat" attitude—with so many out of work, the jobless were less likely to see themselves as failures.

A turnaround in the economy also causes chains of social distress. Companies overwork employees to meet consumer demand, and many people returning to work find that their skills have become obsolete.

MILITARY SPENDING

A 1982 study of major capitalist countries showed that the two nations which, in the last twenty years, spent the greatest percentage of their gross national product on military expenses—the United States and the United Kingdom—also had the slowest rate of productivity growth. On the other hand, the two nations that had the highest rate of growth—Japan and Denmark—spent the lowest percentage on the military.

The study, *World Military and Social Expenditures* by Ruth Leger Sivard, also reported that nearly two-thirds of the nations of the world—including the United States and the Soviet Union—spend more money on the military than on health.

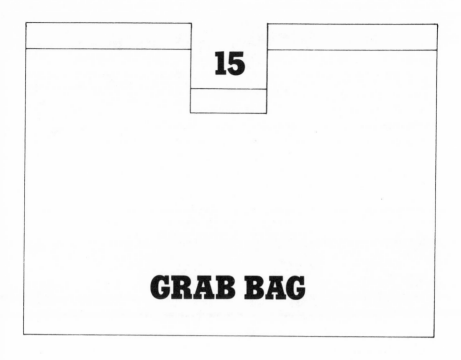

15

GRAB BAG

THE KILLER YO-YO

Yo-yos were first used as deadly weapons, not as toys.

Originating in prehistoric times in China, the yo-yo later made its way to the Philippines, where it was adapted to lethal ends by jungle hunters. A typical Philippine yo-yo (the word means "to return") was fashioned from a pair of four-pound stones and a twenty-foot vine or a piece of animal sinew. Hiding in a tree, the user would lower the boom on his prey (either animal or human). If the first blow was not fatal, it was easy to quickly reel in the weapon and try again.

In later centuries, the yo-yo came to be used more as an amusement. Today, yo-yoing is bigger than ever in the Philippines. Rural youths labor long and hard making beautiful models from wood or animal horns.

The world's biggest yo-yo was created by an American, Dr. Tom

Among centuries of yo-yo users has been Richard Nixon,
who showed his skill to Roy Acuff *(Right)* and Grand Ol' Opry
audience when he was president

Kuhn. Weighing 256 pounds and measuring 50 inches by 31½ inches,
it was demonstrated in 1979 on an 11,800-pound test line suspended from
an 80-foot crane.

BANNING CHRISTMAS

Can you imagine armed soldiers arresting you in church for the crime
of observing Christmas Day? It happened in England when Oliver Cromwell's parliament banned Christmas in 1644. Those dour Puritans, calling it "the Profane Man's Ranting Day," disapproved of the Catholic im-
plications of Christ's Mass and the worldly pleasures associated with the
holiday.

Not all Englishmen agreed. Riots occurred so often on December

25 that many must have assumed they were part of the religious obser-
vance.

Even some American colonies were affected. In 1659, Massachusetts
passed a law fining anyone caught celebrating Christmas. Throughout
New England, Christmas was suppressed, but—as in England—
defiance was strong. Nevertheless, even though Massachusetts repealed
its law in 1681 (twenty-one years after its repeal in England), Boston's
public schools remained open on December 25 until 1870.

One other time in America the anti-Christmas spirit took hold. In
1918, just before the armistice, World War I caused the Council of National Defense to consider prohibiting gift-giving as an economy measure. However, A. C. Gilbert, inventor of the Erector Set, protested. Allowed fifteen minutes to address the council, Gilbert spoke of the
educational merits of toys. He then produced a bag of toys for inspec-
tion. The dignified men promptly forgot the time limit as they got down
on their hands and knees for a closer look.

THE PANATOMIC CANAL

From the late 1950s to the 1970s, the United States made plans to blast
a canal across the Isthmus of Panama using hundreds of nuclear devices. The project was one of several in the Plowshare Program of the
Atomic Energy Commission.

The plan for one route (five were considered) was to detonate 300
deeply buried nuclear charges with a total yield of 170 mega-
tons—nearly 9,000 times that of the Hiroshima bomb. Construction cost
was estimated at $650 million and would have meant resettling at least
30,000 people. The Atomic Energy Commission exploded nearly thirty
underground bombs to test the practicality of the plan. One gouged a
hole 1,200 feet wide in the Nevada desert.

Project Chariot, another Plowshare operation, proposed excavating
a harbor 1,800 feet in diameter 250 miles north of Nome, Alaska. This
costly experiment would have had little commercial value, being iced
over eight months a year. It was canceled after protests by Eskimos and
Alaskan officials, who were concerned that the blasts would kill caribou,
damage the permafrost, and pollute the oceans.

Other experiments—many with cute names like Gasbuggy and
Gnome—*were* carried out. Their purpose: to study the feasibility of re-
leasing oil and gas reserves from hard-to-reach rock formations using

"contained" underground nuclear explosions. Atomic Energy Commission experts said the projects gave scientists "a strong data base for the resolution of radioactivity questions." They downplayed possible effects of long-lasting radiation, not to mention other problems like groundwater contamination or earthquakes.

Despite such potential hazards, the United States seriously pursued the Plowshare projects for fifteen years. And it spent hundreds of millions doing it.

TEXAS-SIZED BLAST

Texas City, Texas, was once virtually destroyed by explosions more powerful at ground level than the atomic blasts at Hiroshima and Nagasaki.

At 9:12 A.M. on April 16, 1947, the French freighter *Grandcamp*, laden with 2,500 tons of ammonium nitrate fertilizer, caught fire and exploded in a blinding wall of flames and smoke. Nearby, a steel barge was shot from the water like a toy and hurtled 100 yards inland; two light planes were obliterated in the sky. In the business district a mile away, people were hurled through doors by violent concussive drafts.

But the *Grandcamp* was only the beginning. Next, the nearby Monsanto chemical plant blew up, and soon oil refineries, tin smelters, and tanks filled with chlorine gas, sulfur, and nitrate were ablaze all along the two-mile waterfront. Chunks of metal and human flesh rained everywhere. In Galveston, ten miles away, the blasts shattered windows. Some of the explosions were audible 150 miles away and were picked up by seismographs in Denver, 1,000 miles away. At 1:11 the following morning, the *Grandcamp*'s sister ship, *High Flyer*, also exploded.

The final toll: 462 dead, 50 missing, 3,000 injured, and $55 million in property damage. "In four years of war coverage," wrote Associated Press correspondent Hal Boyle, "I have seen no concentrated devastation so utter, except Nagasaki."

TSUNAMI—THE MONSTER WAVE

A tsunami is a massive wave triggered by an earthquake or volcanic eruption. History has recorded less than 300 great tsunami. One of these struck the port of Arica in Peru (now Chile) on August 8, 1868, 4½ hours after an earthquake had devastated the town, killed most of its 10,000 inhabitants, and unearthed a large cemetery of mummies, who rose to the surface in the seated positions in which they had been buried years before.

The U.S.S. *Wateree* was anchored offshore when its lookout spotted the approaching tsunami. The 234 crew members clutched their lifeline as the fifty-foot wave swept over the ship. The *Wateree* managed to rise to the surface and ride the crest of the wave, which carried the flat-bottomed craft three miles up the coast and two miles inland.

When the sun rose, the crew discovered that their boat had been deposited in the middle of a desert, 200 feet from the Andes Mountains. Miraculously, no one on board had been killed. The *Wateree* was undamaged, but it was impossible to return the ship to the sea. Sold at auction to a hotel company, the U.S.S. *Wateree* was subsequently used as a hospital and then as a warehouse before seeing its final service as an artillery target during the Peruvian-Chilean War of the Pacific in 1879.

AMERICA'S GREATEST EARTHQUAKE

No, it wasn't the one in San Francisco. It happened in Missouri on December 16, 1811. If it occurred today, owing to the increased population of the area, it would do ten times the damage of the San Francisco earthquake of 1906.

A pioneer, Eliza Bryan, described it: ". . . about two o'clock in the morning, a violent shock of earthquake accompanied by a very awful noise resembling loud but distant thunder, but hoarse and vibrating, followed by complete saturation of the atmosphere with sulphurous vapor, causing total darkness."

Eliza lived in the Mississippi River town of New Madrid, sixty-five miles northeast of the earthquake's epicenter. The shock was felt over nearly a million square miles, as far north as Canada. Chimneys fell in Cincinnati, 400 miles away. The Mississippi stopped, rolled backward, then surged ahead in huge tidal waves, uprooting trees, leaving boats stranded, and sinking islands—including Island 94, with a contingent of river pirates. Naturalist John J. Audubon observed that "the earth waved like a field of corn before the breeze." Sand geysers blew through holes in the surface. Huge fissures yawned.

For more than a year afterward, smaller earthquakes rumbled. Engineer Jarad Brooks rigged pendulums that registered 1,874 shocks during the first three months, including eight that he classified as violent. The earthquakes changed the course of the Mississippi and created islands, domes, lakes—and "Earthquake Christians."

Unknown to most people, the earthquake was not an isolated event. The five-state region below St. Louis is earthquake-prone. Its most recent shock occurred in August, 1981.

THE CASE OF THE OOZING CEILING

On August 8, 1919, something strange happened at the rectory at Swanton Novers in Norfolk, England. The pungent smell of sandalwood oil invaded the rectory, piquing the curiosity of the Rev. Hugh Guy and his wife. Soon patches of gasoline, paraffin, and water began to form on the ceilings of the seventy-year-old house. The patches would condense and then drop in showers onto the breakfast table, floors, kitchen stove, bathrooms—everywhere. These bizarre phenomena continued, forcing the couple to move out their furniture (which was being ruined) and, finally, themselves. Sometimes the dripping gasoline was mixed with paraffin, sandalwood oil, and alcohol, sometimes paraffin fell by itself, sometimes water also fell. After each shower, the ceiling was completely dry, with no sign of discoloration.

Finally a plumber was called in, the ceilings and walls were torn open, officials came to investigate, and stories appeared in all the major newspapers, but no dampness or explanation of any kind could be found. The stuff was now falling at the rate of a quart every ten minutes; more than fifty gallons in all were collected.

To further complicate matters, the dripping and oozing and pouring seemed to follow fourteen-year-old servant girl Mabel Phillips into any room in which she slept or worked. Oswald Williams, "an illusionist," was summoned and pronounced young Mabel responsible. As a practical joke, he said, Mabel had been throwing water on the ceiling. She was fired, though she claimed to be innocent, saying to the end, "I have not played any tricks whatever. I deny that I have done so." Williams and his wife allegedly threatened and slapped Mabel, who brought charges against them, but the case was dismissed.

No one yet has been able to explain how Mabel managed to dump fifty gallons of gasoline, paraffin, sandalwood oil, alcohol, and water onto the ceilings, and no "normal" explanation has ever been found.

JINX OF THE PRESIDENT'S BOX

Four people shared the presidential box in Ford's Theater on April 14, 1865. Two were later murdered by madmen; the other two became insane. The four were President and Mrs. Lincoln, and Major Henry Rathbone and his fiancée, Clara Harris. Rathbone, a War Office attaché, was the stepson of Sen. Ira Harris of New York. Clara was the senator's daughter.

Shortly after 10:00 P.M., John Wilkes Booth slipped into the box and shot Lincoln, who died the next morning. Rathbone received a serious

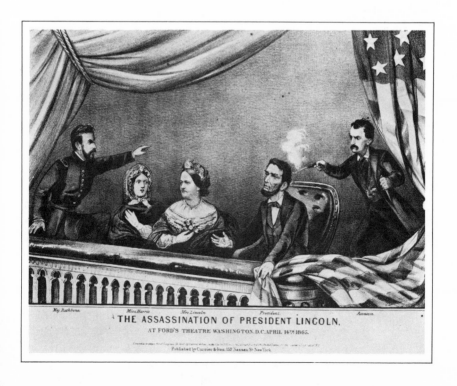

THE ASSASSINATION OF PRESIDENT LINCOLN.
AT FORD'S THEATRE WASHINGTON D.C. APRIL 14TH 1865.

Published by Currier & Ives. 152 Nassau St New York.

knife wound trying to stop Booth. Ten years later, Mary Todd Lincoln, the President's widow, was certified as a "lunatic" in Cook County, Illinois, and was committed to a mental institution for a year.

In 1883, Henry and Clara Rathbone were in Europe supervising the education of their three children. Henry had been growing increasingly morose, irritable, and jealous of his wife. Ordinarily quiet and agreeable, he had become subject to violent and dangerous fits of temper. During their last visit to the States, he had threatened to kill Mrs. Rathbone. But she decided to remain with him for the sake of their children and accompanied him to Hanover, Germany.

On Christmas Eve, shots were heard from the couple's bedroom in Hanover. The servants broke down the door and found Mrs. Rathbone on the bed, lying in blood. Her husband, near death, was bleeding from five wounds in the chest. A smoking revolver and bloody dagger lay on the floor.

Mrs. Rathbone died without regaining consciousness. She was buried in Engesohde, Germany. Rathbone recovered physically, but his mind was gone. He rambled incoherently and seemed unaware that he had shot and stabbed his wife and himself. He was committed to an insane asylum in Hildesheim, where he died on August 14, 1911. He was buried alongside his wife.

SOAP AND SLAVERY

Cleanliness played a part in the British government's decision to oppose slavery in the nineteenth century.

Early in the century, Britain developed a great demand for West African palm oil, used to make candles, lubricants, and soap. Missionaries and traders traveling up the Niger River, doorway to West Africa, thus began persuading tribal leaders to sell palm oil rather than men, since it was more profitable. In 1807, Britain abolished the slave trade (though it continued to flourish for fifty years).

Meanwhile, getting clean became an obsession. In 1840, Queen Victoria had her railroad compartment equipped with a washbasin. Six years later, the first of several acts was passed providing public bathhouses so the poor too could bathe with hot water and soap. By 1853, British soap production totaled 136 million pounds a year.

The connection between slavery and palm oil was succinctly put in a Liverpool candlemaker's advertisement: "Buy our palm-oil candles to contribute to abolition of the slave trade." Ending slavery had become good business.

THE TREE THAT ATE ROGER WILLIAMS

The body of the great seventeenth-century religious emancipator Roger Williams was eaten by a tree.

Williams died in 1683 and was buried in a poorly marked grave in the backyard of his home. Fifty-six years later, a workman accidentally broke into the emancipator's coffin while excavating a nearby grave, exposing the bones. In 1860, a descendant of Williams, Stephen Randall, ordered workmen to exhume the remains from the Providence, Rhode Island, plot and transfer them to a more suitable tomb. But the excavation yielded only a few badly rusted coffin nails and scraps of rotten wood. Not a bone was found.

The workmen, however, did find something extraordinary: the ramifying root of a nearby apple tree lay exactly where the remains should have been, and it had taken the shape of Williams's body, from head to heels. As it grew, the root apparently had encountered Williams's skull and followed the path of least resistance, inching down the side of his head, backbone, hips, and legs, molding itself closely to the contours of his body. The corpse itself was gone—absorbed into the tree through the roots. The tree had eaten Roger Williams.

The human-shaped root was removed for safekeeping and today is on display at the Rhode Island Historical Society in Providence.

THE SMALLEST COUNTRY IN THE WORLD

The world's tiniest country is the Sovereign and Military Order of Malta (SMOM), a walled enclave about half the size of a football field. Located in central Rome at 68 Via Condotti, it is the only nation in the world small enough to merit a street address.

SMOM came into being in 1048 as the Knights Hospitalers, an order of monks who tended a hospital for pilgrims in Jerusalem. During the First Crusade, the Hospitalers cared for the wounded and accepted gen-

SMOM's biggest
tourist attraction—
its keyhole view
of three nations

erous donations from the wealthier crusaders. As the assets of the order
grew, so did its military might, and the Hospitalers dedicated themselves
to killing Moslems as much as to healing the sick. Between 1219 and
1798, the order was known by a variety of names and headquartered
successively on the islands of Cyprus, Rhodes, and Malta. It turned up
at its present digs in Rome in 1834.

Although it remains independent, SMOM is not much of a power
these days. Recent estimates give its population as eighty (ruled by a
grand master). As in 1048, its principal business is good works—running
hospitals, clinics, and leper colonies throughout the world.

Drop by SMOM next time you're in Rome. Its biggest tourist attraction is the keyhole in the main gate of the Priory of the Cavaliere dei
Malta on Via S. Sabina. Peek through it for an exquisitely framed view
of the basilica of St. Peters. This is the only keyhole in the world through
which you can see three countries at once—Italy, the Vatican and, of
course, SMOM.

THE WORLD'S MOST CHANGEABLE GOVERNMENT

When Bolivia's president Gen. Celso Torrelio Villa resigned under pressure in mid-1982, it marked at least the 190th time that country had changed rulers in the past 157 years. Unstable? No other government in the world even comes close.

Since it became independent from Spain in 1824, Bolivia has weathered at least sixty major uprisings, dozens of minor ones, and countless political assassinations, including that of President Gualberto Villaroel, who was hanged by a mob in 1946.

Nicknamed "the Tibet of South America" because it is mountainous, landlocked, and small, Bolivia (pop. 5,425,000) has a history of poverty, underdevelopment, and inept rule. It is bordered by five nations and claims the rare distinction of having warred with all of them—and never won.

Bolivia also has had its share of creditable rulers, the most notable being its first, Simón Bolívar, after whom the country is named. But there were dictators like Enrique Peñaranda, the illiterate general who rose to the presidency in 1940 and whose mother is supposed to have said, "Why, if I had known Enrique would be president, I would have sent him to school."

The nineteenth century was an especially disruptive period for Bolivia, as the country saw a succession of corrupt military dictators who plundered the national coffers and generally ground the people into the dust. The most infamous was Mariano Melgarejo, a murderous, swaggering tyrant. In 1868, he tied the British ambassador—seated backward—to a donkey and paraded him through the public square of the capital in disgrace. When Queen Victoria heard of the outrage, she ordered up a map and crossed Bolivia off. "Bolivia," she announced, "no longer exists."

In July 1982, Gen. Guido Vildoso became president, leading a junta known for its corrupt and repressive rule. However, like many Bolivian leaders, his reign was brief, and by October he was replaced by Hernan Siles Zuazo—after three elections which Zuazo had won had been annulled by the Vildoso regime. Zuazo is the tenth president in four years. When he will be replaced is anybody's guess.

A HOUSE DIVIDED CAN STAND

The front door of the Haskell Free Library and Opera House opens onto the town of Derby Line, Vermont, in the United States, while the back door leads to Rock Island in Quebec. Because the building lies on the international line, the audience in the second-floor opera house sits in the United States and is entertained by a cast performing in Canada.

This international arrangement has occasionally presented problems. In 1935, when 33 percent of a new U.S.-built furnace was going to rest on the Canadian side, a hefty import duty threatened the installation. Officials in Ottawa issued a special exemption. During World War II, the U.S. alien control acts required Canadian patrons of the opera house to carry passports along with their tickets through the main door. This continued until the structure was declared neutral territory.

The building's unique location might have led to a Beatles reunion. The group considered meeting there to talk at a time when John Lennon, a U.S. resident, feared that, because of a drug charge, he wouldn't be readmitted if he left, and Paul McCartney and George Harrison were barred from the United States as "undesirable aliens" due to their British drug convictions. After the meeting was arranged, the musicians canceled it, fearing they'd be mobbed by fans.

MEET THE UNITED NATIONS

There are 157 members of the United Nations, ranging from China, with a population of more than 950 million, to the Seychelles, a small island group in the Indian Ocean with just 65,000 inhabitants. Only one out of three member states has a democratic form of government. The remaining two-thirds are ruled by dictators, royal families, military officers, and one-party governments.

The largest nations that do *not* belong to the UN are South Korea (40 million people), North Korea (20 million), Taiwan (18 million), and Switzerland (6.5 million). The most recent country to be admitted is Antigua and Barbuda, an island nation in the Caribbean with a population of 74,000.

THE HOLLOW EARTH

Congress once voted on a bill to send an expedition to the center of the earth. Although the bill was defeated, it did receive twenty-five favorable votes.

It was in 1823 that Kentucky Congressman Richard Johnson (later vice-president under Martin Van Buren) tried to get funding for the expedition into the earth's interior. Johnson was one of the thousands of Americans who believed in the popular "hollow earth theory" advocated by Captain John Cleves Symmes.

A respected veteran of the War of 1812, Symmes described the earth as a group of hollow, concentric spheres, with an opening at the North Pole 4,000 miles in diameter and an opening at the South Pole of 6,000 miles. It seemed reasonable to him that this inner earth was inhabited. An expedition would prove his theory, and instead of dropping over the polar hole's edge, explorers would sail over a curved rim and down the inner side of the planet. There, they would find a "warm and rich land, stocked with thrifty vegetables and animals, if not men . . ." In 1818 Symmes mailed a brochure to American and European scientists, requesting support. He included a medical report that confirmed his sani-

Captain John
Cleves Symmes

ty. No response came, so Symmes contacted his congressman, Richard Johnson. When Symmes died in 1829, he had not seen his theory proved or disproved.

By the 1920s, many aerial expeditions had flown over the poles without sighting Symmes's openings to the world within. Geologists have since learned that beneath the earth's crust there are indeed concentric spheres—of solid rock and iron. And at the very center is a hot core of molten iron and nickel.

TALL TALE FROM OUTER SPACE

Space travel can make you taller. When U.S. astronauts Gerald Carr, Edward Gibson, and William Pogue returned from an eighty-four-day mission aboard Skylab 3 in 1974, each measured almost two inches taller than when he'd left.

A daily fluctuation in height is normal for earthbound humans too. The disks in the spine contract each day from the pull of gravity, and by evening an active adult may find himself as much as an inch shorter. A night's rest allows the disks to stretch out again, and the lost height is restored.

But the Skylab 3 crew experienced no such daily shrinkage. In a weightless environment, the spinal disks absorb additional fluid from the surrounding bloodstream, forcing the spine to expand—hence, the astronauts' growth. Within a few days after landing, however, they had shrunk to their normal height.

THE EMPIRE STRIKES—OUT

Hawaii, the fiftieth state of the United States, has a tiny British Union Jack in the upper left corner of the state flag. It's a reminder that the islands once were—unofficially—part of the British Empire.

When explorer George Vancouver visited the big island of Hawaii in 1793, he was eager to declare it "under the dominion of Great Britain," according to Archibald Menzies, the naturalist on the expedition. Meanwhile, Hawaii's King Kamehameha saw the opportunity for British protection of his dominion. So on February 25, 1794, the Hawaiians were accepted as "people of Britain." Eleven guns boomed, the British flag was raised, and the six-foot-six Kamehameha was given an engraved brass plate. While it was understood that Britain would not interfere in island affairs, Vancouver felt he had gained "an addition to the empire." In 1810, when Kamehameha conquered the other islands of Hawaii, they too became part of the unofficial British protectorate. The cession of the islands to Britain was never formally or legally recognized in London, much to the disappointment of Kamehameha. The political status of Hawaii remained unclear for years, even with Kamehameha III's establishment of a written constitution for the islands in 1840. Soon after that, he negotiated recognition of Hawaii's independence from the United States, Britain, and France. But in 1898, the United States annexed Hawaii, and in 1959 it became a state.

Mausoleum in Manila's China Cemetery has all the comforts— including cool Cokes

CITY OF THE DEAD

In Manila in the Philippines is a cemetery where the dead are housed in greater comfort than the living people in surrounding neighborhoods.

The Chinese Cemetery of Manila reflects the great respect that the Chinese have for their ancestors. The streets are lined with private mausoleums that have the outward appearance of houses in an affluent suburban community.

We were allowed inside one mausoleum belonging to the founders of a wealthy merchant family. Besides the coffins of the deceased couple, the two-story building contains a bathroom, kitchen, dining room, well-stocked pantry, and two large bedrooms.

Every Saturday morning, fifty descendants gather at the mausoleum to honor the dead couple. Then they have lunch and spend the afternoon socializing. Once a year, during the Festival of the Dead, family members spend the night with their dead relatives.

THE MULTIPURPOSE MUMMY

Mummies, those preserved bodies of ancient Egyptians, have been used over the past 800 years in many bizarre ways—as medicines, paint additives, paper, and even as the silent stars of striptease shows.

Beginning in the twelfth century, "powdered mummy" was prescribed in various forms as a medicine for all kinds of illness, from epilepsy to ulcers. When exporting mummies from Egypt for this purpose became illegal in the late sixteenth century, a black market was created. Entrepreneurs sometimes simulated mummies by slicing the muscles from fresh corpses, packing them with asphalt to mimic the resins used in the embalming process, then pickling them for a few months. As late as the 1970s, mummy reportedly was sold in a New York City pharmacy at $40 an ounce.

During the Renaissance, many artists added powdered mummy to their paint pigments. They hoped the ancient embalming substances would prevent their own works from cracking with age.

In the 1850s, when contraband mummy bandages often could be obtained more cheaply than ordinary cloth rags, manufacturers used them to make paper. But this presented problems. At one paper manufacturing factory, the workers had trouble flattening the ancient bandages, which kept popping back to their rounded, mummy shape.

Augustus Stanwood of Maine also used mummies during the Civil War rag shortage to make paper, which unfortunately was brown because he could find no way to bleach the resin-coated cerements. Stanwood's brown paper was routinely used by grocers to wrap food until a cholera epidemic was traced to his Maine mill, where the workers had been handling the infected mummy wrappings.

Earlier in the nineteenth century, British surgeon and lecturer T. J. Pettigrew, a mummy fancier, unwrapped several mummies before large audiences—a kind of academic striptease.

NEW ENGLAND MUMMY

Between the graves of Charlotte Moody and Caroline Mead in Middlebury, Vermont, may be found the grave of an Egyptian prince who died 3,375 years before Columbus discovered America. The tombstone of the Egyptian prince reads:

> Ashes of Amun-Her-Khepesh-Ef. Aged 2 years. Son of Sen Woset
> 3rd, King of Egypt and his wife Hathor-Hotpe. 1883 B.C.

Henry Sheldon of Middlebury, an oddities collector, purchased the embalmed corpse of the young prince from a New York dealer in 1886. After Sheldon's death in 1907, the miniature mummy was stowed in the Sheldon Museum attic. There it remained until 1945, when the museum curator stumbled upon the decayed and leaking remains.

George Mead, president of the museum's board of trustees, decided to give the little prince a Christian burial. He had the mummy cremated in his neighbor's furnace. The ashes were interred in Mead's family plot, and the headstone was erected—3,828 years after the death of Amun-Her-Khepesh-Ef.

ONE INCH OF THE YUKON

It was the most unusual breakfast cereal premium ever offered: a legal deed to 1 square inch of land in Canada's Yukon Territory, free in each box of Quaker Puffed Rice and Puffed Wheat.

The Quaker Oats Company made the offer in 1955, when it sponsored a children's TV show called "Sergeant Preston of the Yukon." Determined to go beyond the standard sort of cereal box giveaways, the company paid the Canadian government $10,000 for a 19.11-acre tract on the Yukon River, twelve miles north of Dawson, in the heart of Sergeant Preston country. Quaker then passed title on to the Klondike Big Inch Land Co., Inc., which subdivided the land into 21 million square-inch plots, for which individually numbered deeds were printed and packed into 21 million boxes of cereal.

There is no record of any deedholder journeying to the Yukon to inspect his holdings, although one man wrote Quaker maintaining that he had collected 10,000 deeds, enough to give him title to a 75-square-foot plot. (It didn't, however, since his tiny land parcels were not adjacent.) Ultimately, the Canadian government reclaimed the land from Quaker for $37 in back taxes. The deeds themselves are prized today by collectors and are worth $25 to $40 each.

The deeds were such a successful advertising campaign that Quaker Oats soon made a follow-up promotional offer: 1-ounce packages of

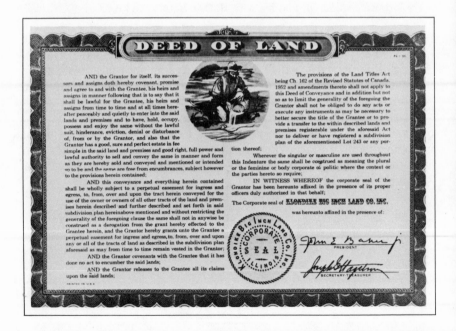

"bona fide Yukon dirt" that could be sent for as premiums for the purchase of puffed cereal. The Yukon dirt was collected and shipped to an orphanage in Alaska. There, the children divided it into 1-ounce packages, which became premiums.

ICE PALACES

It was the biggest building in St. Paul—fourteen stories high on an acre of land. And it was made entirely of ice.

It was the ice palace of the 1888 St. Paul Winter Carnival. Although the annual event is still held in the Minnesota capital, there has never been another ice palace like that one. Made of 55,000 blocks of ice and lit by electric lamps, it also was the scene of the social event of the season—the wedding of George Brown and Eva Evan. More than 6,000 guests attended.

The Brown-Evan wedding wasn't the first to be held in a palace of ice. More than 150 years earlier, Prince Michael Golitsyn of Russia had

taken an Italian Catholic wife, to the intense displeasure of Czarina Anna Ivanovna. Although the prince's bride soon died, the czarina remained bent on punishing him. She had a vendetta against the prince and his family, who opposed her rule; she also had a vicious sense of humor. She ordered an ice palace built in St. Petersburg in the winter of 1739, completely outfitted with ice furnishings—dishes, toilets, tables, even a four-poster ice bed. When all was finished, she selected the ugliest woman she could find to be the prince's second bride and forced the couple to parade about town on an elephant before the wedding. Accompanying them was a procession of freaks.

The procession made its way to the ice palace, where "the Bridal Pair of Fools" were stripped and sent to their icy nuptial chamber. Then all exits were sealed. The couple survived the frigid night, and nine months later, the prince's wife gave birth to twins.

QUAINT SAINTS

The Catholic Church has 2,500 saints. In 1969, the Vatican did a housecleaning and dropped the feast days of more than 200 saints from its liturgical calendar—in some cases because it was not known if they had really lived, or because they were of local interest only. Saints whose feast days have been deleted or made optional retain their full status as saints, and continue to be venerated. Among those deleted were St. Christopher, patron of travelers; St. Valentine, patron of sweethearts; and St. Vitus, patron of epileptics. The feast day of St. Nicholas of Myra, patron of pawnbrokers and brewers (and prototype of Santa Claus) was made optional.

But consider the wide choice of saints who are still listed on the calendar. There is, for one, St. Matthew, patron saint of tax collectors. According to the New Testament, Matthew took his first step toward saintliness when Jesus saw him collecting customs and told him, "Follow me."

St. Simeon of Stylites is the patron saint of pillar (and by extension, flagpole) sitters. At the height of his career, Simeon sat atop a sixty-foot pillar. He remained there for thirty-six years, preaching and converting the heathens below to Christianity.

A patron saint of the toothache? Apollonia was a deaconess at a church in Egypt where an anti-Christian riot erupted in A.D. 249, and three of her teeth were kicked out. Threatened with burning, she voluntarily entered the flames. St. Apollonia's emblem shows a forceps gripping a tooth.

Other fascinating patron saints abound. St. Martha, patron saint of housewives, is usually shown holding a soup ladle. St. Brendan, who supposedly discovered America 900 years before Columbus, is patron saint of sailors. St. Jerome, who helped compile the Latin Bible, is patron saint of book collectors.

Honorable mention in our quaint list goes to St. Druon (or Drogo), patron saint of hernias and ruptures.

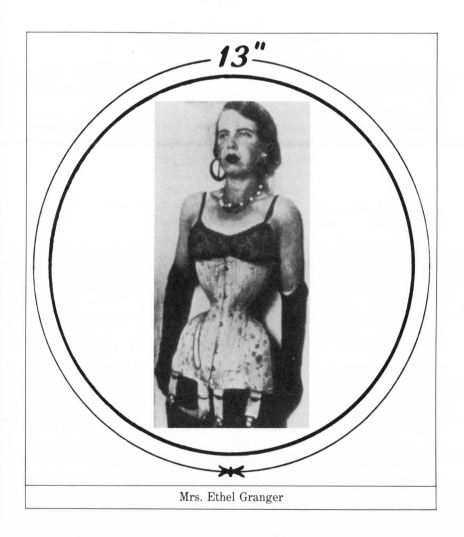

Mrs. Ethel Granger

WHAT A WAIST

Tastes in waists come and go, and over the centuries men and women have favored the abundant, round belly and its extreme opposite—the tightly corseted wasp waist.

The smallest known waist in recorded history—thirteen inches—belonged to Ethel Granger of Peterborough, England. Ethel's unusual story has been recounted in David Kunzle's book *Fashion and Fetishism*. The man behind the remarkable waist was Ethel's husband, William Granger, a crafts teacher and amateur astronomer. Relentlessly and methodically, William urged his wife into ever tighter corsets, which she removed only to bathe. Periodically she rebelled, but always gave in to please her husband. Even in her hometown, Ethel could barely walk down the street without causing a traffic accident and gathering a crowd. (Undoubtedly, her size three shoes with five-inch stiletto heels added to the showstopping effect of the thirteen-inch waist.) In 1957, the couple went public, causing a sensation throughout England. William Granger, a large, rotund man, said of his own hefty waist, "I've tried corsets meself, but it didn't do much good."

Perhaps the most extraordinary thing about Mrs. Granger was, until her death at age eighty, her continuing good health. She ate heartily and enjoyed physical labor—when she helped her husband build an observatory, she shoveled 6 tons of wet cement.

STAMP OF VANITY

Acting solely on his own authority, a Canadian postmaster once ordered the printing of a postage stamp bearing a portrait of himself.

He was Charles Connell, postmaster general of New Brunswick. In 1860, as the province was switching from British shillings and pence to Canadian dollars and cents, it fell to Connell to order a new set of postage stamps. The artwork was standard for the most part: the latest locomotive was depicted on the 1-cent stamp, a portrait of Queen Victoria was on the 10-cent stamp, a steamship was on the 12½-cent stamp, and Edward, the Prince of Wales, was on the 17-cent stamp. But the 5-cent stamp showed Connell himself.

The governor of New Brunswick didn't care for the Connell stamp, and the postmaster resigned under pressure—but not before buying up all 5,000 sheets of the stamp, which he is said to have thrown into a huge bonfire in his garden. Connell kept a few stamps for himself, however, and some have since fallen into the hands of fortunate collectors.

Today, the Connell issue is worth a good deal more than the stamp hastily printed to replace it. In London in 1963, a pair of the stamps went for £1,400 (nearly $4,000).

COUNTERFEIT SEASHELLS

Chinese forgers once did a brisk business selling counterfeit seashells to gullible Europeans.

Native to the southwest Pacific, the Precious Wentletrap is an exquisitely formed shell bearing unique ladderlike markings. In the 1700s, Dutch merchants introduced it to Europe, where some collectors prized it even above the rarest jewels. Precious Wentletraps soon commanded prices that only the rich could pay.

In the nineteenth century, as demand for the shell outstripped the supply, Chinese forgers began manufacturing counterfeits from rice-flour paste and selling them to unsuspecting traders. They certainly looked real, and it was only when collectors washed them—and watched in horror as the shells dissolved in the water—that the ruse was exposed.

These days, a real Precious Wentletrap will bring only about $7.50. But the nineteenth-century fakes—if you can still find one—are worth far more.

MEETING OF THE MINDS

Some of Cornell University's finest brains aren't found in lecture halls, but in jars.

They comprise the Wilder Brain Collection, housed mostly in a basement laboratory on the Ithaca, New York, campus. The first such collection in the United States, it was begun in the 1890s by the Cornell animal biologist Burt Green Wilder to study the relationship between brain structure and the mind. At its peak, the collection held some 650 specimens, but dissections and other factors have whittled the holdings down to 122.

Although Wilder accepted the brains of all sorts of people, he prized those of "well-known persons of marked idiosyncrasies," especially college professors. And he often distributed brain bequest forms at Cornell alumni dinners. The collection today includes the brain of Wilder himself, who died in 1925.

THE PEOPLE'S CHOICE: NONE OF THE ABOVE

A Louisiana gubernatorial candidate lost his place on the ballot in 1979 when he legally changed his name to "None of the Above."

He was born Luther D. Knox and established his candidacy under that name. But some time before Election Day, he made the name change and requested that it be reflected on the ballot. When the Louisiana attorney general turned him down, None of the Above took his case to the Louisiana Court of Appeal. In a suit officially listed in court records as *None of the Above* v. *Paul J. Hardy, William J. Guste, Jr., and Douglas Fowler,* the plaintiff requested that the attorney general's rebuff be declared unconstitutional. The court held no: a state has every right to protect voters from candidates whose names are fraudulent, confusing, or frivolous. None of the Above's name, of course, was all of the above.

More recently, a candidate for Parliament in Liverpool, England, legally changed his name from John Desmond Lewis to Tarquin Fintimlinbinwhinbimlin Bus Stop-FTang-Ole-Biscuit Barrel in time to be thus identified on the ballot. "This is ridiculous," Liverpool Mayor William Bullen protested. "He may think it's a joke, but an election is a very serious matter." The mayor's pique was understandable: it was his job to read aloud the full names of all candidates as he reported the outcome of the election on nationwide TV. Lewis compromised and ran under a more manageable, but still mysterious name, "T-Tan." He won 223 votes but lost the election.

A TEST OF GENIUSES

Many people have heard of Mensa, the organization for people with high IQs, but there are several societies that are much more exclusive. Whereas 1 out of 50 people qualifies for Mensa, only 1 out of every 2,500 can pass the two entrance exams of the International Society for Philosophical Enquiry. Here are some sample questions from the W87 test, one of the exams.

1. Rearrange the letters to form a proper word.
   s u o u s i n d i n g e
2. Fill in the missing number.
   29-11-2
   73-10-?
3. Fill in the missing word.
   Examples: Autumn (fall) Trip
   Season (spring) Coil

   Question: Argue (. . . . .) Partition

Information about the organization is available from the International Society of Philosophical Enquiry, Box 3282, Kingsport, Tenn. 37664

For the answers to the sample questions, see below.

3) Argue (fence) Partition
2) 73-10-1
1) disingenuous

ANSWERS:

KNITTING: FOR MEN ONLY

You may think of knitting as women's work. But centuries ago, men worked as professional knitters.

Knitting probably originated in the Middle East around A.D. 200 and was carried around the globe by male sailors and merchants. In medieval Europe, entire families knitted to supplement their incomes, especially during hard times. Male herdsmen, farmers, cart drivers, and fishermen knitted wool stockings and other garments while on the job. Knitting

Cyril Smith, former member of British Parliament, knits during a debate

was considered a highly prized skill of brides-to-be, but women were not allowed to make a living at the craft.

When the knitting and hosiery guilds were established in the fifteenth century, only men were admitted. The entrance requirements were exacting. After serving a six-year apprenticeship, a craftsman had thirteen weeks to complete four projects: a small carpet bearing an original, approved design that depicted animals, birds, flowers, and foliage in their proper colors; a beret; a wool shirt; and a pair of hose decorated with ornate Spanish clocks. If the projects were approved, the applicant was admitted to the guild as a "master knitter."

THE VANISHING-URANIUM CASE

In 1968, a Liberian freighter carrying 560 barrels of uranium valued at $3.7 million mysteriously disappeared at sea somewhere between Antwerp, Belgium, and its scheduled destination in Genoa, Italy. More mysterious still, the German-built freighter showed up two weeks later at the Turkish port of Iskanderun with a new name, a new crew, and a new registry—but no uranium.

Oddly, the episode was kept secret for nearly nine years. In April 1977, the *New York Times*, the *Los Angeles Times*, and Paul Leventhal, a former U.S. government authority on nuclear weapons, all broke the story. The CIA, said the accounts, had looked into the case of the vanishing uranium; so had the intelligence agencies of at least three other nations. Officially, the investigations drew blanks. But some insiders had a pretty good idea—off the record—about who had swiped the precious ore: Israel.

It was not an implausible theory. In 1968, Israel had needed hard-to-get uranium to fuel a powerful and highly controversial nuclear reactor built in 1957 in the Negev Desert. Israeli officials denied the whole thing, but *Time* magazine offered another explanation a month later. The freighter, the magazine said, actually had been owned by Mossad, the Israeli intelligence service. Israeli intelligence agents had purchased the uranium covertly from West Germany, *Time* alleged, and then staged a phony midocean heist to conceal the deal from both the United States and the Soviets. Nobody, of course, ever found the missing uranium.

DISAPPEARANCE OF THE *POET*

On October 24, 1980, the U.S. freighter *Poet*, bound for Egypt with a cargo of yellow corn and a crew of thirty-four, suddenly disappeared without even sending a distress signal. It was never found, nor was the crew.

A U.S. House of Representatives committee held hearings in 1981 to investigate the disappearance. It was established that 7½ hours after leaving Philadelphia on October 24, the *Poet* sent a message reporting a speed of fifteen knots on a course directly toward Gibraltar, with November 9 as its estimated date of arrival at Port Said. Later that day, Third Mate Robert Gove called his wife by ship-to-shore telephone. He reported no problems on board. That was the last communication from the ill-fated ship.

Two days later, on October 26, the *Poet* should have radioed again, according to routine practice. It did not. Its owner privately attempted to communicate with the freighter but waited until November 3 to alert the Coast Guard, which conducted a fruitless ten-day air search covering 300,000 square miles.

Two possible explanations to come out of the House hearings were that the *Poet* was hijacked in an underworld scheme to trade its cargo for heroin in Iran, or that it was carrying secret explosives to Egypt for the U.S. military. The official decision, however, was that the ship was probably lost in a sudden storm at night, before the crew could send a message. But no debris was ever found, and the mystery remains unsolved.

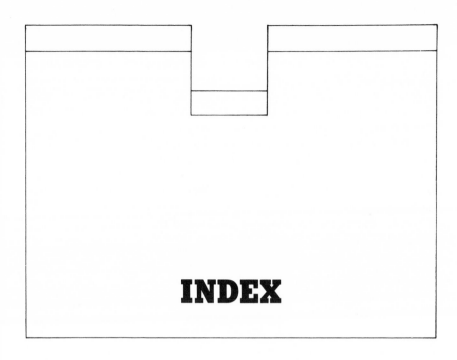

INDEX

Anne, queen of England, 34–35
Antheil, George, 201–2
Anthony, Susan B., 306
Ants, doctor, 102–3
Apollonia, 350–51
Appendectomy, in submarine, 231–32
Appert, Nicholas, 252–53
Appleseed, Johnny (John Chapman), 30
Ara, Pedro, 5
Arawak (language), 189
Arizona, Colorado River rights dispute in,
    86
Armstrong, Neil, 225
Art
    forgeries in, 20
    largest painting in, 284–85
    one-subject painter in, 284
Asta (singing dog), 96
Atkins, George, 321
Atlantic Ocean, row boat trip across, 299
Audubon, John James, 11–12, 336
Auschwitz, 169
Austro-Hungarian Empire, proposed res-
    toration of, 170–71

Babbage, Charles, 207
Baboon, as railroad assistant, 90–91
Bacon, Mary, 25
Bacon, Roger, 177
Bailey, James, 134–35
Baldwin, Henry, 108–9
Baldwin, Mark, 292
Ballet Mécanique (Antheil), 201–2
Bank, unguarded, 325–26
Banvard, John, 284–85
Baptiste, Jean, 116
Barbary States, 136–37
Barks, Carl, 195
Barrow, Alaska, climate in, 57
Barrow, Clyde, 215, 259–60
Barrymore, John, 236
Bartley, James, 33
Baseball
    1890 strike in, 291–92
    largest crowd in, 291
    three-sided, 293
Bats, bombs carried by, 171–73
Battey, Robert, 230
Baxter, William, 208
Bayes, Nora, 290
Beard, as crime, 36–38
Beatles, 342
Beer
    flood of, 238
    with shoe polish, 244
Beetles, carrion, 101–2
Behan, Brendan, 236

Behlen, Charles H., II, 243
Belmont-Gobert, Mme., 152–53
Bender, George H., 68
Benga, Ota, 26–27
Ben-Gurion, David, 36
Benjy (singing dog), 96
Berger, Henry, 283
Bernard, Tristan, 181–82
Berry, James, 113–14
Bialowieza National Park, Poland, 169–70
Bible, censored version of, 178–79
Bill of Rights, final ratification of, 82–83
Birger, Charlie, 111–12
Black, Hugo, 24
Blacks
    all-black town maintained by, 73
    as combat pilot hero, 48–49
    as cowboys, 3–5
    drum music outlawed for, 65–66
    emancipation of, 13
    as Pilgrim, 72
    pre-Columbian American, 58
    in race-riot bombing, 60–61
    as slaveholder, 45–46
    as slave prince, 80
    white Afrikaners and, 21
Bligh, William, 110–11
Block Island, R. I., climate in, 57
Blücher, Gebhard Leberecht von, 142
Blue jeans, invention of, 317–19
Blue people of Kentucky, 243–44
Blyth, Chay, 299
Bólivar, Simón, 83, 341
Bolton, Harvey, 308
Boniface VIII, Pope, 45
Bonnie and Clyde, 215, 259–60
Booth, John, 337–38
Borah, William E., 139
Bordagaray, Frenchy, 293
Borglum, Gutzon, 25
Boston Curtis (mule), 103–4
Botha, Louis, 21
Bottineau, Etienne, 38
Bouchard, Hippolyte de, 83–84
Boxer Rebellion, 148
Boxing matches, first female, 288–89
Boyle, George, 222
Boyle, Hal, 334
Brachhausen, Gustav, 320–21
Bragg, Braxton, 150
Brains, preserved in jars, 353–54
Brandeis, Louis, 320
Braun, Wernher von, 162
BRAVO H-bomb test, 128–29
Brazil, germ warfare in, 82
Breakfast cereal
    sex drive and, 263–64
    Yukon giveaway in, 348–49